Disarming the Playground

VIOLENCE PREVENTION THROUGH MOVEMENT & PRO-SOCIAL SKILLS

Training Manual

Rena Kornblum, MCAT, ADTR

Cathi Teeter McCutchan

Published by:

Wood & Barnes Publishing
2717 NW 50th
Oklahoma City, OK 73112
(405) 942-6812

Cover Art by Blue Designs
Photography by Robyn Lending Halsten
Copyediting & Design by Ramona Cunningham
Interior Illustrations by Delores Kroutil, Art House

Printed in the United States of America
Oklahoma City, Oklahoma
ISBN # 1-885473-49-4

Acknowledgements

This book would not have happened without the support and help of many wonderful people. First is Deborah Thomas, director of Hancock Center, my boss, adopted grandmother of my children, and good friend to my family. At work, whenever I have a new idea or a direction I want to explore, her response is "Go for it, try it." Any time I am discouraged or frustrated she is willing to talk, treat me to dinner or bring me something to lighten my load. Deborah, you are an inspiration to all of us at Hancock Center both in your ability to support our growth and your energy to pursue your own.

Next, certainly, is Cathi Teeter McCutchan, a dance therapist who was my right hand assistant providing computer know-how, design skills, and her own professional ideas while working with me in the field as well as in the office. It was wonderful to be able to tell Cathi what was in my head and have her produce it visually on the computer. Cathi relocated across the country part way through our work but continued to travel here once a month to spend three or four twelve hour work days with me. Even after a long commute she was always organized, open, and ready to work. Now a new mother, I wish her all the best.

My husband Joseph Schmitt was also indispensable. This book has taken three years from the initial request to Hancock Center for support to its release by the publishers. During this period the house has been neglected, meals have been more haphazard and I have been preoccupied. Not only has Joe tolerated the dust bunnies and clutter with constant restraint but he also read and reread my manuscript for grammar, wording and comprehension even when incredibly busy with his own business. He has been both supportive of the difficulty one can have coming up with the right words and a wonder at helping me express myself more clearly.

Then there are my two youngest children, Benjamin and Keri, who have lived at home during the process of writing this book. I am amazed and appreciative of their willingness to be quiet and give me space to work, as well as their support of my becoming an author. They even made me special cards and a special dessert when Wood 'N' Barnes accepted my book. Thank you so much.

It was my brother, Allan Kornblum, who initially encouraged me to put the curriculum on paper, as well as developing a video, so that more people could learn about it. He also volunteered his time to help me find a suitable publisher and has offered continued emotional support during this process.

There is Barbara Thompson, principal, and the staff and students at Lapham Elementary School who inspired this curriculum. Barbara has continually encouraged and supported my work at her school. She has been very creative obtaining funding and has incorporated my curriculum fully into the school's daily life. Of course, Barbara could not be the principal she is without a staff of dedicated, skilled and caring teachers who have gone out of their way to encourage me, work with me, fill out my endless paperwork demands, etc. And the teachers, of course, would have no work without the children who make the school and this curriculum come alive.

My colleagues at Hancock Center have provided endless support and expertise. Dance therapist, Jeanine Noyce, reviewed sections of the book, tested some of the activities and developed adaptations that have been included in the curriculum. Robyn Lending Halsten, also a dance therapist, took still photos and videos of the curriculum, again offering professional advice that was always supportive. Dori Regnier kept me up to date on the financial picture. And the rest of the staff as well as Hancock Center's board have provided both support and encouragement.

There are many other people who have given of their time to help and encourage me as I wrote this book and the truth is, without them I couldn't have completed it. Lori Frank helped me connect with Wood 'N' Barnes. Dianne Dulicai, Rebecca Rosenberg, and Karyn Schwoeble Johnson read the original manuscript and gave excellent feedback and suggestions. And countless friends, family and colleagues have given encouragement.

The people at Wood 'N' Barnes also deserve my thanks. As a first book it meant stepping into the unknown, much like putting your child in someone else's care. My child was treated with respect, gentle humor and lots of encouragement.

My deepest thanks to everyone,
Rena Kornblum

Rena invites readers to send in anecdotes and/or adaptions of the curriculum they develop or problems they see. You may contact her at rbkornbl@facstaff.wisc.edu

Publisher's Acknowledgements

Welcome to a timely and terrific curriculum.

As with most projects we undertake, *Disarming the Playground* has touched a place within. Violence and its pervasive, inescapable presence in our world touches us all in some fashion. Any of us with children are on guard for them as they encounter the poor boundaries and unchecked anger of some of their peers. We collectively examine, in the media or within our own families, the issues that create the climate and how we might educate our children to live safely in it. We feel that *Disarming the Playground* makes a significant contribution toward that goal.

When Rena originally forwarded her manuscript to us, we knew from the start that it was something we wanted to be involved with. It came to us as an exhaustive single volume, full of great interventions just right for achieving the goals Rena set. In our initial response to Rena, we suggested a format that we felt would best suit the real life application of a curriculum such as hers. One piece, the Training Manual, would be used by the instructor/professional to understand the program and offer guidance behind the appropriate delivery of the strategies and concepts in each session. The other piece, the Activity Book, would be used "in the field" for on-hand facilitation of the creative and innovative interventions.

Repetition within the text is by design. It is our intention for you to have done your "homework" in the office by reviewing the Training Manual and then head to the "field" with the Activity Book to deliver this powerful curriculum to the population with which you are working.

It has been common for us to hear the words "I wish we had a program like this when my children were younger" or, "Our society has never needed a book like this more than right now..." Both of those statements ring true for anybody exposed to this well examined and delivered curriculum.

Before closing, I'd like to thank Rena and her contributors and supporters at The Hancock Center. Their vision, hard work and consistent efforts to develop this program have resulted in a tremendous vehicle for delivering the messages of violence prevention to today's children.

We wish you all the best in disarming your playgrounds!

David Wood, Publisher

Video Information

Disarming the Playground: Violence Prevention through Movement and Pro-Social Skills, Training Videos One & Two suppliment the Violence Prevention through Movement Curriculum developed by Rena Kornblum. They illustrate materials presented in Chapters Two through Eight allowing you to see children engaged in the activities, and they briefly discuss some of the concepts. The videos are designed to be used one unit or activity at a time. Also available to assist you in implementing the curriculum is *Moving toward Peace*, a short video that presents an overview of the curriculum.

Training Video One covers: Spatial Awareness, Self Control & Stress Management, Awareness of and Response to Tense or Dangerous Situations, and Movement Strategies for Dealing with Conflict and Aggression.

Training Video Two covers: Developing Empathy, Anger Management, Use of Props to Augment the Curriculum, and Decreasing Prejudice, Violence, and the Use of Weapons.

Videos are available from Wood 'N' Barnes Publishing & Distribution, 800-678-0621.

# Foreword

We have all heard stories about an increase in violence in our schools and in our communities. Many parents are at a loss as to how to control aggressive behavior in their children, how to teach their children to stand up for themselves appropriately, and how to protect their children from danger. Teachers have seen an increase in the numbers of children who have not learned to accept limits and who are impulsive in the way they handle their feelings. Over the course of more than twenty years of therapeutic work with children and families, I have experienced this increase in difficult behaviors firsthand.

This book presents a movement-based curriculum for violence prevention. The activities are fun and exciting, allowing children to develop safe ways to use their strength, social awareness and creativity. They can be used as presented in this book or they can be adapted and changed as desired. Parents, teachers and mental health professionals can use the activities described. Although it is presented as a curriculum, activities can be used separately to address specific skills. It is my hope that people will feel free to use this book to further the goal of a peaceful society.

As a dance/movement therapist, using a combination of movement, discussion and creativity to work toward change, I am seeing more and more of my clients come to therapy with issues of pain and rage. Many have been physically or sexually abused, and some are already acting out this pain on others. As a therapist, I could affect only a small number of children at a time. While I consider this work essential and fulfilling, I had been looking for a way to affect a larger population. In January of 1995 a door to that opportunity opened.

In a collaboration between Lapham Elementary School in Madison, Wisconsin and Hancock Center for Movement Arts & Therapies where I coordinate children's programming, I, along with a colleague, Jeanine Noyce, introduced a program of school based dance/movement therapy groups for children who had witnessed or experienced trauma, domestic violence or physical or sexual abuse. The school staff had seen an increase in the number of angry, "acting out" and withdrawn children who were unable to focus on learning. In a bold step, not unlike our nationwide school nutrition programs, which have the philosophy that children who are hungry are not going to learn, the school's principal, Barbara Thompson, sought to provide treatment for some of these children as an integral part of their daily program. She felt that if their emotional needs were addressed, perhaps they would have more energy available for learning. The first groups were started in January of 1993.

Two years into the program, the physical education teacher, who was very experienced, asked if I would be willing to work with an entire class that was having major anger management issues. My weekly movement work with this class gave the children healthier ways to vent their anger, provided experiences using strength in a safe, cooperative way, and helped them develop skills to ignore disruptive classmates. These experiences resulted in less disruption in the classroom overall. The experiment of teaching these movement skills to an entire class had been successful and led to requests for movement sessions with other classes.

During the following school year I worked with several classes expanding a variety of movement activities to address issues, which the teachers, students and I felt were important. The result of that year's work was the development of a curriculum called "Violence Prevention through Movement." This curriculum uniquely covers many of the issues addressed in the "Student Anti-Victimization Education" (SAVE) program, a city-wide program here in Madison, in addition to other issues that, as a dance/movement therapist, I felt were essential.

Why include movement in a violence prevention program? Dance/movement therapy has been shown to have a positive effect on socialization, emotional expression, self-esteem, tension release and the development of a positive control over one's body actions (Ritter and Low, 1996). Since violent acts are a series of movements our bodies have learned to use to represent our inability to control emotions like anger; it follows that learning different movements to express or react to anger can prevent violence. It has long been accepted that our first sense of ourselves is a body sense. When this body sense develops in a way that is harmful to one's self or others; reeducation of the body is the solution.

As children develop new skills in movement, they increase their awareness of internal sensations. At first these sensations may only be recognized and used in the movement sessions. Part of the curriculum is designed to help raise children's awareness of these sensations in everyday situations so that they can consider alternative behaviors outside the prevention classes. For example, children can learn to become aware of their arousal level while doing exciting movement activities in prevention classes. Once they are aware of how arousal feels at different levels they can begin to transfer this to other situations. They can be taught to use calming strategies early in the arousal cycle so they do not become combative.

You will find the Violence Prevention Through Movement curriculum useful not only for teaching impulse control and anger management to disruptive children, but also for teaching protective behaviors, such as strategies to defuse potentially violent situations. All children experience emotional states of powerlessness, which can range from the simple need to accept healthy limits from adults in charge, to more extreme situations involving abuse. Many children do not develop a wide range of coping behaviors to deal with these feelings other than in a dominant or submissive manner. Surprisingly this includes children who are raised in healthy homes, as well as children with more conflicted backgrounds.

This book contains movement activities presented in a format that can be used by teachers, parents, social workers, dance/movement therapists and other therapists whether they have a movement background or not. It includes a description and rationale of both the movement and verbal skills necessary for violence prevention. Suggested props, effective sequencing of lessons and discussion topics are provided, as well as detailed lesson plans which include step by step directions for all movement activities.

While this program was developed for elementary school children, I have included ways parents might utilize it at home and professionals might apply it in other settings, including special education, psychiatric populations, family therapy, other grade levels and parenting classes. Activities are cross-referenced for skills, age appropriateness, length of lesson, etc.

While this curriculum is presented as a finished piece of work, in actuality, I am always adapting and changing things to meet the needs of specific groups I am working with. This allows me to accept the children where they are and is a part of succeeding in diminishing violence. When I observe good teachers, I always see them adapt their lesson plans to meet the specific issues of their class that day. Since not everyone is comfortable enough with movement to feel that they can improvise, the activities can be used as set down. I recommend that adults planning to use this program first get comfortable with the activities as presented. You may even want to try them out yourself. But once you have used them and feel comfortable, please feel free to adapt things to fit your needs.

Rena Kornblum, MCAT, ADTR, has a Masters in Creative Arts in Therapy from Hahnemann University and is a member of the Academy of Dance Therapist Registered. She is a past faculty member of Hahnemann University in Philadelphia and currently teaches at the University of Wisconsin-Madison. Ms. Kornblum works with children and families dealing with autism, learning disabilities, emotional problems, sexual and physical abuse, violence, and attachment and adoption issues, as well as with senior adults and adults dealing with visual disabilities. She developed the children and family program at Hancock Center for Movement Arts and Therapies where she currently coordinates children outreach programming with a special emphasis on public schools. She often presents workshops and training seminars and is published in several books, including the revised *Dance/Movement Therapy: A Healing Art* by Fran Levy. Ms. Kornblum brings over 20 years of professional experience as a dance/movement therapist with children and families to her work in violence prevention. She has also developed training videos about Dance Movement Therapy and Violence Prevention, and is the mother of four.

Contents

CHAPTER ONE

Overview of Violence Prevention

I. GETTING STARTED

This Training Manual includes a description of both the movement and verbal skills necessary for violence prevention and a rationale for their use. It presents the theoretical framework that supports the *Violence Prevention through Movement* Curriculum, examples of its use with different grade levels in the elementary school, and teaching strategies to help you use the Activity Book successfully. Before delving into the curriculum itself, some background knowledge on violence, violence prevention programs and movement is necessary. Since part of this program involves detailed discussions with the children, better preparation will result in better teaching. This background starts in Part II of this chapter where you will find research cited that documents the common components found in successful violence prevention programs and a description of the movement skills that are necessary for preventing violence. Part III of this chapter introduces information on the roles of bullies and targets and witnesses of bullying.

While the Activity Book contains detailed activity descriptions, the Training Manual contains the theoretical and teaching adaptations as mentioned above. To ease the transition between the two books, some things are repeated. Both books contain a listing of the goals and skills taught in each chapter and an overview of each activity. In addition, some of the real life examples described in the Training Manual are used to enhance Chapter Five, Movement Strategies for Dealing with Conflict and Aggression, and are therefore repeated as part of the activity descriptions in that Chapter.

The core units of the curriculum are presented in Chapters Two through Seven. Each chapter consists of a theoretical introduction to the issues being covered, interspersed with case examples. Following the introduction is an overview of the activities that are used to teach these issues, with specific teaching strategies to help implement them and to troubleshoot any problems that may arise. Illustrated handouts, detailed lesson plans, parent letters, and anything else you need in the actual classroom are provided in the Activity Book. Chapter Eight describes activities using movement props that can be incorporated into the curriculum. Information on purchasing and/or making these props is provided. And Chapter Nine illustrates applications for professionals including dance/movement therapists, other mental health professionals, and childcare workers. The Training Manual is designed to provide the background knowledge and application ideas needed to best utilize the curriculum presented in the Activity Book.

Additionally, while this curriculum is designed as a complete violence prevention program, many teachers, professionals or parents may choose to implement only certain core units in response to specific group needs or time constraints. Movement activities may also be used to augment an existing prevention program. Adaptations for home use as well as several additional resources to assist you in implementing this curriculum are described in the Activity Book. (See Chapter One, Getting Started in the Activity Book.)

II. Violence Prevention through Movement - Components That Make It Successful

One afternoon I was walking home from work on a different path than I usually took. I was thinking about cleaning for a visit from my mother-in-law, when I noticed a truck pulling into a factory driveway. The driver opened the gate and drove in. As I neared the driveway, two large German Shepherds came out onto the sidewalk. I just assumed they were friendly since the gate was still open and no one from the factory was in sight. As I passed the gate, the dogs ran over to me, and it wasn't until one of them opened its mouth to bite me that I realized I was in danger, and I was petrified. There was no one in sight to call to for help. There was no chance of running since the dogs were right there. I could feel myself cringe, shrinking into myself in terror. At that moment I was a VICTIM.

In a split second, I knew I had to save myself. I remembered someone once telling me that all dogs seem to know and fear the action of a person reaching down as if to pick up a stone and threatening to throw it. At that moment I stopped being a victim and became PRO-ACTIVE. As one dog started to bite me I reached for the imaginary stone, put back my hand and pretended to throw it while yelling at the dogs in very loud voice. The biting dog let go of my leg and both ran back inside the gate. I kept yelling at them as if I were the aggressor until they were out of sight.

At that point I quickly finished walking home and collapsed, crying. The police were called to make sure the gate was closed and nothing like that ever happened again. I was lucky it was winter—I had on two pairs of socks, long johns, and heavy pants. Although I had a large bruise that lasted a month, the dog's teeth had not broken the skin. I was also lucky that someone had once told me a way to protect myself, and I had been able to use it. Being pro-active had saved me from serious injury...

Violence prevention requires three major skills: the ability to be pro-active, the ability to manage anger, and the social skills necessary to get one's needs met without hurting others. All three of these, in turn, require the integration of the mind (deciding what to do in a tense situation) and the body (implementing that decision) in order to be successful. Many prevention programs neglect addressing the body component.

Many body skills are necessary, for example, when dealing with an approaching bully. Two of these, the timing of the intervention and the body attitude used for the intervention, require the knowledge of how to appear assertive as well as the ability to change from being scared to being mobilized and pro-active. The ability to manage the physical arousal of anger in a safe way requires more than an awareness of anger triggers. It requires the body experience of calming techniques practiced in different environments: a playground, a hallway, and a classroom.

The physical experience of moving with others in synchrony and of having spatial boundaries respected are just a few of the other body level skills involved in helping children learn to get along peacefully.

Violence Prevention through Movement is a comprehensive curriculum, utilizing body and mind as equal partners in developing the skills necessary for creating a safe world. It teaches protective and pro-active behaviors, tailored for the aggressors, the targets, and the witnesses of aggression.

In the course of researching material to validate the program, we discovered a wide range of supportive data and some fresh ideas that we were able to incorporate into the program. One particularly helpful article presented the results of an extensive survey conducted by a team of researchers to discover the elements necessary for a prevention program to succeed (Dusenbury et al., 1997). They studied school-based programs around the country in order to determine which approaches offered the most promising results and found nine essential components that the successful school-based prevention programs had in common. These are summarized on the following pages.

1. PROGRAMS NEED TO HAVE A COMPREHENSIVE, MULTI-FACETED AP-
PROACH, meaning that family and community, as well as the school, all
need to be involved. A successful program addresses both specific interventions such as peer mediation to deal with a conflict as it happens as well
as global strategies such as learning anger management. Norway made decreasing school violence a national priority in 1983 after three child suicides
related to bullying shocked the nation. An intensive program began in all
the schools that was also coordinated with the distribution of educational
pamphlets for all parents. Norway's national multi-faceted campaign resulted in a 50% reduction in school bullying (Olweus, 1994).

2. PROGRAMS SHOULD BEGIN IN THE PRIMARY GRADES AND BE REIN-
FORCED ACROSS GRADE LEVELS. Bullying behavior patterns have been observed in children as early as age two (Beane, 1999). Since bullying patterns
are learned behaviors and quickly develop into habits, the older a child becomes, the more difficult change will be (Beane, 1999; Fried & Fried, 1996).
It is therefore important to begin prevention work in the early grades and
continue it as the children get older. Another consideration, based on age,
is the willingness of children to talk about why they are picked on or teased.
Teachers and principals have reported that, in the case of racism, younger
children are more inclined to admit they are teased based on skin color. By
the time children reach middle school, the effects of racism have become
more ingrained, and the children may have replaced "hopeful anger" with
"hopeless bitterness" (Fried & Fried, 1996, p. 123).

3. PERSONAL AND SOCIAL COMPETENCY NEEDS TO BE PROMOTED. Competencies needed include anger management, problem-solving skills, ability
to resist peer pressure, effective communication, and a sense of social
perspective, to name a few. Courtesy, compassion, respect, and caring
should also be emphasized. Research has shown that most bullies are individuals lacking empathy, and most victims are individuals lacking appropriate self-assertion skills (Rigby, 1997; Kocs, 1998). Programs that attempt to
counter early antisocial behavior, by encouraging cognitive development and
the acquisition of social skills, have been shown to reduce behavioral problems while increasing problem-solving abilities, at least in the short term
(Kellerman, et al., 1998). This competency gives children the skills needed
to be able to handle themselves in the world today.

4. INTERVENTIONS NEED TO BE AGE-APPROPRIATE. Risk factors and social
situations that tend to cause conflicts change at different stages in devel-

opment. This needs to be taken into consideration when planning for different grade levels.

5. INTERACTIVE TECHNIQUES SUCH AS ROLE-PLAYING FACILITATE SOCIAL LEARNING. Programs that present material solely from a theoretical perspective have trouble keeping students engaged. Interactive techniques give students the experience of practicing some of the concepts. This, of course, is a major part of the movement curriculum, not simply trying things out while seated or standing in place, but rather utilizing the gross motor skills that would actually be required in a life-threatening situation.

6. A CULTURALLY SENSITIVE PERSPECTIVE IS NEEDED. Racism and sexism go hand-in-hand with the overall bullying problem in schools (Hoover and Oliver, 1996). This data emphasizes the importance of adapting the presentation to reflect the ethnic identity of the children participating in the prevention program.

7. TEACHER AND STAFF TRAINING IS IMPORTANT IF THE PROGRAM IS GOING TO BE REINFORCED PROPERLY. Teachers need to have a chance to practice the techniques and learn the vocabulary needed to enforce and reinforce the program in the classroom, hallway, and schoolyard.

8. A POSITIVE SCHOOL CLIMATE SHOULD BE PROMOTED through structural elements such as effective class management, well-lighted halls and stairs, and buildings that are well-maintained and attractively decorated. These elements give students the sense that the environment they are in is respected, well cared for, and safe.

9. FOSTERING NORMS AGAINST VIOLENCE, AGGRESSION, AND BULLYING ARE ESSENTIAL if a prevention program is going to be implemented effectively. A culture where peace is the norm has to be established by the school. Students have to know that violence won't be tolerated.

The movement curriculum presented in these volumes, *Violence Prevention through Movement Training Manual & Activity Book,* incorporates the first eight components of a successful program. Each school must satisfy the component for fostering norms against violence, aggression, and bullying. Many schools have already adopted a zero-tolerance policy for aggression or weapons. All too often, however, the zero-tolerance policy tends to be too rigid with a punishment structure that does not allow for discretion. Everyone has heard of ludicrous situations where children are suspended or even expelled because of the lack of flexibility. My son came home just two days ago with a story about a child who was suspended for having a plastic, half-inch, key chain gun. It was not real. It did not shoot. I could understand taking it away for the day and letting the child know he was never to bring it back to school again, but suspension?

Another situation calling for common sense can arise around children with certain disabilities. Some children with severe neurological problems strike out physically or verbally as a result of their disability. A school has to take a stand against violence, but it should be a compassionate stand.

In 1996, Lapham Elementary School in Madison, Wisconsin made a commitment to do something about violence and bullying. Classrooms that were free of any violence for a week were given ribbons to hang on the classroom door to signify their success to the whole school. The students also were given extra recess if their class earned a ribbon. Among the programs instituted was a school-based therapy program and the *Violence Prevention through Movement* Program, both done through a collaboration between Lapham School and Hancock Center for Movement Arts & Therapies. This program has now been expanded to three schools and receives funding through United Way®.

Violence Prevention through Movement is multi-faceted and comprehensive in scope. Class discussions focus on sibling and family as well as on peer relationships. Families are also included through correspondence and progress reports. Many children begin this program in kindergarten or first grade and have had more than one exposure to it by the time they finish elementary school. It has been my experience that children who participate in the movement curriculum only once do not feel secure in their ability to remember what to do under pressure. Many children at Lapham Elementary School have now had the opportunity to experience this program for two or three years in succession and have reported an increase in their ability and sense of confidence to handle problems as they arise. However, children encounter different issues as they get older and need the chance to develop new strategies and skills to deal with them. Movement activities in this book are planned from a developmental perspective and change with the needs of the children and teachers. Social skill-building is incorporated into the curriculum along with problem-solving, anger management, decision-making and resisting peer pressure. All of the lessons are presented in an interactive format, and the children participate sometimes as a whole group and other times with a small group or a partner. The children typically hear about a technique, see it demonstrated, and then try it out themselves.

Cultural awareness is promoted by verbally processing some of the differences and similarities in movement choices and how some of these choices are influenced by culture. Respect for different choices is demonstrated by the leaders and is incorporated as part of the expectations in the program. Teachers participate along with their classes, reinforcing the lessons and monitoring application of the newly learned techniques in the classrooms and on the playground. The curriculum's potential for promoting a positive school environment is best illustrated by a case vignette.

> In one fourth grade classroom with a new teacher, the issue of peer pressure arose. There were a few "class clowns" and a number of children who were happy to join in any time one of the clowns acted up. It was considered cool by the students in this class to act goofy, causing the new teacher a lot of difficulty. During a movement activity, which required resisting pressure from a Spandex cloth being pulled on by the rest of the class, one of the students who regularly and easily got sidetracked, gasped, "resisting is hard work." This was a turning point for the teacher and the students as they explored how difficult it was to resist pressures of all kinds. The teacher shared with her students how she felt both physically and emotionally exhausted trying to keep them focused. She was asked to explore what would happen if she permitted some release time inbetween activities, while her students practiced the art of being able to stop themselves quickly when allowed to be goofy for a short period of time. The students were also able to look at why they felt it was cool to act goofy during academic activities and what it would take for them to shift that pattern to recess time. As a result, the teacher reported more of a sense of relaxed control with her class.

The *Violence Prevention through Movement* Program provides a unique approach to violence prevention. It is unique because it teaches nonverbal as well as verbal communication skills. It involves the body as fully as the mind. This program has twelve movement skills that form the core of its curriculum.

1) SPATIAL AWARENESS is always the first skill presented. Since all physical violence involves an intrusion into someone else's space, spatial awareness is an integral part of the program. Children become more aware of their own and others' spatial needs. They learn to identify their comfort zone in relation to other people.

2) ASSERTION is the ability to present oneself as strong and capable. This skill is as important in everyday interactions as it is in dangerous situations. And it is as important for the aggressor as it is for everyone else since aggressive children need help defining their boundaries. Children

learn to assume a strong stance with knees bent and legs slightly apart. They learn to say "Stop!" or "No!" with assertion of body, face, voice, and posture in order to appear unafraid and impenetrable.

3) PRO-ACTIVE STRATEGIES are important as a resource when direct assertion is not effective. Some children, even after months of practice, are not able to assert themselves credibly. Participants are taught a repertoire of verbal and nonverbal strategies that tend to neutralize aggression or conflict such as distracting, changing the subject, being friendly, or using humor. They learn various ways of using words and movement to divert potentially dangerous situations and are given the chance to practice them. The full list of strategies developed in our pilot study was made into a rhythmic chant and into rhyming phrases to help children remember them.

4) ENERGY MODULATION deals with awareness of arousal and how to move from one energy state to another. Many children, particularly those with ADHD, and also some of those who have experienced trauma, cannot feel when they are becoming agitated or losing control. Children will not be able to control themselves and think of alternative behavior options if they are not aware of becoming agitated in the first place. Before children can learn to calm down, they must know when they feel tense. The awareness of tension or arousal can be developed through exciting, high-energy activities, and this awareness can then be related to situations outside the movement sessions. Children are taught the difference between high-energy that is in control versus high energy that is out of control. They also practice moving between high energy and low energy states using imagery to help them. Learning the movement phrase called "the 4 B's of Self Control" integrates the skills practiced in this unit.

5) RELAXATION, or the ability to calm down, is essential when in danger. Settling enough to be able to think clearly enables one to come up with a protective strategy in response to a situation. Agitation is a physiological state that can lead to aggression. Stopping the process of becoming agitated prevents the mounting tension that can result in an explosive release of energy. Children practice relaxation techniques, including breathing and imagery, to help them calm down. They experiment with the different body sensations associated with tension and relaxation. They learn abdominal breathing as a quick way to settle oneself when getting agitated.

6) SELF-CONTROL AND ANGER MANAGEMENT are necessary both for helping bullies learn to stop bullying (to develop appropriate outlets for anger)

and for everyone to develop the impulse control necessary to resist inappropriate behaviors such as picking up a weapon or resorting to violence. Children are taught to recognize angry feelings inside themselves and are shown healthy ways to release that anger. A four-part movement phrase called the "4 B's of Self-Settling" is taught and practiced. Children play games that increase impulse control. Discussions, which relate all these activities to bullying, supplement the movement activities.

7) GROUNDING, or the ability to stand one's ground, is an important part of violence prevention, both because it affects the ability to assert oneself, and it enables one to resist peer-pressure. Activities using resistance such as tug-of-war games help to develop this skill.

8) EARLY WARNING SIGNS are signals in the body that alert one to dangerous situations. Many individuals who have been attacked later report that they had an earlier sense that something was not "right," but they ignored it because they could not pinpoint the cause of their discomfort. Children learn to be aware of these "uh-oh" feelings, body cues that warn them of danger, and learn to trust these cues. They also explore the timing involved in becoming aware of danger and trying a pro-active strategy.

9) IGNORING SKILLS are required to maintain an inner focus despite being surrounded by turmoil. Classroom behavior can deteriorate quickly when children are unable to ignore the distracting behaviors of others in the room. Inner focus is also necessary in order to avoid escalating a tense situation, such as feeding into teasing behaviors. Children practice several techniques of ignoring and decide which one works best for them. The steps, involved in successfully utilizing ignoring techniques, are presented as the "ABC's of Ignoring."

10) REFOCUSING is the ability to settle oneself after danger signals prove to be unfounded or after being distracted, and it enables one to return to the task at hand. Children are given the opportunity to apply their relaxation and ignoring skills in this unit.

11) ATTUNEMENT OR EMPATHY is the ability to read the feelings in others' faces and bodies as well as their words with accuracy and understanding. It also involves the ability to show that you understand and care about the other person's feelings. The inability to interpret nonverbal cues can lead to misunderstandings, creating a greater potential for violence. Unfortunately there are many children who have not learned to read nonverbal

cues. Children with ADHD or emotional problems are at risk for problems in this area. Preschool is the time when children are most sensitive to developing these skills, which speaks to beginning prevention in early childhood programs as well as elementary school. Learning to interpret someone else's feelings is the first step in developing empathy, a skill necessary for ending abuse or violence and for establishing a broad range of relationships. Children practice mirroring activities, matching intensity, and "feeling" role-plays.

12) SYNCHRONIZING THE EXPRESSION OF FEELINGS means that a person's feelings are consistently displayed through tone of voice, facial expression, body posture, gestures, and words. If a child is not able to express his/her feelings so that other children can recognize and understand them, misunderstandings will arise, which can lead to alienation or arguments.

13) GENERAL BODY AWARENESS increases one's repertoire of strategies. Children experience moving in a variety of ways and are taught to pay attention to how these movements feel. Body awareness is an integral part of every other skill in this program.

14) SOCIAL SKILLS such as the ability to resist peer pressure, positive problem solving, empowerment, and being able to deal with isolation give children resources to utilize in difficult situations. Movement activities that practice handling situations, such as not getting my way, how to join a group, how to occupy one's self when alone, and feeling comfortable taking a stand, integrate many of the movement skills listed above.

The core movement skills described above are not necessarily taught in the order presented. For example, body awareness is taught throughout the curriculum. The lesson plans presented in the following chapters will develop and expand upon these core movement skills. Toward the end of the curriculum, integration of the above skills is reinforced through dramatic movement themes. These themes utilize animal imagery and require the children to apply protective behaviors and safety rules in the face of imaginary dangerous situations.

In addition to the movement skills described above, verbal skills are also an important part of the process and are integrated throughout the movement program. They serve to process reactions from the movement experiences, share stories from life that illustrate the application of new techniques, and brainstorm alternate solutions to problems. They also serve as a source of feedback.

Discussions include a broad range of topics. Some of them test a child's ability to handle some situations alone and identify when to get help. A list of people each child could approach for help is developed in one discussion. Problem-solving actual situations the children have experienced and giving examples of people successfully coping with threats are important topics. Other topics range from brainstorming alternative conflict-resolution strategies and exploring the definition and causes of bullying to taking a look at the responsibility of individuals to others being bullied and discussing feelings evoked by the movement activities. Children are given practice in verbal techniques to deflect teasing. They also practice saying phrases to help themselves maintain the ability to think in a crisis, for example, "Breathing and thinking will get me through this."

Prevention classes last anywhere from 30 - 60 minutes with 45 minutes or more being ideal. Every session starts with a movement warmup that works on body awareness and grounding. The core of the session alternates movement skill building with verbal processing. Sessions frequently end with a unifying activity to calm the children before they return to their classrooms.

While the *Violence Prevention Through Movement* Program was developed with the idea that weekly sessions would be offered over twelve to fifteen weeks, some classroom teachers have been able to commit to only four to six weeks. In these cases, the teacher is asked to identify the most significant issues the class needs to tackle so that the curriculum can be customized.

In summary, violence continues to be a problem in our society at large, and much attention has recently been focused on preventing violence in schools in particular. In order to make a significant impact in preventing violence, communities need to make a commitment to teach new skills, starting at the earliest school level. My goal in presenting this curriculum is to offer a comprehensive, skill-building program that is applicable to all ages.

Professionals who teach prevention need to have an understanding of the roles of bullies and targets and witnesses of bullying. This knowledge helps with verbal processing as well as with the development of movement activities. Therefore, this chapter, which describes these roles, precedes the movement curriculum.

III. INSIGHTS INTO THE ROLES OF BULLY, TARGET, AND WITNESS

In a therapy session, a fourth grade girl reported that each day at recess a larger boy from her school would chase and threaten her. She wasn't really afraid of being hurt, she said, because her friends knew about the situation, and they positioned themselves between her and the boy to stop him from beating her up. Nevertheless, she didn't like being chased every recess and felt powerless to stop it. The therapy session was spent practicing some pro-active choices such as ignoring, being assertive, and changing the subject. She chose the technique of changing the subject by being friendly. The next recess, instead of running away, she complimented him on his running speed and offered to time him running across the playground. That was the last day he chased her. She was then able to play with her friends at recess instead of being protected by them.

In our current cultural climate, children are literally bombarded with images of violence. This exposure is not only in the media. It occurs in our schools, playgrounds, and homes. According to the U.S. National Institute on Justice report on "Crime and Violence in Our Schools - an Overview of the Statistics" from February 1996, "Nearly three million thefts and violent crimes occur on or near school campuses every year. This equates to almost 16,000 incidents per school day, or one every six seconds." In addition, "Every school day, 160,000 students skip classes because they fear physical harm." Clearly, developing a child's repertoire for dealing with confrontation or his/her own aggressive impulses may enable that child to avoid becoming a bully or becoming the target of one. Developing this repertoire is a necessary prevention strategy for all children if we as a society hope to have a significant impact on safety.

BULLIES
Bullying is the form of violence that occurs most often on or near school grounds. It is any form of behavior that causes physical or psychological distress. Bullying behaviors range from obvious direct actions (e.g., hitting or calling someone a hurtful name) to subtle indirect actions (e.g., spreading rumors or excluding a peer). Bullying always involves an imbalance in power that can be on a physical and/or an emotional level. While an imbalance in physical power is obvious, as when one child towers over another, an imbalance in psychological power can be difficult to detect. Hence, the mystery of why some people are not able to defend themselves from physical or verbal attack when the aggressor is the same size or even smaller than the target. Imbalances in power can also be based on level of authority (a fourth grader threatening a first grader) or on numbers (a group of children threatening an individual).

Bullying can be intentional or unintentional. Most people know and recognize the intentional bully. This is the person who has most likely come from a violent or neglectful family situation. These children may be the targets of violence at home or are imitating what they see others do. Early neglect and abuse creates a cycle of rage, arising from unmet needs. Children who have not experienced empathy to their own pain rarely show empathy to others. When children's needs are not met emotionally and physically, their feelings of helplessness create a desire to gain power. Belittling or dominating others often satisfies this desire. Since their lack of empathy results in feeling no guilt when they cause pain in others, power gained at the expense of others makes them feel good. This good feeling becomes permanently associated with domination and, ultimately, with malice. Again, in many cases, the intentional bully has been the target of bullying behavior, has witnessed violence at home or in the community, or has been neglected without violence, leading to an accumulation of rage.

The role that family interactions play in the development of intentional bullying behaviors is profound. Parents themselves may have been bullied as children and repeat the behavior with their offspring. Many adult members of dysfunctional families lack the same skills that the children are being taught in the prevention program. This underscores the need for active involvement of families in school prevention programs so that they can learn new skills and expand positive behaviors at home.

One should also be aware, however, that intentional bullying - the desire in an individual to cause pain in others and the resulting pleasure in seeing that pain - can also develop when one is filled with anger or impotence because of a physiological problem, for example, a learning disability, communication disorder, or impulse control problem. A child can have an intact, healthy family but have a neurological make up or have endured enough rejection by classmates to cause the need for dominance in some manner. This type of child may lack an outlet for frustration. Bullies sometimes select such children as targets; at other times they become bullies themselves.

Another less understood reason for becoming an intentional bully can be a combination of genetic make-up and environmental guidance. Some children are born with a strong aggressive drive. Observations of infants support strong personality differences. As early as preschool there are some children whose level of aggression goes beyond the average, even when there is no aggression or other disruption at home. Some families are successful at channeling the strong aggressive drives of their children into outlets such as sports. In other families, parents feel less able to help their children out of negative cycles of aggressive outbursts. These feelings of helplessness can fuel even more violence. In order to feel safe, children need to have a sense that the adults in charge can contain their impulses. And safe control is necessary to learn to direct aggressive feelings along healthy avenues.

The unintentional bully is the person who causes real pain in others but does so without awareness of the impact of this behavior. The un-intentional bully is not acting out of rage or malice but rather out of the desire to be included as part of a group or as part of what is seen as a game. Teasing someone is seen as fun. This seemingly happy, well-adjusted child is mindlessly gaining pleasure from inflicting pain on others. Groups of children who exclude one child on the playground provide a good example of such behavior. In a third grade classroom I worked with a few years ago, 90% of the children felt bad about being excluded on the playground during recess. Many of them had cried at home or regularly complained to the teacher and often felt they weren't liked or weren't as good as the other children. But when asked, 80% of them admitted to excluding others. Obviously many of the children were both being excluded and also excluding others. This was a class of predominantly bright, well-adjusted children. It was the last place I thought I would encounter a high percentage of bullying. Indeed, 90% of these children had never initiated a physical fight with the intent to hurt (except, as they admitted, with their siblings). Even though most of the children in this class hated being excluded and knew it made them feel bad, they didn't seem to realize the impact of their own behavior. They were aware that they felt some pleasure at their power to keep someone out of whatever group they formed that day, but they seemed unaware of the extent of the damage it was doing to their classmates. After much brainstorming, the class agreed to try not to exclude anyone at school for a month. (Several children refused to make the deal if they had to extend it to home as well.) They learned that they could set boundaries for themselves in a friendly way, for example, they could say, "I made plans to play a special game with so and so this recess, but you can play with me next recess." At the end of a month, I met with the class again. Exclusion just didn't seem to be such an issue any more. The teacher reported very few complaints and the children felt that the issue had resolved itself. While some excluding incidents still occurred from time to time, our work on this subtle form of bullying seemed to eliminate it as a major issue for the remainder of the school year.

While everyone is mean once in awhile, and we all have a bully somewhere inside of us that hopefully we have learned to control, bullying is a pattern of ongoing, negative behavior, played out when an imbalance of power exists. (In the above example of the third grade classroom, the imbalance existed as a group against an individual). Being the bully or the target of a bully can become a long-term pattern that causes negative results lasting into adulthood (Rigby, 1996; Fried &

Fried, 1996; Webster-Doyle, 1992). Interventions are needed to stop these patterns. To the child being teased, it doesn't make a difference whether the bullying is intentional or not. The pain is the same. But the intervention used to deal with bullying is different when it arises from a lack of thoughtfulness than when anger is the precipitating cause.

Targets

Targets of bullying are on the receiving end of the negative behavior described above. It is difficult to say why a person becomes a target. It is not as simple as the widely held belief that children who are different (e.g. too big, too short, has a lisp, has a physical disability, belongs to another culture) are chosen as targets because of their easily visible differences. Targets frequently display vulnerability or the inability to stand up for themselves. It is this vulnerability that makes them an easy mark, not visible differences. Complicating the issue even further, some children are targets in one environment (the child abused at home) and bullies in another environment (at school). While these children need help in controlling their bullying behavior, they also need support and empathy for their target role.

Sometimes targets are sensitive kids who have difficulty interpreting social cues (Nowicki and Duke, 1992). These children can't tell when something is meant to be funny and when it is meant in a mean way. They are vulnerable even in a "safe class" because all children tease sometimes. Teachers and classmates tend to get annoyed at the endless complaints about what they perceive as minor incidents. And while sensitive children need training in "reading" non-verbal behavior, it is important for the adults and the children working and playing with this type of child to remember that social bantering is acceptable only when all parties involved are having fun.

The following story will serve as an example of bullying behavior from both perspectives—the bully and the target.

> At the end of the 1994-1995 school year a mother (who was visiting school that day) asked her academically gifted kindergartner why she was avoiding a boy from her class during recess. The child explained that for months this boy had been blocking her exit from the school bus until she kissed him. Being afraid of missing her stop she would comply. She had tried waiting until he got on the bus so she could choose a seat far away from him. But then he would switch his seat. When asked why she didn't call out to the bus driver or get up and switch her seat, she said these things were against the rules. This child had been miserable for months but did not want to break the rules or tattle.

According to Ken Rigby in *Bullying in the Schools And What To Do About It* (1996), several studies have shown that results of being bullied in school have long range consequences for many people. These possible effects include lingering low self-esteem, depression, less success in achieving ongoing intimate relationships and a tendency for adults who were bullied in childhood to have children who also are bullied.

When we look at the above incident, it is important to recognize that the little girl was not the only victim. Why did this boy, who was also a kindergartner, although larger and stockier than the girl, behave this way? He had in his short life been witness to and victim of significant violence. He felt powerless to change these things, and his family felt powerless to change his increasing violence. Research shows that by age 30, one in four individuals who were bullies as children will have a criminal record (Fried and Fried, 1996). This boy, as well as others like him, also need help if incidents of bullying are going to be stopped. They need a repertoire of behaviors that will enable them to feel powerful safely. They need to be taught empathy for others and how to have others accept them. Fortunately, in our example, both of these children did get help. Sadly however, many more incidents of bullying take place regularly by other children who need help. It is important to realize that most bullying takes place out of the sight of adults, and much of it goes unreported.

WITNESSES

The anecdote above can be used as an example of two prevention themes. The first is the knowledge that rules can be broken when safety is at stake. The little girl on the bus could have called out or switched seats as a way to draw attention to her problem. Kindergartners and some first graders have trouble with the concept that breaking rules can sometimes be okay. When asked what they would do if their teacher fell unconscious to the floor, most kindergartners, and about half the first graders I have asked over the years, say that they would walk quickly to get help because running in the halls was against the rules. I was taken aback once when a bright second-grader calmly said, "I would buzz the intercom. Then I wouldn't have to walk or run." (There's always one in a crowd.) Through the above story, the children are led to explore why the little girl needs to get up and get help. This also leads to a discussion of when one can handle a problem alone and when there is a need to involve an adult as well as clarifying the difference between reporting unsafe behavior versus tattling.

The second theme is about the role of the witness. This little girl was not sitting alone on the bus. Nor was her stop one of the last. Surely some of her friends or classmates saw this behavior happening each day, yet no one helped her. (Even though the boy in this story was a kindergartner, many children were wary of him because of the intensity and unpredictability of his aggression.) This true story is used to introduce the concept of the witness during violence prevention sessions. Discussion focuses on what her friends could have done and why they didn't act. This leads into movement role-playing, where all of the children practice being active witnesses.

Violence prevention programs, in general, need to include nonviolent methods to deal with danger, reach the bullies or aggressors to help stop the danger in the first place, and develop the powerful role of the witness (Fried & Fried, 1996). Witnesses are an integral part of a prevention program because "...they can be powerful change agents and because of the price they pay for witnessing cruelty. Children who are spectators in the arena of bullying will not be unscathed. The conflict they experience can lead to feelings of sadness, anger, guilt, and shame. If they support the bully, they are an accomplice to the crime; if they stand up for the victim, they are at risk to become the next target; if they remain silent, they may carry a burden of guilt for many years" (Fried & Fried, 1996, p.110).

COMMUNITY COMMITMENT

We have seen that bullying can be malicious or thoughtless, that some children are both bullies and targets depending on the situation, and that to have an impact on violence, the needs of the targets, bullies, and witnesses must be taken into consideration. A community's commitment to ending violence is also an essential element. Indifference by the adults in charge gives nonverbal permission to bullies that they can operate unchecked. Children living in a home where sibling aggression is not held in check by parents are at risk for increasing levels of violence at home and in the community. A school without a public commitment against bullying (i.e. where reports of teasing or tormenting are met with the reaction of "kids will be kids") can be the cause of a child's continuing role as a target for bullying. There are several cases cited in which long term bullying that was not stopped by the adults in charge led to both murder and suicide (Fried & Fried, 1996; Hoover & Oliver, 1996). Life as an unending target of verbal and physical harassment simply became unbearable. As adults, we often have the option to leave an unbearable situation, but most children do not. A policy of non-tolerance for violence and harassment by school or community leaders is a necessary part of keeping this kind of behavior from escalating.

Spatial awareness is an important part of preventing violence. The ability to re-spect the spatial needs of others is the first skill taught in the *Violence Prevention through Movement* Program. This chapter emphasized the need for our whole society to be involved in violence prevention. The next chapter introduces spatial awareness as a skill that can easily be worked on at home as well as in the schools and in the community.

CHAPTER TWO

Spatial Awareness
Proximity to Others and Implications for Safety

An old woman was walking down a street in New York City one afternoon carrying two bags full of groceries. Two men came up from behind, one on each side of her, into her space. While she couldn't see them until they were next to her, she had a clear sense of danger as they were approaching.   No one else was around, and there was no store or other safe haven in sight. As she couldn't run away, it looked like she was going to be robbed or attacked. But as they reached her, she took a deep breath, smiled, turned toward each of them and said, "Oh, I'm so glad to see you. My arms are getting so tired. I don't know what I would have done if you hadn't come along. Here, you take this bag (as she handed a bag to one of the men), and you take this one (as she handed over the other bag to the second man). You saved me. Thank you." The two men automatically took her bags and walked her home. As she stood in her doorway with her bags on the floor inside, one of the men couldn't resist asking her if she knew what they had planned to do to her. "Of course I did," she said as she closed and locked her door.

Proximity deals with the distance between people or things in relation to space. In general, larger distances allow for more strategic choices in hostile or dangerous situations while near distances can create a vulnerability to physical contact. All physical violence involves an intrusion into someone else's space. This makes spatial awareness an integral part of any violence prevention program.

This chapter will explore proximity to others and its role in both violence and protection. Areas of spatial use will be discussed, especially those that are important in maintaining and developing healthy relationships. The emphasis is on developing relationships, because people who become bullies are often unaware of how to develop healthy relationships. A description of spatial activities that will teach children effective self-protection strategies will also be covered.

An overview of the goals covered in this chapter follows:

 ## Maintaining Space: Developing the Ability to Maintain One's Own Space without Intruding on Others.

> Learn the concept of space bubbles (small, medium and large) as a way to discuss and visualize space.

> Practice the different types of movement required in small, contained spaces versus larger areas.

> Experience moving while maintaining different size space bubbles.

> Learn positive strategies for controlling one's body to contain the impulses involved in spatial intrusion.

> Apply these strategies to a variety of in-school behaviors such as lining up, walking in the hallways, and sitting together in a circle or cluster.

> Apply these strategies to other situations such as recess and free play.

> Practice moving from larger spaces to smaller, crowded spaces.

> Increase the ability to maintain a sense of personal space, even in crowded situations.

 ## Spatial Needs: Increasing Awareness of and Respect for One's Own and Others' Spatial Needs.

> Increase a sense of one's own preferences or comfort level regarding personal space.

> Gain awareness of the range of other people's spatial preferences.

> Explore ways to respect these preferences while preserving one's own needs.

> Learn that no one's space should be intruded upon without permission.

> Experiment with ways to protect one's own space safely.

Appropriate Distancing: Learning Appropriate Social Distancing for Different Situations.

> with strangers

> with authority figures such as teachers, principals, etc.

> with friends and family

SPECIFIC MOVEMENT SKILLS TAUGHT:

> Learn to be visually oriented in space.
> Learn what to do with one's body parts while moving and while still so as not to invade someone else's space.
> Learn to request more space politely if just feeling crowded and firmly if being touched or a polite request is ignored.
> Discover one's own spatial preferences and how these might differ in various circumstances and how these differ from other people's preferences.
> Maintain an awareness of one's own and others' space and understand that others have spatial preferences that may differ from your own.
> Learn a safe distance to stop someone when they do not appear to be friendly.
> Maintain an awareness of "Uh oh" feelings (discomfort) that develop when danger is sensed.
> Learn movement strategies necessary to maintain one's own spatial boundaries in different situations to maintain impulse control in relation to space.
> Apply concepts about space to real life such as walking in school hallways and lining up at various times during the school day.

DISCUSSION TOPICS:

> Why is it important to be aware of your space, and what is the role of spatial preferences in conflicts? How does spatial awareness relate to violence prevention?
> How do you need to modify your movement to avoid getting too close or bumping into another child who is moving in a different direction or in a crowded space?
> Who likes moving in a small space and who prefers a large one? How does your preference for big or little space transfer to your interactions with others?
> How do you feel when someone approaches you? Where is that feeling in your body? What feels uncomfortable and what feels good?

> What made it difficult to say "stop" before an approaching person got too close?
> What can you say and do if you feel uncomfortable? What can you say or do if you feel someone is in your space?
> What are tactics children can use when they're in the classroom and they cannot choose the size of their space bubble (e.g. they may need to move next to someone who doesn't invade their space or learn to ignore spatial intrusion in certain circumstances)?
> Discuss the problems the children think they have with space and what their strategies are for solving them.
> Discuss proximity norms and how they vary in different cultures and in different relationships (close friends, family, teachers, principal, etc.).
> Discuss the importance of increasing distance in potentially hostile situations (e.g. when someone is angry, if the approaching person is a stranger).
> What kind of space does one need for walking in a line or while working in your classroom?
> What do you need to do in order to stay in your own space?

People carry a sense of their personal space wherever they go. (Different cultures vary as to the size of that space.) The extent of this space is flexible depending upon the situation. It can be as small as the area just surrounding the skin, or as large as the arms can reach in all directions (Hall, 1966). In some situations people need a space that extends beyond their reach to feel safe. Spatial invasion occurs when a person moves uninvited into another individual's personal space, that space being as large as the individual defines it for his/her own sense of safety (Nowicki and Duke, 1992). A lack of respect, a sense of violation, and a loss of control over safety may be experienced when an individual's personal space is invaded. Personal space is intricately tied to the sense people have of themselves, their relationships with others, and their perception and trust in their environment.

Spatial intrusions can be malicious, accidental (due to a lack of awareness), playful, necessary for medical reasons, or can be an attempt to define the limits within a relationship. All forms of violence involve an intrusion into another person's space. Any intrusion, even a playful one, can be interpreted as aggressive if it is unwanted. Verbal abuse, though not physical, is also perceived as a violation of one's personal boundaries or space.

Spatial isolation is the opposite of intrusion, and it too can cause violence. The ability to share space with others and to maintain a healthy sense of self are key ingredients in developing nonviolent relationships. It was a sense of extreme isolation that precipitated the shooting incident at Columbine High School during the spring of 1999. Violence was the mode of making contact. The isolation was caused by exclusion from the mainstream. Such exclusion is felt as a form of bullying and, therefore, as a form of violence. The response to this bullying at Columbine was a tragic intrusion with bullets.

Sometimes a person can feel invaded or abused but may be confused as to why they feel that way. An example of this occurred in one of my first prevention classes.

A first grade boy kept bringing up the issue of being tickled to the point of tears by his mother. The class related many similar incidents with siblings and friends. They expressed how difficult it was to be appropriately assertive when they were laughing or crying. Together we decided that an effective strategy might be to work out a safety code, a special word that would indicate that they really wanted the tickling or excited roughhousing to stop, even when they couldn't use a serious voice. We agreed that this special word had to be worked out ahead of time and used only when needed. After I was finished working with this group of children I wrote a letter to their parents about the safety code and the children's concerns about aggressive tickling.

A chance meeting with the mother of the boy happened later in the year. We spoke about the tickling. She told me that this was her form of discipline. She said she would never spank her children because that would be abusive. Instead, when her son wouldn't listen to her, she would tickle him until he cried. It was the only way she knew how to get him to be obedient. Since prolonged tickling against someone's will is abusive, I expressed this concern to her. She agreed to look into other forms of discipline. Intensive tickling is invasive and disrespectful of one's body boundaries. It is also very confusing because tickling is thought to be a fun activity. In this case, it was regularly being done to the point of pain.

This incident reminded me of my youngest son's dislike of being tickled. As a preschooler he was comfortable expressing this dislike to adults, yet many adults refused to believe him and tickled him anyway. I was amazed at how many adults did not take a child's (my child's) requests seriously. It often took my reaffirming that his dislike was real before the adults would stop. This tickling was not ongoing nor was it intense, but had I not stepped in and helped my child protect himself, he would not have developed a sense that his right to protect his body from uncomfortable touch was valid.

Spatial intrusion is a key ingredient in violence. People who are violent have a lack of respect (if the intent is malicious) or a lack of awareness (if the intent is accidental or careless) for personal boundaries. Therefore, the development of spatial awareness and respect for other's spatial boundaries needs to be an integral part of any violence prevention program.

What are the hallmarks of a healthy individual coping with, or functioning within, a variety of spatial situations? Healthy individuals are able both to share (merge) and to separate their space with people they feel close to. They can allow others to touch them (at appropriate times), and they are able to touch others. They are able to take part in the general give and take of relationships in public and personal space.

The healthy use of space requires the development of several skills. Individuals must be able to protect their own space. They must learn to be comfortable or tolerant of different spatial situations. For children at school, some of these situations might be sitting at circle time, being on a crowded bus, walking in a line, playing in the schoolyard, or being alone. All people need to develop an awareness of and respect for the different spatial preferences and needs of others and a sense of the cultural norms (of whichever culture they are living in) for public and personal space. An individual's safety requires the development of a sense of when one's space is being intruded upon and how to make one's space look larger and less penetrable.

> Lining up to walk down the hallway and waiting while being lined up are prime times for fights to begin in elementary school, particularly in the early grades. One first grade class participating in prevention sessions could not line up or walk down the hall without at least one major conflict arising. A good example of this occurred one morning while the class was coming in from recess. The teacher was leading the line, and the children directly behind her were evenly spaced and following each other. However, as the children farther away from the teacher entered the hallway, they were straggling and yelling at each other. One boy appeared to be trying to pull another boy's pants down. Then a child from the end of the line ran up to another child and jumped on his back, punching him. The two children fell, rolling to the floor, one of them instantly wailing. Two adults were required to break them up. A trip to see the principal did not uncover what exactly had provoked the fight.

These types of incidents were common in this class, leaving the teacher feeling exhausted and overwhelmed at times. Being able to maintain a safe space while moving through the room, as well as while moving in a line, became the first theme addressed with this class during prevention lessons. The following series of activities can be used to develop and practice the skills described above.

Maintaining Space: Developing the Ability to Maintain One's Own Space without Intruding on Others.

Purpose:
> Teach children to be visually oriented in space.
> Develop an awareness of one's own and others' space.
> Develop an ability to move through varying spatial circumstances without intruding into another's space.
> Understand and develop the ability to use movement strategies necessary for maintaining one's own spatial boundaries in different situations.
> Gain a sense of connection to the ground and to one's self when sitting and walking.
> Gain awareness of one's own spatial preferences.
> Develop skills to request more space, politely if just feeling crowded and firmly if being touched or if a polite request is ignored.
> Transfer the concepts about space to real life applications such as walking in school hallways, lining up at various times during the school day, and sitting in clusters.

 Activity 1, Maintaining Space: Maintaining Space while Sitting

Overview: Children will sit in a circle with just enough room between them for their hands to touch the floor without touching their neighbors' hands. A rhyme will be taught, with accompanying actions, that defines the children's space and connects them to the floor and to feelings of control. "Space on my left. Space on my right. Now we sit, nice and tight."

Children put their hands to the left and then to the right to make sure they have space.

Teaching Thoughts: This activity helps children become aware of the spacing of the class as a whole, as well as their role in helping to make sure that everyone has an equitable amount of space. It also works on giving children a sense of control that decreases spatial intrusion while sitting in a circle.

When first teaching this activity, young children enjoy doing it at different tempos. Start out medium. Repeat going faster and faster if you choose, and then end by

The children then link fingers and put on their seat belt.

doing it in slow motion to calm everyone down. The concept of the hands making a seat belt creates a connection to the ground and aides in self-control.

You can use this rhyme any time you want to help your class settle down during a circle activity. Once you have played with the different tempos a few times, only do that part once in a while, almost as a treat, to keep the children's interest in the spacing and control.

Activity 2, Maintaining Space: Maintaining Space while Traveling

Overview: Children will be asked to move around the room in a variety of ways while maintaining a space as large as their hands can reach. They will then be asked to move in a much smaller space without touching anyone.

Teaching Thoughts: This activity increases the children's spatial awareness while traveling. This is a very different skill than maintaining space while sitting still. There are really three parts to this activity, maintaining space with a large space bubble, maintaining space in a crowded area, and learning about spatial preferences.

With the large space bubble, the goal is to increase awareness of others while moving with more and more complexity. Otherwise, some children will lose their sense of space as soon as they get involved in doing anything but walking. I start out simply with walking in different directions both forwards and backwards and also to the side. Moving backwards requires control and is something I usually do with every class but particularly with classes that have problems with impulse control. It makes them aware of the space behind them, that they wouldn't notice ordinarily, and forces them to move even slower than usual.

Children maintain their space while moving through a small space. They must narrow their bodies and move slower, weaving around each other.

If children need more grounding, have them move through the room, still maintaining their space bubble and add making noise with their feet or traveling close to the ground. Traveling sideways usually begins the process of speeding up since it leads to sliding and galloping. Increasing speed with skipping, dancing, running, etc. increases difficulty of maintaining space. Since most children want the freedom to go faster or move with more complexity, they try hard to keep their space. If they are not up to the challenge, slow the speed down again.

I frequently use the large space bubble activity as a five-minute warm-up during other class times. I will then add moving with different feelings or with different body challenges that allow for more creative expression.

Moving in a crowded space necessitates self-control. Identifying what is required so as not to be intrusive gives children cognitive and body strategies to use. Be aware that some children feel uncomfortable in a cramped space. Discuss potential strategies such as staying close to the outer part of the space to help them handle their discomfort. Bring up using words instead of pushing to get more space.

Discovering that some children hate the crowded areas and prefer to stay on the edge of the small space while some children like being right in the middle of the crowd allows the introduction of different spatial preferences. Sometimes fights start because of these different preferences. Teach children to understand and respect these differences. Help decrease the potential for this issue to provoke aggression by teaching children polite ways to ask for more space. Have the class make an agreement to give more space when asked. Explore a policy of giving permission for a child to move to a new spot when feeling crowded. Give the children who need closeness something like a stuffed animal to hold onto, a wall or chair to lean against or something concrete to do with their hands. Maybe allow them to sit very close to you or even lean on you sometimes. It is important for children who crave physical closeness to have times during the day when they can be that close. It is also important for them to learn how to settle themselves in their own space when it is not time for that closeness.

 Activity 3, Maintaining Space: Moving Inside our Space Bubbles

Overview: Each child makes up a gesture that takes place in a small space bubble, the class repeats the gesture and says the child's name. These can then be done in sequence. Then children make a gesture in a large space. Again the class repeats each gesture.

Teaching Thoughts: This is a good activity to learn names and to acknowledge each child by having the whole class do their movement. It is also a different way to explore what can happen in each size space bubble. Medium gestures can also be done. Include a discussion as to the different size space bubbles and situations in which the children might need to use each one. (Use accompanying Space Bubble Handout)

 ## Activity 4, Maintaining Space: Moving into Crowded Spaces with Control

Overview: Children practice moving from a large space to a small space without crashing or touching anyone. They learn that when moving into a large space, they can move quickly, but when moving into a small space, they need to slow down.

Teaching Thoughts: Children maintain their attention during this activity by the difference in speed between quickly moving to a large space and slowly coming back in to a small space. This activity can be done at one time or reinforced throughout other space activities. Children are constantly shifting from moving through space to gathering together for discussions. I usually do this activity a few times in a row to introduce the concept and then reinforce the concept by reminding the children of it as we continue to move in and out of small and large spaces.

 ## Activity 5, Maintaining Space: Personal Space Imagery and Control in a Crowd

Overview: Children explore how to maintain their space when sitting in a crowded area. Positioning and imagery are used to develop the self-control to keep from invading another's space and to develop a sense of protective spacing, like a force field, which provides a feeling of safety in close spatial settings.

Teaching Thoughts: This activity might have to be done over a few periods. Some children get very anxious in a crowd and can only tolerate working on it for short periods of time. Ask the class for volunteers for the first cluster of children. Tell them they will be sitting very close to each other and ask who thinks they can tolerate it. Allow the more anxious children to sit on the outer edge of the cluster so they have some open space next to them.

Activity 6, Maintaining Space: Following the Leader in a Line

Overview: Children will explore the kind of space they need for walking in a line and practice what they need to do in order to stay in their own space.

 Activity 7, Maintaining Space: Lining Up

Overview: Students practice getting in line. They explore ways to get enough space in line without intruding on others.

Children put one hand in front and one behind to check their space.

Then they buckle their seat belt of control so they are ready to go.

Thoughts in general for this section:

Some classes do not need all the activities in this section. Cover the activities important for your class and then implement the space challenge.

Spatial Needs: Activities for Increasing Awareness of and Respect for One's Own and Others' Spatial Needs.

Purpose:

> Become more aware of one's own spatial preferences and how it may differ in various circumstances.
> Become aware of their "Uh oh" feelings (discomfort) when people get too close to them.
> Learn that people have different spatial preferences.
> Learn to respect these differences while taking care of one's own needs.

Activity 8, Spatial Needs: Approach and Stop

Overview: Children approach each other in a variety of ways and take turns stopping each other at a distance that feels safe or comfortable. Discussions center on an exploration of spatial preference.

Children approach a classmate and stop themselves between half an arm's length to a little more than one arm's length away. Everyone checks their own and their partner's comfort level.

Teaching Thoughts: Children need to be able to stop quickly when the "boss" tells them to, otherwise it is not safe. The class may need some guidance if the children have trouble coming up with reasons to stop the "movers" further away when they feel uncomfortable with closer distances.

Certain reactions from the bosses and the movers create tension and indicate the need for discussion before proceeding further in the activity. Sometimes, for example, the mover doesn't want to come closer but the boss doesn't say stop. Sometimes the boss says stop before the mover gets to take a step. And, sometimes the boss never says stop and may even turn to one side so that the mover will go past them.

Activity 9, Spatial Needs: Preferences in Space

Overview: This activity has the same basic movement component as Maintaining Space Activity 3: Maintaining Space while Traveling. It is the discussion afterward that relates it to this theme.

Appropriate Distancing: Activities for Learning Appropriate Social Distancing for Different Situations.

Purpose:
> Teach children common distances used for friendly dialogue.
> Learn when to share space bubbles and when not to.
> Teach children safe distances to stop someone who does not appear friendly.
> Learn that different approaches allow for different spacing.
> Learn that different circumstances require different spacing.

> Learn to recognize the distance of one full arm length away, a common distance for standing face-to-face with another individual.

Activity 10, Appropriate Distancing: Social Distancing

Overview: Cultural norms for proximity (personal space) will be presented. How these norms vary in different cultures and different relationships (close friends, family, teachers, principal, strangers, etc.) will be discussed. Children practice recognizing and stopping themselves and others at the distance of one arm length away, a good distance for most face-to-face interactions.

The children are divided into two groups. The children on the line are the bosses. Each boss has a partner. The boss tells the approaching partner when to stop.

Activity 11, Appropriate Distancing: Safe Distancing

Overview: Children work on recognizing safe distances for strangers and hostile interactions.

Note to Teachers Regarding Space Problems in General:

Identify where most of the problems occur with regards to spacing. Common problem areas include:
- sitting at desks
- sitting in a circle for quiet time
- lining up and walking in hallways
- moving around the classroom or on the playground

Consider these specific strategies for dealing with space problems in the classroom:
- Positioning (e.g. have children sit in boy-girl-boy-girl arrangement).
- Structured sitting (e.g. crossed legs, hands on knees).
- Give concrete actions to child (e.g. Say, "Keep your hands in your pockets" rather than "Don't touch anyone").
- Become aware of and accept a child's ability to stay on task.
- Use visual cues to make spatial distancing concrete (e.g. assigning specific places to sit such as carpet squares or tape on the floor to mark off appropriate spacing for sitting or for lining up).

• Use a rhyme such as "Space in front and space behind, buckle up to walk in a line." Or "Space on the left, space on the right, now we sit, nice and tight."

Note to Parents Regarding Space Problems in General:

In the home, children do not have to line up in between activities, but proximity is still an important issue. Fights are often instigated by some type of spatial intrusion. Playing games in the home to develop awareness and respect for personal space adds to peace within the family as well as in the community. In addition to the activities above, I have provided two additional ideas that work in the smaller scale of the home situation.

The first idea involves providing safe places for children to utilize during exciting play. These spaces help children who are getting overexcited, scared, frustrated, or upset by giving them a place that no one can invade. This is empowering. Below is a description of this idea at work in my home.

My children used to like to play fantasy games involving wild animals and other wild things. We developed a space rule, which required people playing to have their own safe space. No one was allowed in that space without permission. Even a monster or a robber could not attack or rob someone in their safe space without permission. Anyone who was feeling overwhelmed could retreat to their spot. These spaces might be as small as a chair, but they still provided security. Neighborhood children who came over to play were instructed to find their safe space. Children who did not respect this rule were not allowed to play. Once this rule was instituted, fights decreased tremendously. The respect for each person's space had some carry over to other aspects of our family too.

Requiring people playing fantasy games to have a safe space is not really an activity but more of a structure to use to make fantasy play safe. Parents have to help children pick their safe space and teach them to follow the rule of no intrusion without permission. Even with safety zones, this type of play can get over-stimulating, and an adult needs to be watching or listening, even if from another room.

The second idea is related to Spatial Needs Activity 1: Approach and Stop. The small environment of home allows more in depth exploration of personal space preferences. Individuals practice approaching family members from different directions: from the side, diagonally, straight on, or from behind. Different approaches feel different to people, and some allow for more closeness than others do. Designate one person as the approacher and the other as the approached. The approacher moves toward the approached in as many different ways as possible. The approached is supposed to pay attention to which approaches feel good and which don't. The approached can even ask the approacher to move in certain ways. This can be done while the approached stands and, again, while sitting. Everyone should get a chance to try both roles. Children can be quite creative about the various ways to approach someone. After doing this activity, family members can try to use the approaches that feel the most comfortable to each other. Finding the ones that both people like are the best.

I worked with a family consisting of a single woman, who had lived alone for many years, and a fairly new adopted older daughter who was very spatially intrusive. The more the daughter tried to come into the mother's personal space, the more the mother felt invaded and pushed her away. After doing the above activity, the mother realized that she felt very accepting of her daughter when approached from the side instead of straight on. The daughter agreed to try approaching her mother in this way to get affection. This one realization had a major impact on their relationship.

CHAPTER SUMMARY

In summary, this chapter explored the role of personal space or proximity on violence within the home, community and schools. Activities were presented that: develop children's awareness of their own and others' space; decrease spatial intrusion; develop children's awareness of their own spatial preferences and how they may differ from others; and increase awareness of appropriate social distances. Class readiness is measured by the following:

- Children can maintain their space while lining up.
- Children can maintain their space while waiting and walking in a line.
- Children can maintain their space (decrease in spatial intrusiveness) during class time.
- Children can maintain their space (decrease in spatial intrusiveness) during playtime.
- Children can adjust to the spatial needs of the group (e.g. switch places or move over when needed and use words to request more space).
- Children can demonstrate an understanding of appropriate spatial distancing (e.g. when someone is friendly vs. not friendly, close friend vs. acquaintance, stranger vs. authority figure/adult).

While not every child in the class has to be able to demonstrate these skills before moving on, the majority of students in a class should develop these abilities. Since one of the skills taught in this unit is how to request more space politely and firmly, once most of the children get the idea of space bubbles and maintaining personal space, they can cue the intruders or the more impulsive children. As the class gets better at watching space, children can adjust to the more impulsive children by moving when they feel uncomfortable or accommodating them by leaving them a larger amount of space. Usually a classroom is ready to move on after two to four weeks, but more difficult classes can take longer. One class worked on space and self-settling skills for most of a semester. While the activities were varied to maintain interest, this particular class really benefited from this extended work.

After two or three lessons, I frequently challenge a class to be space detectives, to watch their use of space (see space detective handout). The classroom teacher has to be willing to prompt the children before lining up, sitting in a circle, etc. to remember their spatial skills. A point is earned on a chart (see space challenge sheet) each time the class is successful. We decide how many points a week designate success and permit the class to earn a special activity or a treat. The class has to earn these points successfully for two weeks in order to get their reward. After two weeks of being prompted consistently before each spatial transition, the class is challenged to continue earning space detective points with more minimal prompts. Change either to general reminders instead of saying the rhymes each time or gradually fading the reminders to once in awhile instead of consistently preceding each space transition.

There are particular classes that continue to need reminders and cueing throughout the year. If the class has so many impulsive children that there is not a big enough core group to act as models, you, as the teacher, may have to continue to prompt.

> *It took two months of hard work to develop a structure that helped a class having a very high proportion of children with special needs gain control. I sadly watched things fall apart in the second semester when the teacher pulled back on the structure because she felt that the class should be ready to use these skills more independently. She was not willing to accept that they needed the structure reinstated.*

Once the children have begun to master the strategies in this chapter, techniques for developing self-control are introduced. Without self-control, the targets and witnesses of bullying are not able to keep themselves from retaliating. With self-control, the bullies might be able to stop themselves. If we are going to have an impact on violence, the aggressors need new skills too, skills to resist the lure of gangs, weapons, etc. The next chapter deals with self-control and stress management.

CHAPTER THREE

Self-Control & Stress Management
Modulation of Energy—How to Stay Alert & Calm

It was the last month of the school year, and I had only four weeks to work with a second grade class that had a reputation for being unruly, to say the least. The teacher and I decided that her group would benefit from spending the full month on self-control and energy modulation. We spent two weeks experimenting with changing energy levels from calm to wild and back to calm again. The class learned to move through the 4 B's of self-control: brakes (catch the wildness and stop short), breathing (deep abdominal breathes), brains (tell yourself that you are going to calm down), and body (calm your body down and feel your heart rate slow down). A movement phrase that accompanies this is described later in this chapter.

After two weeks of working on a skill, I like to challenge a group to practice it outside of my class. I offered this particular group a surprise if they successfully used the 4 B's ten times a week for two weeks. The following week I heard two stories about their practice. In the first story, the school was having a tornado drill and all the classrooms were in the hallway. It was loud and distracting and many children were having difficulty. One of the students from the class in question called out to her classmates, "Let's use what Rena taught us." Everyone from that class calmed down immediately. The rest of the teachers and students stared, wondering what had happened.

The second story happened later in the week during art. The class was having a bad day. Again, they thought of using what I had taught them. The art teacher later told me that they had caught the wildness and put on the brakes, but it had slipped out of their fingers and taken over again. Oh well, so much for progress. By the end of our four weeks together, however, this class had changed remarkably. There was no more tattling, and during most days, the teacher was able to get the group settled with a gentle reminder of the 4 B's. Needless to say, this group earned their surprise.

This Chapter deals with regulating excitability and controlling impulses. Some children, particularly those with ADHD or other neurological problems, cannot feel that they are aroused. (It is important to realize that brain research is now showing that trauma and abuse can cause physical changes in the brain structure, creating such neurological vulnerability.) They need movement activities that create a high level of arousal in a safe situation before they can become aware of the sensation that arousal creates in their bodies. This chapter and Chapter Six present activities that explore where and how children feel arousal. Once they are able to recognize their feelings of arousal at high levels of intensity, only then will they be able to develop an awareness at lower levels. A child cannot be expected to regulate him/herself if unaware of internal body sensations. Once this skill is developed in movement, the goal becomes relating it to events in everyday life and expanding awareness to these events. Some children need more intensive movement work than is available in prevention classes. Individual or small group dance/movement therapy is recommended in those cases.

 ## Energy Modulation: Learning How to Stay Calm and Alert

> Develop more awareness of energy and excitement levels.

> Gain more general body awareness.

> Learn the difference between being excited in-control and excited out-of-control.

> Learn to recognize the early body signals of excitement or agitation.

> Learn the body sensations of feeling calm.

> Distinguish between calm energy and no energy in movement and feelings.

> Learn what energy level is needed in different situations.

> Learn specific techniques for calming down such as the 4 B's, abdominal breathing, and relaxation.

> Practice switching from one energy level to another.

> Practice energizing techniques for use when sluggish.

> Practice using self-talk to sustain calm, alert energy.

> Gain mastery over focusing techniques such as the 4 C's to aid attention and concentration.

> Practice sustaining calm, alert energy while moving.

SPECIFIC MOVEMENT SKILLS TAUGHT:
> The movement skill and strategies involved in modulating energy.
> Learn to move using high energy while maintaining control.
> The steps involved in calming down after being excited and in high energy.
> Learn to stop short as a way to control self when overexcited.
> Learn abdominal breathing and how to add breathing after stopping short.
> Learn to sustain calm, alert energy.
> The importance of and how to utilize self-talk.
> Relaxation techniques.
> Learn the 4 B's of Self-Settling.
> Monitor internal sensations of excitement to know the body cues related to in control, relaxed, calm-alert, and over excited.
> Learn to sustain a feeling of being connected to the ground, to being down to earth, settled.

DISCUSSION TOPICS:
> What are the different body sensations related to tense vs. relaxed or frozen vs. melted?
> What does it feel like in your body when you are in control of your movement, your body?
> How is it different from being out of control? How can you tell when you are in control vs. out of control?
> What are the characteristics of high energy in control?
> Discuss the effects and purposes of abdominal breathing.
> What is the difference between calm energy and no energy?
> How do people change their energy level and when might they want to do so?
> How do you remind yourself to stop and breath when you are not in prevention class? What body cues act as a reminder?
> Discuss the importance of self-talk in affecting mood and behavior.
> What thoughts and sensations did you have during relaxation or while doing the 4 C's.
> What does developing attention and connection to the ground have to do with violence prevention and resisting temptation?
> How does stress affect your body? What can you do to relieve that stress?

Most violence occurs when a person or group is agitated or physiologically aroused. Agitation, or stress, is a physiological state that prepares the body to stand and fight or, alternatively, to flee danger. This state reflects the body's primitive reaction to circumstances that are perceived as scary, threatening, stressful, exciting, irritating, or dangerous. While the fight/flight reaction is still important for our survival, we are no longer living in the prehistoric conditions in which such a reaction was essential. Fighting or fleeing are no longer our only options nor are they appropriate in many situations. Our physiological reactions, however, have not kept pace with our changing culture. As a result, many people find themselves aroused (i.e. racing pulse, shallow breath, raised blood pressure, suppressed digestive system, tense muscles) much more often than is healthy for them. The consequences of this are seen in an increase in the frequency of psychosomatic ills such as headaches, irritable bowel syndrome, insomnia, nausea, or depression (Davis, Eshelman, & McKay, 1995). We also see this in widespread difficulty in controlling arousal, manifested in an increase in violence. "As our anger builds, it is as if each annoying event acts as a mini-trigger to sustain and intensify the anger we are feeling. When feelings of anger get to a certain point, they are extremely hard to contain" (Elias, Tobias, & Friedlander, 1999, p. 222). When there is not enough time between stressful events for us to regain a calm state, several of our body systems, such as our immune system, are compromised. Our bodies keep releasing stress chemicals to keep us alert. The end result is one stress piled on top of another, making us ready to explode over trivial incidents. And once we are in the "explode mode" it is very hard to regain control.

> Joann is two-years-old. She has been shopping all afternoon with her mother and has missed her nap. By the time Joann and her mother get home, it is time to make supper. Joann is understandably tired and cranky. Mom puts Joann on the floor to play and starts dinner. Joann starts whining. She wants to be picked up. Mom tries to engage Joann in a television show, but that doesn't work. Then the dog runs by and knocks Joann down. Whining turns into crying. Mom tries to comfort her but has supper cooking on the stove. Within fifteen minutes of coming home, Joann is in the middle of a full-blown tantrum. Nothing Mom does can calm Joann, who cries herself out in about thirty minutes.

Joann had one stress after another and finally fell apart completely. Had Mom been able to foresee her child's crankiness and either not shopped as long or had some finger foods to give the toddler immediately upon coming home, the tantrum might have been averted. Paying attention to changes in tone quality, excitement level, tiredness, etc. can help parents predict and avert many potential disasters. This same premise is at work in older children and adults. Paying attention to inner arousal and outer reactions that indicate rising levels of stress allows one a chance to do something about it. If these indicators are ignored, violence may be the price. Self-awareness of arousal levels, the ability to calm down through relaxation and cognitive control, and skills in physical release of tension are all essential components of a violence prevention program.

Before elaborating on the techniques involved in obtaining these essential skills, there are several questions about the topics of self-control and arousal that need to be addressed. Why do some people seem to become agitated so easily while others are able to stay calm through almost anything? Does genetics determine excitability? If so, why try to do anything about it?

Genetics clearly does play a major role in one's temperament. "Temperament describes a range of different characteristics that include not only our typical energy level but also our speed in adjusting to new situations; the intensity of our emotions; our sensitivity to sights, sounds, smells, feelings, and tastes; and more" (Kurcinka, 1992, p. 25). There are nine traits that work together to form each child's inherited temperament: 1) intensity, 2) persistence, 3) sensitivity, 4) perceptiveness, 5) adaptability, 6) regularity, 7) energy, 8) first reaction, and 9) mood.

Most parents will agree that some babies are calm and easy going from birth while others are intense and moody. To some extent, your inborn temperament has an impact on who you will become as an adult. Jerome Kagan, a developmental psychologist at Harvard University, believes that fearful or intense people are born with a neurochemistry that is easily aroused; they have a low threshold for stimulation. But being born timid does not mean you will become a timid adult; your outcome is not chiseled in stone. In Kagan's studies, one-third of the children who started out timid were no longer in that range by the time they started kindergarten (Goleman, 1995, p. 221-223). Parents and teachers can have a major impact on the social-emotional skills a child acquires. "The emotional lessons of childhood can have a profound impact on temperament, either amplifying or muting an innate predisposition. The great plasticity of the brain in childhood means that experiences during those years can have a lasting impact on the sculpting of neural pathways for the rest of life" (Goleman, 1995, p. 221).

Unfortunately, this sculpting can be detrimental as well as beneficial. Childhood neglect and abuse can actually change brain functioning, making a child more excitable and less able to function cognitively. Children living in a violent household may need to stay aroused in order to stay safe. As a result, someone brushing past them, or even events happening outside their personal sphere, can be interpreted as hostile or threatening. This over-arousal has a direct impact on aggression.

The latest brain research indicates that emotional trauma effects the structure of the brain, making it more vulnerable to arousal, among other issues (Goleman, 1995). Is the structural damage permanent? Is there any point to working on self-settling? No one knows if brain damage is permanent. But if negative experiences can influence the brain structures, one can reasonably assume that positive experiences can also. The focus of this chapter, however, is not how easily children can become aroused but rather how skilled they can become at settling themselves when aroused. And growth in this area is possible for all children, no matter what their temperament or background.

The child who is easily aroused is at risk for becoming either a bully or a target for bullying. Easy arousal can lead to a child's behavior escalating, resulting in frequent violent outbursts, hence, becoming a bully. Or other's awareness of this tendency toward easy arousal could result in intentional provocation by a bully, hence, being a target. Lastly, the easily aroused child could influence an intervening adult or another child into an equal or greater level of arousal, hence, putting the interaction at risk for a violent outcome.

Let's look at several examples of typical situations where elementary school children may become aroused or angry and explore the different potential outcomes depending upon the skill level of the children involved. A common cause for fights in elementary school is cutting in line, or "budging" as it is locally known.

> Sammy was a child who was easily aroused to anger. While he was standing in line one day waiting to go to the lunchroom, Rose cut in front of him. Sammy immediately became angry. He pushed Rose while shouting at her. Rose bumped into somebody else, and the whole class fell apart in domino fashion. The result: three children ate their lunches in the principal's office and lost their lunch recess.

> The following week, Rose cut in front of another child, Max. (We won't explore here why Rose keeps cutting. That is for another story.) Max was a fairly easygoing kid. He told Rose to stop, and when she didn't listen, he decided to ignore it. When the teacher came by, he saw that Rose was not in her place and gently moved her back. The result: there was no fight and no one was sent to the office.

Another common area for fights to occur is on the playground.

> Morgan was a child who cried and flailed about each time she was teased or was involved in an activity that did not go her way. Taylor had witnessed Morgan's tantrums several times and discovered how easy it was to get a rise out of her. Recess became a constant stress for Morgan as Taylor, along with several other

children, got into the habit of provoking her in order to watch "the show." Morgan became a target and was being bullied. Morgan's helplessness aroused the urge to gain control or power in children who had a lack of self-esteem or a sense of well-being during recess. This example was brought to my attention in a prevention class. After much coaching in staying settled along with pairing Morgan with a classmate who helped her stay calm, Morgan started to respond differently to the teasing and provocation. This, plus some work on empathy, helped Taylor and the other children to try interacting in different ways. These changes did not happen overnight, and on bad days, Morgan's over-sensitivity still caused problems, but there were far fewer tearful trips to the recess teacher.

While we are looking at recess examples, Sammy, the easily aroused child from the lunch line, also provoked others. He experienced feelings of excitement from interacting with older, more powerful children. He both feared getting hurt, physically or emotionally, by them and craved acceptance at the same time. This tension and excitement propelled him to act impulsively and inappropriately, almost inviting bullying. During one recess, Sammy approached Casey, who was two grade levels above him, and made a side comment about Casey's mother. Sammy thought he was just being goofy. But for Casey, it was no laughing matter. It was immediate provocation for a fight. Sammy, of course, was the injured one and had no understanding of why he was beaten up.

Lack of awareness between the cause and effect of one's behavior is, unfortunately, becoming more and more common. Developing the ability to self-settle or relax gives a child, such as Sammy, an extra moment to think before acting. Self-settling skills increase impulse-control.

When children like Sammy go home after a stressful day at school, they are ready to explode at the slightest request of their parents. This explosion may involve behaviors such as swearing, throwing things around, or just intense pouting. This extreme response to a minor demand might outrage mom or dad, who may have been calm to begin with. Parents can become aroused in response to the intensity of their child's reactions. With the whole family in an escalated state of arousal, it is likely that the consequences will be disproportionate to the circumstances, creating a risk for physical punishment. An easily aroused child can create high levels of arousal in the whole household, making it necessary for the parents to learn self-calming strategies to help themselves as well as their child.

Of course, a child like Sammy may come from a home where physical aggression is a common occurrence. And Sammy's easy arousal and drive toward being aroused at school could be a reflection of the hyper-vigilance he needs to maintain his safety at home.

Regardless of the cause of arousal, whether genetic propensities or environmental stressors, the ability to regulate tension in one's body and to calm down when agitated is essential for both physical well-being and emotional harmony. The more able we are to find ways of releasing stress, the more likely we will find peaceful solutions to conflicts.

The self-control developed by learning to manage arousal is a pre-cursor to anger management. In this chapter, we will explore two types of self-control. In one type of situation, children are taught to become aware of growing agitation and can use relaxation or self-settling strategies to calm themselves down before they reach the boiling point. In the second type of situation, boiling is just about to happen, and there is no time for slowly calming down. It is necessary to STOP quickly, to put on the brakes as it were.

To know what intervention is necessary in order to maintain control requires an on-going self-awareness of one's arousal level. As stated in the beginning of the chapter, there are many children who lack the ability to monitor their arousal level because they are unaware of the bodily sensations it creates. Since some of these children need more frequent help than the prevention curriculum can provide, I rely on teachers to monitor external signs of tension in their students and cue them to use different strategies. This has worked well as a stop gap measure and, in some cases, has helped children become more aware of these feelings in themselves.

There are several stages in the arousal or stress cycle, each involving different body sensations and requiring a different type of intervention. The first stage involves doing what you can to avoid or modify certain stressors in the first place. This calls for advanced planning and eliminates the need to become aroused. For example, if I know that there is construction on my route to work, I can either leave earlier or come up with an alternate route. In this stage, you manage controllable stressors ahead of time so that you do not encounter them to begin with.

But what if I do not know about the construction and find myself stuck in a traffic jam? The next stage in the arousal cycle involves becoming cognitively aware of the stressor. While for some people, being late would not be a stressor, for me, it is. (This raises an important point about stress management. Different individuals respond differently to the same stimuli. Each person, therefore, has his/her own set of stress triggers, which must be respected.) Getting stuck in a traffic jam on my way to work and becoming aware that I am going to be late starts out as a cognitive stressor. I am not emotionally or physiologically aroused yet, but I know that I hate to be late. At this point in the stress cycle, I can use "self-talk" to keep from getting aroused. I might say to myself, "It's okay Rena. You are hardly ever late, and you can't do anything about it anyway. Stay calm." I can use rational thought to attempt to control my stress level. If this works, I don't need to do anything else; I have handled a potentially stressful situation.

If attempts at self-talk do not work, the next stage is usually mild emotional arousal. During this stage people can feel themselves beginning to get tense and upset. Still stuck in traffic, let us say that I am worried about my waiting University students, and, instead of staying calm with positive messages, I start playing negative scenarios in my mind. I can feel tension in my head and stomach. (Different people have different areas where they tend to hold tension.) During the stage of mild emotional arousal, relaxation is a good intervention. Now, I don't suggest closing your eyes and lying down while driving, but slow abdominal breathing can do the trick. I have used this tactic many times when I feel myself getting upset with my children. When it works, it helps me to handle those stressful moments without building up to an explosion. The slow, controlled breathing releases the tension and, in combination with positive self-talk, is a very powerful tool.

If mild emotional arousal is not settled and stress continues unabated, the stress cycle progresses to physiological arousal. This is the stage where the "emotional hijacking" described by Daniel Goleman can take place where "a center in the limbic brain proclaims an emergency, recruiting the rest of the brain to its urgent agenda. The hijacking occurs in an instant, triggering this reaction crucial moments before the neocortex, the thinking brain, has had a chance to glimpse fully what is happening, let alone decide if it is a good idea" (Goleman, 1995, p.14). In an emergency or crisis, this "hijacking" is our way to be ready to take action immediately. Sometimes this action saves our life, but it can also cause undesirable behavior such as violence. Whatever happens, at this stage in the arousal cycle physical action of some type is needed before relaxation and self-talk will help.

In developing self-control, non-aggressive physical action needs to be substituted for the urge to fight. If the thinking part of the brain, the cortex, can process and help mediate what action to take seconds after this type of arousal happens, then the ability to stop and wait when your life isn't threatened is a good skill. In some situations, intervening earlier may have prevented this high level of arousal from happening in the first place. Other times the arousal happens instantly with no chance to relax or use self talk before the physiological arousal escalates.

One day, I was driving home from work and got caught in an extensive traffic jam. I talked to myself in order to stay calm and turned on some music to help me stay relaxed. As the traffic was barely creeping along, I decided to wait until I had two or three car lengths in front of me before progressing. This was an attempt to save gas and to relax while waiting. I was paying attention to the music when out of nowhere, I heard a pounding right next to my ear. I turned and there was a very large man pounding on my window, screaming at me to move along and stay with the traffic. I became physiologically aroused instantly. This was the fight/flight syndrome. My heart was pounding, I started sweating, my legs and arms were shaking, etc. I was scared out of my wits and extremely thankful that my windows were closed. I immediately locked my doors. I decided that this was not the time to attempt to change the subject or engage in other interactive strategies. I had recently heard of several shootings concerning road rage and did not want to become a victim.

I would have gladly fled, but all of the side streets were blocked by construction. I, therefore, decided to ignore his presence outwardly but to follow his request. He got back in his truck, and I nervously and meticulously inched forward every time the car in front of me moved until I reached my turn-off. I was angry with this man and had a desire to yell back at him when he pounded on my window, but I controlled myself, knowing that this was not a good idea. When I got home I was too agitated and upset to lay down and relax. Physiological arousal needs a physical release. I achieved release by shaking out my whole body and then going for a long walk.

As pointed out above, one way to eliminate stress is to cognitively recognize a potentially stressful situation and then figure out a way to avoid or modify the stressor. Children can be taught to recognize what kinds of situations lead to a loss of control so that they can either avoid them or learn new skills to deal with them in the future (Elias, Tobia, & Friedlander, 1999; Kurcinka, 1992). But what happens when stress is unavoidable and some type of arousal is inevitable?

A crucial part of stress management is learning how to monitor one's arousal level and learning how to calm down or return to equilibrium after becoming stressed. This relates to violence prevention because over-arousal can lead to acting out in anger or other out-of-control behaviors. And, anger management, of course, has to be dealt with in a violence prevention program. But anger is a difficult emotion to deal with. Its strength can be scary or addictive. It is important first to become competent in dealing with arousal when anger is not involved before trying to teach anger management. For example, if I need to learn relaxation to help me control or cope with migraine headaches, it is not going to work very well if I try to learn it when I am in pain. First I need to achieve a level of competency while pain free and then learn to apply the technique when the pain is just beginning, when the pain has increased, etc. In the same way, when teaching children to manage anger, I begin by teaching them about excitability so that the emotional component is not interfering with learning the skill of self-regulation. In order to do this, I have divided the skills necessary for anger management into three chapters. This chapter deals with regulating excitability and controlling impulses. Chapter Four will include activities to help build awareness of where individual children feel arousal in their body and how to ignore provocation so that anger does not build. And Chapter Six will deal with educating children about emotions and emotional expression, including anger management.

The ability to control excitability is directly related to impulse control, which has an impact not only on violence but on school performance as well. Many teachers have complained about the stress involved in teaching classes in which many of the children have control problems. I use imagery to introduce the idea of energy modulation to children. Storms are natural situations that all children have experienced in which energy builds to a high level and then slowly dissipates. Acting out this energy cycle allows children, who ordinarily have difficulty with self-settling, to gain a sense of what calming down feels like in their own body.

The acting out of the storm happens in self-space (the space around your body without traveling). When this is mastered, animal imagery can be used to extend mastery to general space. The general space is divided into different energy zones (low, medium and high) and the children move as animals or as themselves in these zones, moving from one level of energy to another. After the children are competent at expressing energy modulation in this context, more dramatic elements can be added in the "wild" zone to increase the excitement level. These could include a tornado or even a monster. The children have to return to the calm zone to reach the safety of their home base, and the goal is to be able to stay settled afterwards. (One of the many advantages of a movement-based program is that it allows the experience of self-control to happen on a gross motor level, which is where most loss of control happens.)

Once self-regulation is achieved in play, I introduce the image of an internal thermostat that measures and controls arousal and energy. Sometimes the temperature needs to be lowered in order to calm down and decrease the energy level. Impulsive, excitable children have to deal with this task often. There are also times when the temperature needs to be raised. When that jerk pounded on my window, I had to mobilize, I had to be alert in order to stay safe. Many children have reported difficulties in mobilizing for certain tasks. These tasks sometimes deal with school or home performance (e.g. getting going in the mornings, getting work done on time), and sometimes they deal with safety issues such as being sluggish about recognizing and mobilizing for danger. There are children who just seem unaware of what is happening around them. The thermostat image can be transferred to many situations.

Once these gross motor, creative experiences have been integrated, it is important to challenge the children to utilize this skill outside of prevention class. Bear in mind how hard it is to develop new habits, and be prepared to coach and remind children before their behavior is out of control. Offering some kind of reward gives the children incentive to work on generalizing the skill of energy regulation. The compensation that you as the adult will have when the children do generalize it will make it worth the effort. Success requires cueing and keeping track of the number of times children are successful at settling.

When arousal reaches a certain level, slowing down is not effective on its own. The ability to put on the brakes or stop short must be experienced. I have children practice this by running full tilt across a large area and stopping short at a specific, designated spot. We practice this many times before children can feel that stopping short requires pulling back or tensing certain muscles. The next step involves pretending to be wild and out of control in self-space and then stopping short. The experience of holding the stop gets uncomfortable because it means putting tension in the body. When this discomfort is recognized and linked to the possibility of anger, relaxation is introduced as a way to release the tension. Children are taught abdominal breathing and, when time permits, are also taught one of two relaxation techniques. The concept of positive self-talk is also introduced. A four-step sequence called, "The 4 B's of Self-Settling," integrates all the above ideas. Briefly, the sequence includes BRAKES, which entails stopping with an abrupt movement that ends in an isometric push; BREATHING, which entails abdominal breathing while lifting the arms to expand lung capacity; BRAIN, which entails telling one's self to calm down while gently pushing down on the head with both hands; and BODY, which entails bringing the hands to the chest and feeling the heart beat slow down. (See the 4 B's handout, which illustrates this movement sequence.)

The repetitive sounds and ritualized movements provide a framework for these settling techniques and a memory aid for children to access when outside of the classroom. This sequence is elaborated in Activity 8.

A group of second grade classes had more than its share of distractible children. All four classes went through the energy modulation activities and were taught the 4 B's of Self-Settling. The classes were then given the 4 B's handout and a challenge sheet to monitor their success. After several weeks of work, each class succeeded in meeting its goal. In the following weeks I began to hear stories that children were cueing the class to use the 4 B's, or were simply using it themselves and finding that other children just naturally joined in. But the real highlight for me was when the entire second grade used the 4 B's in the cafeteria to successfully calm down. Several of the children came to my class bubbling over with the news of this event and how successful it had been. Teachers made comments suggesting that this was like therapy for the whole class. One teacher picked the three times during the day that her class frequently had problems and used the 4 B's successfully to prevent these problems. Other teachers have used it intermittently, as needed. All have reported success with it.

One of the ways to decrease the frequency of the need to use the 4 B's is to increase attention span and self-control. An activity called "The 4 C's of Control Time" was designed with this in mind. Children practice being upright and still for longer and longer periods of time. They practice focusing on one thing while they keep their body in control. The sequence for this activity is as follows: CONNECT TO THE GROUND, which entails having the children stand or sit upright and feel the ground or chair under them and feel their body holding themselves up. (Feeling the ground and their body is important because many children with attention problems do not feel them at all when they are still. This is part of the reason they move around so much.) COLLECT YOUR THOUGHTS AND CALM DOWN entails having the children calm their bodies and minds and say to themselves, " I can be focused and calm." Saying positive messages to oneself has a major impact on performance. CONCENTRATE ON ONE THING AT A TIME entails choosing one thing to look at and/or think about while doing this activity. CREATE STILLNESS entails having the children keep perfectly still (except for breathing and blinking) while feeling the floor or chair under them. Encourage them to stay aware of their body and breathing.

I used this activity with the same group of second graders discussed above. Almost all of the children were able to master two minutes of stillness. I found their reactions showed a full range of strategies for self-control. One child described standing there and finding his arm itching. He remained still, and the itch got worse and worse until it felt like a thousand bees were stinging him. He remained still despite the itch, and it finally went away. Then his eye started to itch. He ignored that, and it too stopped. Finally he had no more itches and could relax in stillness. Several children described being restless the first minute, wishing the activity were done, and then finding themselves relaxed and enjoying it during the second minute. (I have a timer that I set for one minute at a time so the children know when they are halfway done.) They were surprised by the change in their perception. Other children described being in a dream-like state in which they imagined different story scenarios. A few children felt the floor lower with them on it, and some felt like they were floating.

> *One teacher in particular has been using the control time activity with her class. She had been going home everyday totally overwhelmed by the unruly and distractible behavior her class exhibited. Three weeks into using the control time, she has noticed a significant improvement. Her class has a long way to go, but they just received their first reward from me for two weeks of using a skill successfully.*

As discussed earlier, some children have a more difficult time with regulating their arousal levels. They get excited or upset more often and more quickly, and it may take longer to regain control. Taking a "control time" is a helpful image for some of these children. Instead of sending them to a time out, which is viewed punitively, a child who has learned the skills in this chapter, may be able to take a control time. Teachers or parents can help children learn to sense when settling is needed by cueing them. Cueing can be done verbally to reflect behavior as in "I notice you are getting loud and antsy. You seem to be getting overexcited. It looks like you need to take a control time." Or cueing could be a code, either a word which could be as obscure as "tree" or as concrete as "control time," or it could be a nonverbal signal such as the adult tugging his/her ear. This code needs to be worked out between adult and child beforehand and works best if it is done before the arousal has gotten to the point of a child being completely out of control. The earlier in the arousal cycle that you, the adult, are able to sense the rising tension and can suggest taking a control time, the greater the chance for success.

A special spot can be set up in the classroom or at home where anyone who is in the process of becoming, or is already, too excited, upset, angry, etc. to function productively, can go to take a control time. The spot should preferably face the wall or at least away from the dominant activities. Some children may need to leave the room to settle themselves.

At school, it can be helpful to have a special spot in the principal's or counselor's office where children could go at their own initiative to calm down. At home you can also designate a special spot, one where no television or video games are available. Needing a control time should not be viewed as being sent to the office for being bad but rather as a positive attempt of a child trying to self-settle. At first you, the adult, may be the one suggesting the need for a control time to the child, but the long-term goal is that the child will take the initiative. At school, you might use a special laminated note (like a hall pass) hung on the wall that a child could grab as needed for going to this spot. Have a system worked out ahead of time with school staff so everyone knows where the child is going and what they need to do before returning to class. When a child is getting agitated, having to explain their attempt at settling to everyone is the last thing s/he needs.

A kindergarten boy, who had emotional and physical problems, was regularly having major tantrums in class. These tantrums made him stand out as different and made it hard for him to make friends. After working on energy modulation with his class, the teacher decided to incorporate a regular control time for him. He was given a chance to go to the nurse's office, where it was quiet, each day after lunch recess. (Coming back from lunch recess was always a difficult time for him since he seemed to get over-stimulated.) This quiet time cut down on his tantrums considerably.

Obviously one cannot assume that this strategy will work for all children who need settling. There are children who would run out of the building or take the laminated pass as a ticket to mayhem instead of going to the designated spot. There are also children who might use it to avoid difficult schoolwork or household chores. There are, however, many children who are able to use help learning self-regulation. A positive system always ends up providing better and longer lasting results.

A few years ago, there was a second grade boy receiving special education services for emotional problems. This boy had major temper tantrums that would become violent. The special education teacher had worked with me for many years and decided to try instituting control times using one of my stretch sacks, which are enclosed sacks made out of Spandex with a Velcro™ opening. (See Chapter Nine for a more detailed description.) This particular child loved to thrash about in the containment of the sack.

A program was set up, allowing him to earn points if he left the regular classroom when he started to have a tantrum and regained control by going to the special education office to use a stretch sack. The main worry was whether he would make it to the office or end up running through the halls. Everyone was pleasantly surprised with his compliance to the program. In addition, even though he was already starting a tantrum, he always took off his shoes before getting into the sack, as everyone always did in the movement class. That meant, even in the middle of a tantrum, the motivation that the stretch sack provided, in addition to the habits developed in the movement classes, enabled him to regain control safely and effectively.

It is helpful to set up rules that make the control space a place just for relaxing or regaining control. Headphones with quiet music could be available, but avoid stimulating material. The child will still be responsible for schoolwork or house-work missed once s/he calms down. A chart or tokens could be set up as recognition for using this system and keeping in control.

Some teachers might choose to have their whole class practice a control time when only one or two children may need to calm down. Everyone can benefit from practicing this skill, and doing it this way can keep the children having problems from having to leave the room or stand out. This may work well only if the control time is requested early enough in the arousal cycle. Teachers can also use the control time for the class after recess or during an exciting day. A parent can call a control time for the whole family when everyone or almost everyone is getting agitated. These group control times can consist of "shaking out" in place, doing the 4 B's and then taking a minute to feel the ground and to be still. For variation, it sometimes helps to turn out the lights, have everyone close their eyes, and do whatever relaxation technique has been previously taught. Alternatively, one could have the whole group (family or class) do the 4 B's together a few times. The point is, after learning methods for self-settling, it takes practice and reinforcement to develop them into practical skills. The more children are given positive reminders or foreshadowing such as "I know everyone is excited about the party this afternoon. Let's use the 4 B's or the 4 C's before each activity today so we can stay in control," the more likely it is that the children will begin to use these techniques on their own when needed.

What follows are a series of activities designed to teach children how it feels to get overexcited and how to regulate that arousal. I have included a lot of activities. They are not all necessary, but many of them build on each other. You combine parts of one with another. Start by learning these activities, and then experiment with adapting them for your particular group's needs. It is important to realize that children will not be able to utilize the 4 B's of self-control if they haven't experienced and practiced some of the self-regulating activities beforehand. Over the twenty plus years I have worked as a dance/movement therapist, I have found over and over again that children need to experience something in their whole body, and play with that experience, before they can make changes in their every-day life. This is one of my favorite units to teach.

 ## Activity 1, Energy Modulation: Statue/Holding Shapes

Overview: Children practice making shapes to represent statues in a museum. The shapes change at the teacher's request as if the teacher is now in a new room in the museum. The children practice holding these shapes for longer and longer periods, up to one minute.

Teaching Thoughts: I frequently do this activity in conjunction with the space unit. During the space bubble activity, when the children practice moving while maintaining a large space bubble, I have them freeze inbetween different styles of moving. I use this pause as a chance to introduce making and holding statues. Combining space and self-control right away helps control problem behaviors. The discipline of holding a shape in conjunction with becoming spatially aware seems to increase the child's investment in the program as well as establishing basic skills that will be used more extensively later in the curriculum.

Activity 2, Energy Modulation: Statues/Freezing and Melting

Children are frozen into interesting shapes.

The statues melt and the children slowly go down to the floor. The instructor wiggles the children gently to see if they are floppy (relaxed).

Overview: The children make statues for a pretend museum. The teacher checks them to see if they can hold their shape, remaining stiff even when gently pushed. One room in the museum has ice sculptures and the heat melts the statues into puddles of water. The teacher checks children by lifting one arm and trying to wiggle it back and forth (is it limp?) or by gently pushing their bodies while lying down to see if their bodies wiggle without tension.

Teaching Thoughts: This activity can also be integrated into the space unit.

Activity 3, Energy Modulation: Introduction to Self-Control

Overview: Individually or in small groups, children demonstrate the ability to move with high energy while staying in control. They can move in any way they choose. Discussion leads to defining the qualities involved in being in control while moving as well as the steps for calming down after moving with high energy.

Teaching Notes: The idea that you can be excited and wild and full of energy all while being in control is a new concept to many children. When I have asked children how they would move if they were in high energy or excited while being in control, I've gotten responses that range from walking around the room to sitting calmly to running in a set pathway. Help children understand that being in control means that they can move in all sorts of animated ways as long as they stay spatially aware and can control where they are in relation to other people and to objects even while excited. They also have to be able to stop when it becomes necessary and switch directions quickly. During recess, high energy needs to be safely discharged. During work time in school, it is good to be able to calm down to help maintain control. The goal of this activity is to help children understand how to be safely energetic and to begin to question how to calm down when it's time to.

Activity 4, Energy Modulation: Learning Abdominal Breathing

Children doing abdominal breathing; the child in front has her stomach and chest both rising.

Overview: Abdominal breathing, in which the stomach gets larger when breathing in or inhaling and the stomach gets smaller when breathing out or exhaling, is demonstrated and then practice. Children then move in high energy and use abdominal breathing to calm down afterwards.

Teaching Thoughts: Throughout this curriculum, teachers are encouraged to re-mind children of this breathing technique whenever necessary for classroom manage-ment. It could also be brought up with par-ents so that children can practice it at home. In addition, discuss with the chil-dren how they can become aware of when they need to self-settle before an adult prompts them.

The instructor places her hands over the child's hands. She has the child exhale and then exerts slight pressure on the abdomen to help the child feel it rise.

If the majority of the children in the class cannot move with high energy while be-ing in control, the skill of self- control will require additional practice time. This practice will need to start with movement activities that do not require traveling such as Activity 5.

Activity 5, Energy Modulation: Energy Modulation in Place (The Storm)

Overview: The cycle of a storm (calm, building energy, peak or intense energy, gradual or sudden return to calm) is used to dramatize the concept of energy modulation. Children will explore the various levels of energy in their own space and will practice matching the intensity of an imaginary storm, which will be created with percussion instruments.

Teaching Thoughts: The imagery of the storm gives this activity containment, which is useful for internalizing the skill of calming down. This activity can be enjoyable for people of all ages. It is a good example of the normal energy changes that take place in nature. It is very empowering for children to realize that, to some extent, they have skills that allow them to control their energy.

Activity 6, Energy Modulation: Energy Zones

Overview: The room is divided into three zones: calm, medium, and wild. The children explore moving from one zone to another so that the observers can tell which energy level they are attempting to demonstrate and if it correctly corresponds to the area in the room that they are moving in. This is followed by a fantasy activity in which the children pretend to be animals of their choosing as long as the animals have all three energy levels in their repertoire of regular functioning. These animals then move in the different zones at the direction of the teacher and, later, in their own timing. Review the concept of wild "out of control" versus wild "in control" movement as well as calm energy versus tired, lethargic energy.

One part of the room is designated as the calm area. The middle of the room is designated for medium energy. The nearest part of the room is designated for high energy. Children move into different zones and change their energy accordingly.

Teaching Thoughts: Children generally love this activity. It can be repeated several times over the course of the curriculum. You can decide how to let the animals move from zone to zone. If your group has very good impulse control, they can switch from zone to zone at their own initiative. For ease in teaching, you may want to have only two zones, calm and wild, with the area near the dividing line being the transition area. Each time this activity is done, it is helpful to discuss what is necessary to calm down and to speed up.

Learning self-modulation is a complex skill. Again, reinforcement by the teacher is very helpful. Every time the teacher is getting ready to do a transition, such as lining up, he/she can remind the class or elicit from the class what the three steps involved in staying calm are (foreshadowing). The teacher can then challenge the class to complete the transition and stay settled. They can also challenge the class to use the technique when excited such as when coming in from recess. Keeping track of the number of times the class is able to do this successfully provides visual feedback and provides reinforcement towards generalizing the skill.

If there are children in the class who are not able to calm down, one of the following strategies may be useful. The child can be given an incentive to move in the wild zone only after he/she can demonstrate calm movements. The child may need to have an adult nearby to cue or redirect them if they start to get out of control in the wild zone. Reminders to breathe and slow down may need to be given as the child moves toward the calm zone. Some children should not be in the wild zone together. You will soon figure out who they are. Also there may be some children who simply cannot maintain control and will need to sit out. Sometimes these children can be given the role of observer and report back to the class what they see. In some classes, where there are many children who are out of control, you may need to do this activity with half of the class at a time while the other half observes. If your class is not able to manage that level of excitement, start with Activity 4 instead.

Activity 7A, Energy Modulation: Putting on the Brakes, Part 1

Children run to a designated spot where they have to stop short and feel the tension in their bodies.

Overview: Children will run at full tilt to a specified spot in the room and then stop short and freeze. The children are to stop short without slowing down in preparation but also without sliding or crashing and falling. This is repeated until children can feel that stopping short requires pulling back or putting tension in their body.

Activity 7B, Energy Modulation: Putting On the Brakes, Part 2

Overview: Children are instructed to get very wild in their own space, without traveling, and freeze on cue. They then stay in that position until they feel the discomfort of holding that amount of tension. After feeling a desire for release and its connection to aggression, they are then reintroduced to abdominal breathing and explore it as a way to release tension and settle.

Teaching Thoughts: Sometimes children feel too self-conscious to move wildly. The running activity (7a) does not evoke the same self-consciousness. If one or more of the students in a class do not exhibit enough impulse control to give you a sense of confidence that they would be able to stop short safely, you may need to modify the activity. When only one or two children lack control, you may be able to deal with the situation by having them stand or move next to you or even next to other very solid students. If this does not work, you may need to pull those students aside to practice with them separately while the rest of the class is doing a fun movement exploration. Another approach, especially if the whole class has difficulties, is to have each child demonstrate individually, then in pairs, then in trios or slightly larger groups. This will either build the ability to do these activities as a class or develop the skills in smaller groupings with a rotating part of the class always acting as observers. Yet another approach is to designate individual spots on the floor using masking tape to help children with impulse control problems maintain their own space, even if they can't freeze when told. The rest of the class then gets to practice their ignoring skills, which are introduced in another chapter.

Activity 8, Energy Modulation: The 4 B's of Self-Settling

Overview: Children learn a movement phrase to go with the words, "brakes," "breathing," "brains," "body" that can be used as a self-settling technique in various situations, both inside and outside of the classroom. The technique is reinforced with an accompanying handout, which may be posted in a prominent place and referred to regularly.

Children catch the energy and do an isometric push to contain it.

Teaching Thoughts: In order for children to integrate the use of this technique, adults must be willing to cue them at appropriate times and positively reinforce its use. If done correctly, this sequence does calm people down. If children are still wiggly

Children take 2-3 slow deep breaths.

Children take another deep breath and tell themselves they can calm down.

after doing the 4 B's once, have them do it again. Make sure they squeeze their arms together with strength, and supervise their breathing to make sure it is slow and full, involving the abdomen.

Activity 9, Energy Modulation: The 4 C's of Control Time

Overview: Children stand in their own space, trying to feel the ground and their body, and they are instructed to find one thing to focus on or think about. Using self-talk, they are then expected to stand perfectly still for from one to five minutes. A mnemonic phrase (called the 4 C's) elaborated below, is used to help them master the steps involved in the process. The technique is reinforced with an accompanying handout, which may be posted where the children can easily see it and refer to it (see handout).

Teaching Thoughts: In a gymnasium, this can be done with everyone having a large space bubble. When in the classroom, have them stand next to their chairs. While children prefer to do this activity sitting, they tend to slump over and lean on their arms when doing so. The goal is to instill the discipline of remaining upright, and children are more used to doing this while standing. Once children can be still for at least a minute while standing, you can have them try it while sitting upright with their hands in their lap, feeling the seat or the ground underneath their bottoms. It is important in this activity to feel your body and the ground while staying still. Sometimes activities such as acting out a storm in place are needed to help establish the feeling of the feet being attached to the floor before doing the 4C's.

The teacher has to decide whether to model staying still or to survey the room to assess how children are doing. Both serve their purpose. If one or two children are having difficulty, and, as a result, they act in a distracting manner, instruct the class to practice their ignoring skills and challenge them to complete the task successfully. Have an adult stand next to or near the child you predict is going to have the most trouble staying still. Many times, you can hook the class in by challenging them with the difficulty of the task.

While this activity may be very difficult for children with ADHD, I have been pleasantly surprised to see that most of them can succeed at this task for at least a minute. The more these children practice focusing, the better their focusing skills should become. Children can learn to strengthen and increase their attentional abilities. There may be some children who cannot do this for a whole minute at first. Design the activity for success – if 15 seconds is possible, make that the initial goal. If these children are in a full class group, don't penalize them for not making the class goal; praise the whole class instead. Keep challenging the children who have difficulty to increase the amount of time they can hold still. It is important to maintain a positive environment and attitude about gaining control. In one kindergarten class, there were several (6 out of 15) children with disabilities. At first, the class had a great deal of difficulty staying still for one minute. After three weeks of practicing and praise, all but one could manage it. The teacher could not believe how well they did, and the children felt a great deal of pride in accomplishing this.

Activity 10, Energy Modulation: Grounding while Sitting in the Stretch Cloth

Overview: The children sit in a circle holding on to the stretch cloth in front of them like it is a rope. Children are instructed to pull side to side on the cloth, gently at first and then with more force. The goal of the activity is for every child to maintain their balance for a count of ten while everyone is pulling. Children are encouraged to discover what they need to do on a physical level in order to keep their balance.

Teaching Thoughts: This prop is exciting, and things can get out of hand quickly. I usually precede stretch cloth use by letting the class know that I am very strict about following rules with the cloth because of its potential danger. Anyone pulling when I am giving directions or when it is not part of the activity will be sent to a time out. The cloth is like a giant rubber band, and I would suggest experimenting with small groups before using it with your whole class. (Read the section on stretch cloth use in Chapter Eight before doing any of the stretch cloth activities in this chapter.)

Not all classrooms are ready to start stretch cloth use with a pulling activity. I first need a sense that students have enough control that they will not pull too hard. Some classes need to do trust exercises or make waves with the stretch cloth before they are ready for pulling. There are an infinite number of activities that can be done with this prop.

(See Chapter Eight for stretch cloth ideas.) All classrooms can do some type of activity. It is always popular, and I hold it out as a reward at the end of a period if a class co-operates. I have also used it longer than usual as a reward for generalizing skills outside our group.

Activity 11, Energy Modulation: Grounding while Standing in the Stretch Cloth

Overview: For this activity the children stand in a circle inside of the stretch cloth. With knees bent and hips back, they are told to lean back together, letting the cloth support the class. When this is accomplished, add a gentle rock side to side to let them feel connected by the cloth and affected by their neighbors' movements. You can add a pulling and resistance component if your class is cooperative. Children gently pull side to side and then gently twist and move forward and backward, paying attention to how everyone keeps their balance.

Teaching Thoughts: Same as Activity 10.

Activity 12: Energy Modulation: Storm in the Stretch Cloth (for pre-school to second grade)

Overview: This activity is done with children sitting in a circle inside of the stretch cloth, imagining it is a boat. The ride starts out calm, but the weather soon begins to turn cloudy and windy. It gets worse and worse until there is a big storm. When the thunder and lightning strikes, everyone hides under the cloth by pulling the upper edge and ducking under it. Eventually the storm passes, the day is pleasant again, and the children can safely come out from under the cloth.

Teaching Thoughts: I have several variations to the ending of this activity. Sometimes I just wait a minute or two and declare the storm over, we all come out from under the cloth and breathe a sigh of relief. In another variation I ask a child to peek out and decide if it is safe or not. In a third variation, we decide the boat is broken, and we fix it together so we can start again.

Activity 13, Energy Modulation: Relaxation Techniques

Progressive Relaxation Overview: Children are taught a physical technique for releasing muscular tension. The facilitator may have the children focus on particular parts of the body (like arms and hands) or may guide them to relax the entire body. This type of relaxation can be done sitting or lying down and works best when accompanied by soothing music. The facilitator may create his or her own script or follow the sample provided.

Guided Imagery Overview: Children are introduced to visualization as a technique for releasing stress. A script with concrete imagery is provided so children can practice "seeing with the mind's eye" as well as introducing more abstract

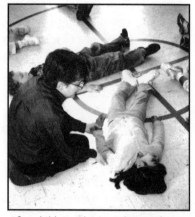

After children relax I might test their arm to see how relaxed and floppy it is.

Teaching Thoughts for Guided Imagery: The guided imagery techniques used in Activity 13B teach children an alternate strategy for relaxing their bodies. These techniques introduce children to visualization skills and engage children's imagination to reduce reactions to stressful situations. While most children are immediately able to tap into their imaginations and will easily pick up visualization skills, some children may have difficulty and become frustrated. Focusing on a picture related to the imagery can help some children. Others may require very concrete imagery. The facilitator can help the children to build their visualization skills by providing lots of descriptive adjectives and by asking the children questions such as how large or small is the object they see? What is it made of? What shape is it? What color? The facilitator can also acknowledge outloud that this may be difficult and then encourage the children to keep trying. For children who have attention disorders, consider giving them the option of drawing a picture of what they see during the imagery if they are not able to sit still for the whole time.

The guided imagery in Variation A is more concrete, which may be helpful to children who have trouble visualizing. The approach in Variation B is more open-ended. It allows each participant to find an image, which relaxes him or her. To develop this exercise more fully, whichever approach you take, ask the children what they were able to see in their mind's eye, and, if time permits, allow them to draw a picture of it.

In Activity 13B, having children draw the special place shortly after doing this exercise helps them remember little details about it. Having a small laminated picture of this placed in one's pocket so that it can be pulled out at a moment's notice has helped some people to control their anger. It can also help people to feel an immediate sense of relief or relaxation. For one father I worked with, counting to ten to control his aggression had not worked but an immediate image of a relaxing place did.

Parents' Summary about Self-Control and Stress Management

The importance of the role of the family in establishing self-control cannot be over-emphasized. From early childhood on, parents can help children learn to delay gratification and find positive ways to settle themselves when upset. The ability to resist impulses is one of the fundamental skills needed for violence control. In a study done at Stanford University in the 1960's, four-year-olds were offered two marshmallows as a treat if they could wait until the researcher ran an errand. For those who could not wait, they could have only one, but they could have it right away. These four-year-olds were studied again when they were graduating from high school. The differences between the group that could wait versus the group that needed immediate gratification were significant. The group that could wait as preschoolers was described as "...more socially competent, personally effective, self-assertive, and better able to cope with the frustrations of life. They were less likely to go to pieces...they embraced challenges and pursued them instead of giving up even in the face of difficulties. They were self-reliant and confident, trustworthy and dependable ...And, more than a decade later, they were still able to delay gratification in pursuit of their goals. The third or so who grabbed for the marshmallow, however, [needing immediate gratification] tended to have fewer of these qualities, and shared instead a relatively more troubled psychological portrait" (Goleman 1994 pgs. 81-82).

Some additional activities for improving impulse control will be explained in the following chapter. But self-settling is an important part of impulse control. In order to delay gratification, children need to learn to use self-talk and not to let enticing things get them overexcited. (There are adults who have trouble with these skills as well.) It takes practice to build character, and this practice needs to happen at home as well as at school to have an impact on society as a whole.

Chapter Summary

In this chapter, we have dealt with self-control and energy modulation. We have looked at ways to calm down when getting excited, ways to "stop" and then self-settle when the arousal level gets too high, and the importance of paying attention to one's internal thermostat. We have also been introduced to relaxation techniques as well as abdominal breathing. This chapter has many activities; not all of which need to be done in order to teach the skills of self-settling, but abdominal breathing, energy modulation, the 4 B's, and the 4 C's should not be missed.

The goals in this section are to improve energy modulation, develop grounding skills, and learn abdominal breathing and positive self-talk. In addition, children learn the 4 B's of self settling (Brakes, Breathe, Brain, Body) and the 4 C's of control time (Connect to the Ground, Collect Your Thoughts, Concentrate on One Thing, and Create Stillness). They learn to monitor internal sensations of arousal (thermostat imagery) and are introduced to relaxation techniques. Indications of readiness to move on would be seen in the ability to use the 4 B's of self-settling first with and eventually without teacher cues. There would be an increase in impulse control and attention span, and an ability to take a control time and use it effectively. An improvement in the ability to handle minor stressors would also be seen.

The next chapter deals with awareness of and responses to danger. This includes learning when and how to ignore provocation and other distractions, and provides activities to practice recognizing early warning signs of danger, as well as the timing necessary to respond to them. Included in learning how to ignore is also how to attend to or focus on what is important, whether it is simply schoolwork, or the inner focus needed to keep from becoming provoked. This combination of ignoring and attending skills often leads to increased attention spans, as well as improved impulse control.

CHAPTER FOUR

Awareness of & Response to Tense or Dangerous Situations

One day, many years ago when I was still in college, I was sent to deliver some papers from Philadelphia to Washington, D.C. I was walking back to the train station when I got an uncomfortable feeling that someone was following me. I was not sure why I had this feeling, but since it was not a common feeling for me, I thought I was probably right. Because I was not positive, however, I decided to test the situation. I stopped to adjust my shoe. The man stopped too. I went into a museum I was passing and walked through the gift shop. When I left the museum, the man did too. This convinced me that my feelings were correct. I was not petrified because I was walking down a public street with other people and figured I could get help if I needed it. (Of course if I knew then what I know now about big cities and the possibility of no one helping me, I might have been more scared.) Anyway, after several blocks of feeling uncomfortable, I finally turned to him and said in an assertive voice, "Why are you following me? I don't like it." The man was immediately defensive. "Why would I follow you? I have children of my own. I would never follow anyone." "Then stand there until I'm out of sight, or I will call the police," I said. He immediately agreed to do this, and with relief, I continued to walk to the train station.

This chapter covers three main skills, the ability to ignore provocation or distraction, the ability to sense and respond to danger, and the ability to tell which of the two skills is needed in any given situation. While it might seem at first glance that these skills are unrelated, or at least deserve to be presented separately, the idea of developing a prevention curriculum arose from the need to be aware of danger signals while ignoring provocation. When an outburst is occurring, either something verbal that is directed at you or something not directly concerning you, there are times when ignoring it is the best strategy. But, what might have started out as a good plan, may not remain one. And an awareness of when the nature of the situation changes can be crucial to the outcome.

An overview of the goals covered in this chapter follows:

Alerting: Alerting the Senses to Early Warning Signs in the Body that Signal Potential Danger

> Learning to pay attention to inner body cues, increasing children's ability to use their senses.

> Learning what early warning signs are and developing awareness of individual body cues.

> Learning how early warning signs can be used in prevention.

> Learning to trust the body's alerting system.

> Illustrating that different people interpret the same cues differently.

> Learning that further checking may be needed to tell whether or not someone is friendly.

> Increasing the ability to think and move in scary situations.

> Improving the timing needed for protective interventions.

Scanning: Increasing the Ability to Scan the Environment

> Increasing children's ability to attend to others, increasing their awareness of others.

> Developing the ability to move with control and to scan the environment at the same time, increasing observation skills.

> Learning multi-focusing skills.

> Improving attention span and impulse control.

> Improving the ability to move from an inner focus to an outer one.

Ignoring: Ignoring Provocation

> Developing individual focusing strategies to use under duress or provocation.

> Developing individual focusing strategies to use for classwork.

> Increasing ability to evaluate situations after alerted to determine if action is needed.

> Learning to refocus on the task at hand when things are safe.

> Learning to ignore distractions and provocations that do not interfere with one's safety.

> Learning to use positive self-talk to aid in ignoring skills.

> Developing and practicing various ignoring strategies using the "ABC's of Safe Ignoring."

> Connecting the ability to ignore with the ability to resist temptation.

SPECIFIC MOVEMENT SKILLS TAUGHT:

> Develop the ability to focus on and rely on inner body cues that alert one to danger.
> Learn specific cues that alert you–learn your early warning signs.
> Learn how to use senses to be alert to the environment.
> Develop the ability to use a multi-focus to scan the environment visually and kinestheticallly.
> Learn how to maintain attending skills over time.
> What strategies work for ignoring provocation.
> How to move between an innner and outer focus.
> What strategies work for resisting temptation.
> Learn the ABC's of Safe Ignoring.

DISCUSSION TOPICS:

> What are early warning signs? How do they help us? Talk about the role early warning signs have in keeping us safe.
> Have children discuss their own early warning signs as you do different activities.

> Allow children to share times they might have felt early warning signs as long as the incidents are not private.
> How did you scan the environment and still keep track of yourself in space?
> How does scanning relate to violence prevention?
> What are some strategies that are helpful when trying to ignore?
> What are important things to pay attention to and what should you ignore?
> What is the difference between tattling and reporting?
> How do you ignore something that is not dangerous but seems unfair?
> What distracts you in the classroom? What types of situations provoke you in class, on the playground, at home?
> What does ignoring have to do with resisting temptation? What temptations do you encounter?

During the 1995-96 school year, I worked with several classrooms for four weeks each, expanding a variety of movement activities to address issues that the teachers, students, and I felt were important. The ability to ignore distractions was frequently requested. Toward the end of the year, an incident occurred that was an impetus for the development of this curriculum.

I was working with a second grade class that had many children with special needs mainstreamed into the group. Since this was the second year this class was together, there was a strong group identity, but there were also frequent outbursts that disrupted the group. Consequently, we were working on developing ignoring skills. A few of the children were instructed to ignore while others tried to get them to laugh. The provokers were allowed to make faces and say and do silly things but were not allowed to touch anyone. During the activity, most of the ignorers did a good job of ignoring, but two of the provokers actually hit them and hurt them. This led us to discuss the question "How do you know when it is safe to ignore and when it is not safe?" I was amazed at how many students did not see the difference in safety between a tantrum occurring across the room from them versus one happening right next to them.

During the same year, another class of second graders was assigned to practice their ignoring skills outside of our movement class. The following week, one child reported successfully ignoring his sister, who had been teasing him, while another child reported that her brother had scribbled all over her homework as she ignored him. One child was happy, the other mad.

These were causes for concern. I was quite disturbed that I might be teaching the children something that would put them at risk. However, as a therapist working primarily in the field of sexual and physical abuse, teaching about early warning signs, physical cues that alert someone to danger, was already part of my work. It seemed to be a natural step to begin using it in movement classes as a complement to learning how to ignore. Furthermore, the children seemed delighted at the idea that they might be able to distinguish when to ignore by using their own body detection system. The violence prevention program had begun to evolve. And thus ends a long explanation of why so many discrete skills are included in one chapter.

EARLY WARNING SIGNS

The ability to sense and respond to danger is a skill that can save your life. Too many people of all ages ignore the early warning signs of danger, the sense of unease they have that something is not right, and in cases of true danger such as kidnapping, molestation, and robbery, they lose the chance to get away before anything happens. Others freeze in fear when the danger is upon them, and they also lose the chance to escape. Gavin De Becker, in an excellent book called *The Gift of Fear*, elaborates on survival signals that protect us. I recommend this book for adults and teens that would like concrete suggestions for keeping themselves safe.

In De Becker's book, he points out the conflict women and children have when they are being enticed by someone who intends to harm them. When women and children are assertive about saying no to an adult, they are thought to be rude or worse. Abductors who lure their victims are skilled at making them feel obliged to accept their help or accompany them. This results in a dilemma as to how to get out of this type of uncomfortable situation. Teenage girls, not wanting to be thought of as "frigid" or "bitchy," may say "yes" to boys when they really want to say "no." A woman in a parking lot may finally accept help from someone who insists over her protests that she accept it. Children may go off with someone who keeps pressuring them, even when they know they should not do it.

> *A seven-year-old girl, who had been enticed into doing sexual acts with her twelve-year-old brother, shared that she did not like it and had not really wanted to do it. When asked what went on in her mind before saying "yes," she said that she felt he would have just kept asking, and she knew that eventually she would have to give in. She just wanted the pressure to stop, and she did not want to hurt his feelings. She was aware of her uncomfortable feelings, but getting help did not occur to her. Even though her brother had not threatened her, she felt that she had to comply.*

Clearly, it is not enough just to be aware of early warning signs; we also need to know what to do about them. The child in the previous example had the power to act on her discomfort but did not realize it. When a trusted member of the family or community tells you to do something that does not feel right, it becomes very confusing.

The violence prevention program does not deal specifically with sexual abuse or incest, but it does inform children that they have the right to feel safe. I frequently ask children if certain activities like chasing or wrestling feel good to them. We have a rule that an activity is okay only if all members participating in it feel all right. Play is supposed to be fun for everyone (West, 1989). If there are uncomfortable or distasteful feelings, then it is not play. This includes play with parents and siblings.

If you have been following the curriculum in the order it is presented, you may be aware that we have already touched on "uh-oh" feelings during some of the spatial activities in the second chapter. During the activity with the boss line and the movers, the bosses were supposed to tell the movers to stop as soon as they (the bosses) started to feel uncomfortable. This was extended to different types of approaches to help fine-tune perceptions. This chapter delves more deeply into these "uh-oh" feelings or early warning signs. It also elaborates on activities that help children get a sense of how and where they feel these signals in their bodies. These activities teach children to trust these feelings of discomfort and act upon them.

The ability to sense and check out danger signals involves moving between an awareness of inner sensations and outer events, between an inner and outer focus. The "uh-oh feeling" is frequently first an unconscious sense that something does not fit the way it should, that something is not right. When this feeling is strong enough, you don't wait around to figure out why you are bothered. You get away. More common, however, is a vague feeling of uneasiness inside, which may or may not get the attention it deserves. Ignoring it, of course, can have devastating results.

When I was in high school, I did a lot of gymnastics just for fun. One afternoon, I was trying to learn a back flip on the trampoline. I made a mistake and ended up flying backward toward the end of the trampoline where spotters stopped me. I was shaken from the experience, so I decided to take a break. After about half an hour I realized what I was doing wrong and decided to try again. I did it correctly but realized that my body was still shaken up from before and needed to rest. Despite my body signals, wanting to make sure I had it down pat, I decided to do it one more time. Well, I didn't make it, and I ended up spraining all the muscles in my back.

Feelings of apprehension are not always indicators of danger. They can also occur when someone is about to take a challenge, e.g. speaking in front of a large group, taking on a project such as this book. Staying safe is not synonymous with living a boring life. Some stress, as long as it is not too much, is necessary for growth and fulfillment. This is where the idea of moving between an inner and outer focus becomes crucial (Peg West, SAVE curriculum, Protective Behaviors).

Inner Focus

People need to be aware of their internal sensations of unease and learn what their individual responses to danger are. Specifically, they need to discover how and where they feel their early warning signs. This helps to develop the inner focus.

The first activity I like to use is one that enhances the senses, a sneaking around game that children of all ages seem to love. Half of the group sits on the floor with their eyes closed, trying to feel when someone is approaching and to catch them at it. The other half of the group sneaks quietly around, going up to but never touching the seated children. Whenever a seated child thinks someone is approaching, the child can open his/her eyes to check. The discovered child moves away, and the seated child closes his/her eyes again. The activity and the discussion that follows it helps children to consider how all their senses give them clues. Everyone, of course, gets a turn in each role.

As adults observing this activity, there are some interesting questions to consider. What does it mean when a child never checks to see if someone is sneaking up on them? How do children who have been abused or experienced violence trust enough to close their eyes? This game, which will be described in the activity section, can be an amazing eye-opener for teachers.

One of the first times I tried this activity, it was with a class containing a second grade child with whom I had worked with in a sexual abuse therapy group. This child had been abducted from her yard and raped at the age of three. Her family had had several other traumas as well. When it was her turn to try and sense when people were sneaking up on her, she never opened her eyes once to check, even when people made noise or fanned the air around her. I had been expressing concern to the school support staff that this child did not seem to know how to keep herself safe, and here was a concrete demonstration of my fear. Thankfully, by the end of the school year this child showed some signs of using protective behaviors. Her whole family, subsequently, came to our clinic to participate in family therapy during the summer. We worked on getting mom to provide

*more adequate supervision and on getting the three children to follow through
on the safety rules that we established and practiced together.*

The strength of our particular program is the totality of the services that were
made available: classroom movement, group therapy, and family therapy. Note
that while this goes beyond the curriculum presented in this book, it clearly demonstrates how effectively a variety of services can work together.

Once children have explored the idea of their senses alerting them, we introduce
fantasy games to try to establish more specifically where in the body each child
feels their "uh-oh" feelings. Children seem to connect readily to the image of
blowing up a balloon. As they imagine it getting bigger and bigger, we pretend it
is about to burst in their face. The children are asked to pay attention to where
the tension builds in their body as they get anxious about the balloon exploding.
Another fantasy that helps children connect to their early warning signs is that of
someone suddenly jumping out of a hiding place and scaring them. The goal in
all of these fantasy games is to help each individual child recognize his/her internal warning signs.

In a third activity to help develop the alerting senses, I approach the children from
behind and have them guess whether or not I am friendly. I might approach the
whole class, small groups of children, or individuals while they sit with their backs to
me. Discussions that follow, regarding their decision, take into account the tempo
of my approach, types of sounds that put them at ease or make them nervous, the
amount of tension in the air, and any other cues they sense. This third activity relates directly to violence prevention, how one interprets and then prepares for
people approaching them. Participants in the prevention classes find it interesting
that the same cue may make one person think I'm friendly and another person think
I'm not. Note that this approach is different from anything we have done so far because the children can not depend on visual cues. Both children and adults may
express a strong desire to turn around and look at me, which of course, is normal.
It adds input to the decision we make regarding our safety. (The interpretation of
facial and postural cues will be covered in the next chapter.)

OUTER FOCUS/SCANNING

Since early warning signs can signal positive challenges as well as danger, it is important to learn how to scan the environment visually and to evaluate what is going on in order to choose the best response for that particular warning sign.
When a person feels a sense of unease, she needs to utilize a multi-focus to take

in as much as possible outside of themself in order to see what might be causing the "uh-oh" feeling inside.

The more involved you are in what you are doing or thinking, the harder it is to pay attention to what is going on around you or inside of you. This lack of awareness makes you more vulnerable to getting hurt. To develop skills in scanning or having a multi-focus, I have an activity that I use as a warmup over several sessions. I instruct the children to move around the room in different ways while watching for someone to stop. As soon as one person stops, the whole class must stop with the goal of everyone stopping in unison. This develops the ability to stay in control of your body while being aware of what others are doing (scanning). The sense of group cohesion increases tremendously when everyone is watching and stops at the same time. As the skill increases, the group is challenged to move faster or in more complex ways while maintaining their scanning techniques. The group cohesion, which develops from this scanning activity, is also helpful toward building a sense of connection to others, a pre-cursor to empathy, which will be discussed in the next chapter.

Another variation of this activity is to have everyone stand in a circle, moving in place the same way. At any point, anyone in the group can change the movement. Everyone has to watch for a change and follow along. Again the goal is for everyone to change together and move in synchrony. This activity adds some give and take because sometimes more than one person starts a new movement at the same time. Since the group can follow only one new movement, someone has to give in without a discussion. Because of this, this activity is more advanced and requires more group co-operation than the stopping activity described previously.

It is important to distinguish a multi-focus from distractibility or lack of focus. Multi-focus is the active awareness of more than one thing at a time. This is necessary for assessing danger and deciding on avenues to safety. Once children have scanned the environment, they must decide if the "uh-oh" feeling signifies danger, is a positive stress or challenge, or is something going on in the environment that distracts them but does not concern them. (This is separate from seeing someone being bullied or hurt and needing to intervene as an active witness.)

If a child assesses a situation and decides that it is not safe, s/he must get help and/or use one of the pro-active interventions that will be taught in the next chapter. In fact, discussions about what children should do if a situation is not safe can lead to an introduction to learning these interventions.

If everything is actually okay when a child checks out an "uh-oh" feeling, he/she can then return to the task at hand or, in other words, refocus. This is a suitable time to incorporate some of the self-settling skills taught in the last chapter, and it also leads to the idea of ignoring. Frequently, things going on in the hallway or the other side of the classroom or playground that do not concern them will agitate distractible children. This can lead to tattling or involvement in fights that started out having nothing to do with the child. The ability to ignore is a crucial skill in violence prevention.

IGNORING SKILLS

The concept of ignoring is an interesting one. No one wants students ignoring their parents or teachers or ignoring their work. In these areas, we actually want them to have better attention or less distractibility. Good social and academic functioning requires the ability to tune out distractions and focus on the task at hand. It also requires the ability to know when it is okay to join in something that looks inviting. But if I block out everything that does not directly concern me, am I being a good citizen? How can I be a pro-active witness if I do not let myself see what is going on around me? Can I lead an adventurous life and still be responsible? If I let everything that goes on around me distract me from the task at hand, will I ever finish anything? Life is full of balancing acts and the ability to balance a single-focus with multi-focus, and distractibility is one of these acts.

Selective attention means that I can attend to what I choose. It means that I can ignore what I need to in the way of extraneous things (background noises and such), and I can choose when to purposely ignore enticing or agitating stimuli such as provocation or a fight that an adult is already handling. Selective attention is what the prevention curriculum works to develop.

The first step involved in developing selective attention is the ability to block out unwanted stimuli. To develop this ability, children practice keeping a straight face while other children try to get them to laugh.

> My first work with a class at Lapham Elementary School was at the request of the gym teacher. She told me that this class was so full of angry children that nothing she tried from her bag of tricks would work. This was a class of first graders, and although I was anxious about whether any of my own tricks would be effective, these were young children. I had worked with children this age for over twenty years. Then the class walked in. One child (remember this is a first grader) was almost as big as I was. Now I'll admit that I am not tall for an

adult, just short of five feet, but usually children do not get taller than I am until the fifth grade. But in walks, actually, in struts this child named Larry. He sits in the circle with his class and blurts out, "So what are we going to do. I bet it's boring." He continued to verbally challenge me throughout the first half of the period, and while I outwardly ignored him, I was rather shocked at Larry's audacity. He was clearly very angry, but it was equally clear that he was movement-oriented. I waited long enough for him to experience his strength safely during some activities, then I challenged him. I told him that he could either have an attitude adjustment in order to become polite, or he would have to sit out for the rest of the period. Well, Larry really enjoyed moving and once the limit was put into place, he became cooperative in our sessions. The teachers, however, understandably continued to see him as a problem for the whole class. His personality was so strong that he was able to set off just about anyone.

This was a class that really needed to work on ignoring other students' misbehavior. Toward this end, I had half of them hop backwards across the gym, trying to keep a straight face while the other half tried to make them laugh. After attempting this several times, we discussed what strategies different students had used. Every student but Larry had added tension to their body. Many students had bitten their lips, kept their eyes averted, gripped tightly with their hands, etc. Only Larry had seemed to be able to ignore effortlessly. When asked how he could do this, he replied that he just kept his mind on other things. (Again, keep in mind this was a six-year-old.) Larry's advanced ability to ignore and his strong personality made him a leader in the classroom. I pointed out to his teachers that he could be a positive leader just as easily as a negative one, but they had to utilize his strengths as well as provide firm but positive limits.

IMPULSE CONTROL

Ignoring provocation is one way to decrease violence. Ignoring temptation is another. Ignoring temptation has to do with impulse control. It is crucial when you think about how easy it has become to obtain guns, drugs, and alcohol. The ability to resist being enticed by something harmful is one of the major skills necessary for ending violence. Anger management, empathy, and impulse control are the skills bullies need to have to stop being bullies. The ability to ignore is intricately connected to impulse-control.

There are several activities that work on this skill. Keeping a straight face as described above is one of them. Maintaining a set movement pattern while others are trying to influence you to change is another. Ignoring children who have secretly been told to break the rules, which the rest of the group has been told to follow, and resisting popping bubbles that are flying all around are two more. It is interesting to see that the strategy needed to ignore intense provocation is that of maintaining focus on something else. Children may practice focusing on their work, picturing a waterfall that washes all the provocation away, looking at their nails with fascination, meditating on an image, etc. To resist temptation, they practice self-control by breathing, self-settling, and self-talk. Teachers often see an increase in attention span and concentration when we finish this unit.

The following series of activities can be used to develop and practice the skills described above.

Alerting: Alerting the Senses to Early Warning Signs in the Body that Signal Potential Danger

Purpose:
> To increase inner focus and reliance on body cues.
> To become aware of how and where each child feels his/her early warning signs.
> To help children key into their senses, to recognize some of the non-visual cues that they use that alert them to potential danger or make them aware of stimuli in the environment.
> To develop trust in their alerting system.

Activity 1, Alerting: Alerting the Senses

Overview: Part of the class sits, eyes closed, with a very large space bubble around each person. Another part of the class tries to sneak up on the sitting classmates. The sitting children open their eyes and check every time they think someone is coming into their space. The sneaking classmate then walks away, and the sitting child closes his/her eyes again. Everyone gets to try both roles. There may also be an observer role.

Half the class scatters throughout the room and sits crosslegged with hands open, palms up, on their lap and their eyes closed.

Teaching Thoughts: If your class is large, you may need to divide it into three groups, observers, movers, and those sitting with eyes closed. Because you will have students with their eyes closed, you have to elicit a firm agreement from your class regarding not touching and really believe they will keep it. Demonstrate this by moving around a seated student, showing what distance should be maintained to prevent even accidentally touching a stray hair. Make sure that you are at least one arm length away from the seated student. If there is a student whose behavior is questionable, you may need to move with that student. Smaller groupings are more manageable. Any touching results in sitting out.

The other half of the class tries to sneak up on the sitting children. If a seated child thinks someone is coming close, he opens his eyes and checks.

It is very difficult for students to keep from giggling or running excitedly from sitting student to sitting student. Be prepared for this reaction and talk about it. If the children begin to get noisy or move too quickly, stop the activity for a second, have them take a calming breath, and start again.

Activity 2, Alerting: Breaking Balloons

Overview: Children have imaginary balloons that they pretend to blow up. The balloons get very large and the children keep blowing until the balloon is about to burst at which point they try to feel where in their body they feel anxious.

Teaching Thoughts: Discussion is a very important part of this activity. Students need to be taught about early warning signs, or "uh-oh feelings." These are the inner feelings people get that warn them of danger. They vary from person to person, some feel butterflies in their stomach, others have itchy feet that want to run away, for example. Our bodies give these signs as part of our own personal safety sensors. They prepare us to flee or take action. You can also discuss how some people ignore these signs and end up in dangerous situations. Some freeze when they are scared. Remind them that this is a time to use the 4 B's or self-talk, saying that you can breathe and think.

Some children will not be able to imagine the balloon, some in each class will think it is funny and not work at it, and some will not be able to feel it in their body. Discuss this after the activity. Could they really picture the balloon getting bigger and bigger? What did their bodies feel like as the balloon was about to burst? Try to get them to be specific as to where in their body they felt the "uh-oh" feeling. Use the worksheet that goes with this activity.

If your students have a hard time imagining a balloon about to burst, they may connect more readily to the idea of someone jumping out from a hiding place to scare them. You could try having the students close their eyes and imagine walking down a lane; they know someone is coming and about to scare them.

Activity 3, Alerting: Friendly or Not, Here I Come
Overview: Children stand with their backs to the teacher at one end of the room. The teacher then approaches the class from behind in many different ways. The class is supposed to guess whether the approach is friendly or not.

Teaching Thoughts: Again, discussion is an integral part of this activity. It is not enough for children to have only the body experience. They must also process and learn that there is a range of possible responses. You cannot always tell if someone is friendly, which is why we caution children to stay away from adults they do not know who approach them. That, of course, is separate from approaching a stranger if they need help. In those cases, the safest strangers are women with children of their own, storekeepers, or police.

Make sure you talk to the children before and after the activity. See what cues they think will work and then check to see if these cues did work or if their thoughts changed after doing the activity.

Activity 4, Alerting: One Step Closer
Overview: Children approach a partner and are stopped at a distance that feels safe or comfortable for that partner (as in the Approach and Stop Activity in the Space unit). The approachees are then instructed to close their eyes and imagine their partner taking one more step toward them. They are then instructed to open their eyes and have their partner actually take that step. Finally, they compare the imagined and real situation.

Teaching Thoughts: After the approachers have taken one more step, ask each approachee what his/her body signs were. Not everyone will be able to tell. You may need to do the activity more than once and have the children scan their bodies to see what is tense. Name the body parts for them to check because if they are already having trouble with body awareness, then they are not going to think of these parts themselves. Ask them to check their heart rates, hand tension, eyes, stomachs, etc.

Scanning: Increasing the Ability to Scan the Environment

Purpose:
> To develop an outer focus thereby becoming more aware of others in the environment.
> To improve visual scanning ability, learning to be aware of more than one person or thing at a time.
> To develop the ability to think and move at the same time.
> To increase the ability to pay attention to others for an extended period of time (increasing attention span).

Activity 5, Scanning: Stopping Together

Overview: Students will walk around the room together. Anytime one person stops, the whole group stops with the goal of stopping as one.

Teaching Thoughts: The purpose of this activity is to learn to scan space visually while moving and to learn multi-focusing skills. Achieving success in these two areas should improve attention span and group cohesion. If your class is very young or has a lot of problems with impulse control, you may want to begin by having the class stop when an adult stops or when a specified person stops. Build slowly on that beginning, next allowing either of two people to stop the group. Then announce that any boy can stop the group and then any girl. We want the children to learn to think and move at the same time; watching only one child does not do that. I have done this activity successfully with four-year-olds and older. Make sure you ask the children to think about how they can watch everyone and still keep track of their space bubble.

Activity 6, Scanning: Follow the Changing Leader

Overview: The group, in a circle formation, begins a movement that is easy to do in a repetitive manner. At any time, any member of the group can change the movement as long as it is also easy to repeat over and over, and the group has to change likewise.

Teaching Thoughts: This is an advanced skill. You may need to do some of the paired mirroring activities presented in the Chapter Six before your class is able to do this one. As necessary, discuss strategies for dealing with more than one student coming up with a new movement at the same time. (All but one of the students has to drop their idea. This takes give and take and may need support from the facilitator.) If things get tricky, discuss how you decide who is going to give-in. Talk about scanning the group to get a sense of which movement is predominant. Make a rule that you have only one turn to initiate a movement that the group follows. This allows more people to have a turn. Discuss how it feels when no one sees your change and picks up on someone else's movement instead. (This works on developing empathy, give and take, and handling disappointment.) Do the activity for a few minutes, and then check in with the group. Make sure no one feels left out. Start again, allowing only those people who have not had a turn yet to initiate new movements.

Activity 7, Scanning: Who is Different?

Overview: The group again moves together in a circle. This time participants try to change the movement very subtly, making it a little bigger or smaller, faster or slower, more or less intense, or in a slightly different direction. Everyone is watching and trying to figure out who is different and how.

Teaching Thoughts: Do not use this activity on the same day as Scanning Activity 6. The scanning activities take a great deal of concentration and should be interspersed among other activities. You may have to begin by assigning specific people to change the movement and having the other students watch for when and how they do it.

Ignoring: Ignoring Provocation

Purpose:
> To learn various strategies that help with ignoring and discover which ignoring strategy works best for each individual.
> To learn how to keep an inner or outer focus as one of these strategies.
> To increase attention span and refocusing ability.
> To increase ability to resist temptation by being able to ignore it or to maintain one's own focus under duress.
> To learn the ABC's of safe ignoring, which connects early warning signs and scanning as assessment to evaluate when it is safe to ignore.

Activity 8, Ignoring: Don't Laugh

Overview: Half of the group, the "ignorers," stand in place and try to keep a straight face while other half, the "distracters," try to provoke them into laughing. A larger class might be divided into thirds with the third group acting as observers. The distracters are instructed to act funny or weird, doing anything they can think of as long as they do not touch the ignorers.

The distractors cannot cross the line, but they are trying to make the ignorers laugh. A physical boundary keeps the ignorers from getting touched or hurt.

Teaching Thoughts: When a class is not sufficiently in enough control to maintain appropriate space (or if you are working in a small space), the leader may have to modify the activity. One modification is to select only a few children at a time for each role. Another modification is to limit the amount of space the distracters can move in such as limiting them to a certain space in front of the ignorers rather than having the freedom to walk around them. This limit can also be imposed for classes where ignoring skills are poor and need to be improved gradually—children can practice ignoring when someone is just behind them, then to their side, then just in front of them, before practicing random distractions. The rest of the children are instructed to be observers, making sure that personal space is not invaded and trying to guess what strategies worked for those children who were able to ignore.

Since excess tension can lead to inappropriate behavior, what ignoring techniques can be used that do not require adding tension? What are helpful things to ignore? What are important things to pay attention to?

Activity 8A, Ignoring: Don't Laugh Doing a Task

Overview: Ignorers are given a movement task to do while attempting to ignore. This is done in four stages. When ignoring in the classroom, children have their work to concentrate on. This variation of Activity 1 works on ignoring but with an added task—something to concentrate on.

Teaching Thoughts: These considerations are divided into each of the four stages of this activity.

During stage one, the children are basically reviewing concentration skills they practiced earlier in the curriculum such as the 4 C's in Chapter 2. If they have not

done any ignoring activities yet, begin by having them look at you without smiling or moving for one minute without anyone providing distractions.

During stage two of this activity, which can happen right after stage one, plan ahead of time what story or information you are going to tell them. This way, you

Some of the children sit in a circle focusing on a thermos in the middle of the circle. The other children move around talking and laughing, trying to distract the focusers.

do not have to think of it during the class. Also, if you already know what you are going to talk about then you can watch the children focus on you while you tell it. Being able to listen through background noise is difficult for some children, but attending is like exercise. The more children practice it, the stronger or better they will get.

Children usually find stage three of this activity hilarious. They love being told to do funny things. Meanwhile, they are working on focused listening while ignoring distractions. Tell them two to four things to do, combining cognitive and physical tasks. Be as creative as you want in coming up with commands. Take into consideration the age and developmental level of the children you work with. Make the tasks slightly challenging so they have to concentrate. For cognitive challenges, you can have the children count by differing amounts, spell things, say the alphabet backwards, etc. Some physical challenges include jumping jacks, hopping on one foot, doing a headstand, touching the four corners of the room, and doing cartwheels. Make the challenge a combination of academic skills plus movement.

Children try to distract the focusers.

For stage three, depending on the size of the class, you may want to switch distracters after one-third or one-half of the class has done their tasks. Otherwise, the children have too long to wait for everyone to go. Only children who are really focusing can have a turn to distract. I judge focusing in the context of the child's skill to begin with. Since most children want a turn to be a pest, the chance to earn that right works as an incentive for children who have focusing difficulty. Wait for a while before calling on them so they can work to practice this skill.

If a child cannot be trusted to distract without becoming spatially invasive, set up specific space boundaries to make it safer. It may be that no distracter can pass a line marked on the floor. The goal is that at some point during the different stages of this activity, everyone gets a chance to distract at least once. Since stage four may be spread over several days, keep track of who has not had a turn yet. Continue using the chance of a turn as an incentive for working on concentration.

Two children try unsuccessfully to distract the seated child.

The fourth stage of this activity involves having the children practice ignoring distractions while they are at their desks. This doesn't happen on the same day as the other stages and often requires several days. When students demonstrate that they can concentrate on you while distracters are bothering them and that they can actually complete a school task, they will really have developed practical focusing and ignoring skills. Children also think this is hilarious to do. I have been amazed at how many children, even those who are contending with ADHD, will work very hard at attending.

Activity 9, Ignoring: Slow/Fast or Curvy/Straight

Overview: Half of the class is designated to move slowly while the other half is designated to move quickly. The fast movers try to influence the slow movers and vice-versa. Each person tries to maintain his/her own moving assignment while trying to influence others to change. In a variation, one-half of the group moves in curvy pathways, and the other half moves in straight ones.

Teaching Thoughts: Some children tend to become intrusive when trying to change someone else's movement pattern. If necessary, stop the activity and discuss the problem. Set a rule beforehand about leaving a large space bubble around each other. If necessary, have the children review moving through the room in a variety of ways while maintaining a large space bubble.

Activity 10, Ignoring: Breaking the Rules

Overview: The group is given a movement task such as moving within certain boundaries. Two or three children are privately told to break the rules. The other students have to learn how to ignore those students and continue with their task.

Teaching Thoughts: I do not do this activity with every class, but I find it useful for those having trouble with tattling and bossiness.

Activity 11, Ignoring: Resisting Temptation

Overview: While you blow soap bubbles all around the area where the children are sitting, they are instructed to focus on their breathing and to ignore the temptation to pop the bubbles. After they learn to leave the bubbles alone physically, instruct them to ignore them visually as well by sitting without moving or even looking at the bubbles.

Teaching Thoughts: This activity works best if you have two or three people blowing bubbles. It is such an unusual activity that it takes the children a little while to get used to the idea. I usually do not tell them about it in advance. I bring out my surprise and challenge them to use the skills they have learned from the 4 C's and ignoring distractions. Discussion is a very important part of this activity. So we often see a ring of children encouraging a fight to continue. The idea of resisting temptation is crucial to violence prevention. The most basic resistance is not joining in bullying or violent behavior. And these days, the discussion that also must happen is resisting temptation to pick up a weapon. In the discussion of weapons, it is important to develop safety plans for those who are fascinated with guns as well as for those who are petrified at the thought of seeing one. Discuss different situations in which children might see a gun. Bring out the obvious, that it is one thing if one's parents hunt, and the gun is always locked up unless it is being used for hunting, and it is quite another thing if a child is visiting a friend and that friend takes out a gun. And it is another thing entirely if children have access to a weapon in their own home because the parents are not keeping it locked securely, if at all. Discussion can elicit a lot of information. Write out safety rules and plans for weapons of all kinds, and relate those rules to this activity of being able to be strong and resist temptation.

Resisting temptation also relates to a whole variety of more common problems such as acting goofy in class because someone else is, snubbing someone because others are, taking drugs or smoking, etc. Depending on the age of the group, different situations will arise, and it is never easy to ignore peer pressure.

For a movement activity that is worth repeating along with this discussion, see Chapter Seven, Activity 1 for the stretch cloth activity relating to resisting peer pressure. Note that I have not done this with children younger than second grade.

Activity 12, Ignoring: The ABC's of Safe Ignoring

Overview: Children are introduced to a formula called the ABC's of Safe Ignoring. This integrates the three areas taught in this chapter: early warning signs or alerting skills, scanning or being able to move from inner to outer focus, and lastly, ignoring provocation by developing impulse control and attention span. The ABC's of Safe Ignoring help children remember and integrate these skills. At the end of the scanning and ignoring unit, this format helps children to remember and use the material presented; it ties it all together. See the two formats available on handouts and decide which is most appropriate for your group of children.

CHAPTER SUMMARY

Looking back at the "Violence Prevention Through Movement Checklist," there are specific goals for each of the three units presented in this chapter. In the early warning signs unit, goals include 1) increasing children's ability to use their senses, 2) teaching children what early warning signs are and where they feel them in their bodies, 3) learning how early warning signs can be used in prevention, 4) increasing the ability to think and move in scary situations, and 5) improving the timing needed for protective interventions.

In the scanning or outer-focus unit, goals include 1) increasing children's ability to attend to others, 2) developing the ability to move with control and to scan the environment at the same time, and 3) improving the ability to move from an inner focus to an outer one.

In the ignoring safely unit, goals include 1) developing individual focusing strategies to use under duress or provocation, 2) developing individual focusing strategies to use for class work, 3) learning to use positive self-talk, and 4) learning the ABC's of Safe Ignoring.

Indications of readiness to move on include a decrease in distractibility, a decrease in tattling, an increase in focus and attention span, more cooperation among students, fewer conflicts, an increase in awareness of early warning signs, and an increase in the use of early warning signs to solicit support in resolving concerns.

The next chapter deals with pro-active responses to aggression. Ignoring is one response to provocation, but it is not always effective nor is it always safe. Other alternatives to aggression are possible with the goal of every child being introduced to at least nine interventions and becoming comfortable with at least three. Nonverbal cues, given during interventions, are taught, and children learn that they are just as important as verbal communication during potentially aggressive situations. Children usually find this work very exciting. I often get stopped in the neighborhood by parents who tell me their children are able to describe in detail what they have been taught and are particularly enthusiastic about having concrete skills to deal with bullies.

CHAPTER FIVE

Movement Strategies for Dealing with Conflict & Aggression
Assertion, Distraction, & Other Pro-Active Interventions

A seventh grade girl walked to a park with four boys after school one day. Once at the park, the boys told the girl she couldn't go home until she had sex with them. "Oh no," the girl said. "I can't have sex with you. I have a boy friend, and he wouldn't like it." The boys left her alone. That same afternoon, they sexually assaulted another seventh grade girl who didn't come up with a pro-active response.

When faced with conflict or danger, what do you tend to do? Our bodies are programmed physiologically to fight back or flee. While that might have worked when we lived in caves, it is no longer an appropriate response to everyday stress. If we wish to stop violence, we have to widen our children's repertoire of coping responses. The International Bodyguard Association, which provides protection for famous people on tour abroad, had an advertisement in the paper a few years back. I asked several elementary school classes what kind of person they thought would be hired. Someone like Arnold Schwarzenegger was the usual response of the children and the teachers. Not true! Instead, the organization wanted to hire women because they were more likely to side step a confrontation than fight it out. Promoting peace in our society means teaching our children a whole repertoire of behaviors that help them to diffuse tension nonviolently. Starting early so these behaviors become ingrained habits would be ideal. This chapter introduces many such behaviors.

Pro-Active: Strategies for Dealing with Conflict and Aggression

> Learning how to appear strong and unafraid.

> Learning how to appear surprised.

> Learning the role surprise has in diffusing anger and aggression.

> Learning the concept of changing the subject.

> Learning the concept of acting "as if" one is strong, friendly, surprised, interested, etc.

> Developing the ability to actually act "as if" in roleplay situations.

> Practicing from five to twenty interventions.

> Becoming comfortable with at least three interventions in addition to assertion.

> Practicing interventions in situations that are not dangerous such as a sibling teasing or a friend being annoying.

> Learning about the role of witnesses in bullying and practicing witness interventions.

> Learning safety concepts such as:
  - It is okay to break the rules, such as running in the halls at school, if safety is at stake.
  - It is okay to lie (telling an attacker you promise never to tell anyone) in order to get away from a dangerous situation. Then it is okay to tell.
  - Always go to a grownup if you see weapons or hear about threats of hurting someone with weapons or feel that your safety or someone else's is at risk.
  - If one grown-up does not believe you, go to another one and another one until someone does believe you.
  - Always make sure the grownup in charge knows who you are with, where you are going, how you are getting there, and when you are coming back.

SPECIFIC MOVEMENT SKILLS TAUGHT:
> How to look and sound assertive to appear strong and unafraid. Learn the front stance. Learn how to make a serious face and lower your voice to sound serious. Learn to widen the body and look in the eyes of the bully.
> How to look and sound surprised.
> How to use the concept of "as if" in the body to change how you appear to others.
> How to think and move even when afraid.
> How to utilize at least four interventions appropriately.

DISCUSSION TOPICS:

> Discuss the roles of bully, victim, and witness. Discuss the range of behaviors that can be considered bullying.

> Discuss the range of interventions a witness can make, e.g. telling the bully to stop, befriending the victim, getting help for the victim, utilizing some of the pro-active interventions that perhaps the victim does not know or is too scared to use. Reinforce the importance of the witness staying safe.

> Discuss safety rules. Make a list that can be sent home and also displayed in the classroom.

> Discuss the concept of redirecting aggression.

> Discuss the advantages of pro-active strategies, but also be clear that there is no guarantee of safety.

> Discuss the emotion of surprise. What facial features and tone of voice communicate that feeling? What kind of timing and spacing is best for the "Hey! Look..." intervention to work?

> Discuss how this strategy can also be used in other types of situations such as siblings who tease or friends who pester.

> Discuss the idea of emergency interventions such as calling "Fire" or wetting one's pants. These are to be used only in truly threatening situations such as abduction or physical attack.

One of the first responses that is taught in this curriculum is how to say "no" or "stop" assertively. Learning to do so will be useful throughout life.

Pay attention to the "play" in the playground on any given day, and I am sure you will see many of the same interactions I observed recently. In the corner of the playground, two boys were chasing two girls. It started out in fun, but in a short time, the girls were ready to stop. They told the boys to stop, but they giggled while they did so. The boys continued to chase them until, close to tears, they went to tell the playground supervisor.

In another part of the playground, a girl kept grabbing hats from her classmates. They responsed by yelling and chasing her. She, however, kept on doing it, laughing all the while. Later, these classmates complained to the teacher. Meanwhile, three boys on the field were teasing another boy about his soccer playing. They were unrelenting until he cried and started kicking them.

Each of these three examples could have been resolved without adult intervention if these children were able to act assertively and confidently. How many adults, including yourself, do you know who have trouble saying "no" or "stop" effectively?

Requests for volunteer work and the pleas of begging children are two situations where parents have often expressed difficulty resisting. Many children, meanwhile, are not able to get their friends to stop pestering them, let alone handle a bully. In middle or high school, the ability or inability to say "no" to peer pressure influences attendance, increases vulnerability to the lure of drugs and alcohol, and decreases the ability to set limits during sexual encounters.

In *The Gift of Fear*, Gavin De Becker, an expert on violent behavior, describes how looking assertive plays an important role in protecting woman from rape and other violent assaults. Violent individuals look for someone vulnerable to victimize. People who furtively check behind themselves when they think they are being followed or look at the ground with tense shoulders indicate to the perpetrator that they are easy prey. Those who can stand straight and look right in the eyes of someone suspicious are less likely to become a victim.

> *When I was attending college on Long Island, I was in a music group that practiced in New York City, requiring frequent travel on subways and trains. One evening, as I was waiting for the elevated subway, I became aware that a man was pushing up against me with his crotch. At first I thought I was just being paranoid, but when I moved over several times so did he, always pushing against me from behind. After a moment of fear I decided that I was not going to let him approach me from behind. I kept looking directly at him. As he would try to approach from behind me, I would change my orientation so I was still looking right at him. After a few attempts, he backed off. I kept looking right at him until my train came.*

Not only has being assertive kept me safe several times in my life, but it also helps me to set limits in all aspects of my life. Children need to see this modeled and learn to do it for themselves. It can be difficult. "Good" children are expected to be cooperative and give into demands placed on them. Certainly these children are easier to live with, but they are not necessarily better able to handle stresses and conflicts.

> *A second grade class I worked with included a boy named Jim who had neurological damage. While waiting in line or sitting next to someone, Jim loved to hug or squeeze other children. This habit annoyed his classmates, and they tried, to no avail, to get Jim to stop. Only one child in the class, Beth, was successful. Upon examination, one could see that Beth was able to say "stop" in a very stern voice. She looked like she meant it, too. The other children had not been able to match her intensity.*

Sometimes saying "stop," even in a very assertive voice does not work. Also, sometimes, personality affects one's ability to be that direct. Fortunately, less direct methods can also be very effective.

In the same second grade class described above, another child, Isaac, decided he wasn't comfortable having to be so stern with Jim all the time. After some brainstorming, we recognized that Jim's squeezing was not being done in anger, or to hurt someone. Jim wanted physical contact with others. Isaac decided that whenever he stood or sat next to Jim, he would initiate friendly physical contact. While saying "Hi," Isaac would ask Jim if he wanted a squeeze. Isaac's approach worked very well, and other children decided to try it too.

Children are taught to be assertive by looking and sounding strong. With knees slightly bent, children take a step forward and a little bit to the side with one leg. This is a front stance in the martial arts and puts a person in a position of balance and strength. The forward leg also makes personal space larger, discouraging someone from getting too close. The voice needs to be short and crisp with the "P" at the end of the word, "stop," accented. A lower rather than higher pitched voice is more effective. Eyebrows need to come closer together and slightly downward. The mouth is in a straight line. I have younger children put one hand out in front of them as they step forward and say "stop."

We practice saying "stop" assertively as a group and then individually while an adult approaches, role-playing a bully.

As a first grade group arrived at their prevention class one afternoon, I noticed that the teacher looked harried. When I asked her what was wrong, she said that during recess, several of her students were screaming as loud as possible into other children's ears. She asked if I could deal with this during our session. This was a very distractible class, and we had spent most of our time together working on spatial awareness and self-calming skills. However, self-assertion had been covered. I asked one of the children who had done the screaming, to approach me as if I was on the playground and he was going to scream in my ear. I knelt on the floor so I was shorter than he was. As he got close to me I put out my hand and said "stop" in a very assertive voice. The children in the class looked at me as if a light bulb had just gone off. We all practiced saying "stop" assertively to partners. The boy who had started the screaming game seemed to have no idea that it hurt. When asked if he wanted to hurt his classmates, his answer was an emphatic "no." He agreed to stop the screaming game as did the other children who had joined him.

After learning about assertion, children are introduced to the idea of changing the subject. They are taught to point diagonally in front of themselves (the bully then has to turn around to see) and say, "Hey! Look at that" and move quickly in the direction they pointed. They have to really seem interested in something. Walking toward it on the diagonal keeps them out of reach of a bully while forcing the bully to turn around and shift perspective. (This differs from pointing to encourage the bully to turn around and then run away as soon as he isn't looking.) The facial expression has to be one of surprise or interest. Eyes should be wide open with eyebrows raised. The mouth is open in an "O" shape, the words "hey look" have to sound excited and be loud enough to slightly startle an angry bully or an overexcited classmate who is being intrusive or even hurtful.

Noteworthy about the distracting technique is its usefulness if a bully gets right into your space. A bully approaches, you mean to say "stop," but you get scared and withdraw physically for a moment. The bully is then just about to grab or hit, but you quickly point and say, "Hey, Look!" and walk away. It's important to realize that it's never too late to try an intervention. There is also, however, never a guarantee that an intervention will make you safe. But pro-active thinking gives you hope and keeps you alert.

On a school playground, there are always things going on that one might pretend to be interested in: someone doing a trick on the climbing frame, something happening in a game, an interaction, etc. Walking toward that happening can bring you close to other people, open the option of interacting with the bully in a different way, or move you away from the bully if the bully does not come along with you.

> One day while in college, I was riding a commuter train. For a period of time, I was alone in the train car with a man in a business suit. He proceeded to unzip his pants and expose himself to me. He kept talking about how beautiful his penis was and asking me to get off at his train stop. At first I was taken aback, even a little scared. Then I took a deep breath to calm down, told myself the conductor would be along any minute, so I was not in immediate danger. I pointed out a train window, saying, "Hey, look at that beautiful scenery." I kept talking about the trees, and he eventually recovered his genitalia.

There are many other ways of redirecting aggression. The old woman with the grocery bags (see beginning of Chapter One) was friendly to her would-be attackers. I frequently ask an unsuspecting teacher to approach me while roleplaying a bully. As the bully (teacher) gets near me, I smile and compliment an article of clothing or his or her hairstyle. The response is almost always shocked surprise.

A first-grade boy, Travis, who was fairly quiet and timid, complained about a boy on the school bus who had been tormenting him regularly. He had tried saying "stop" assertively, but that had not worked. After one of the prevention classes, he asked me to help him come up with another strategy. He was determined to work this out without adult intervention. After thinking over the things we had done in class, he decided to try the friendly approach. (For a shy child, this was a big step, but being pro-active means self-assertion.) The next day on the bus, when the boy started teasing and was about to hit him, Travis said "Oh" in a loud voice. "Do you ever play soccer during recess? We could use some more players. I love soccer." Travis reported back to me that the boy did not answer back, but he did stop the teasing. He didn't seem to know what to do. Travis was thrilled that he had handled the situation himself.

When you point and say, "Hey! Look..." or you act friendly, what you are doing is changing the subject. There are infinite ways to change the subject. Another one that kids find fairly easy to do when approached by a bully is the "What time is it?" approach. As someone is being approached in a hostile manner, they ask the bully what time it is in a somewhat frantic manner. Whatever the bully answers, even if the bully does not know the time, the targeted person says something like, "Oh my gosh! I've got to get going. I'm going to be in big trouble. I promised my mother I'd be home." You then walk or run toward home, school, or a friend's house (whichever is nearer) as fast as you can.

A fourth grader shared with her class an incident that happened on her way home from school. Two middle school boys had jumped out in front of her. She didn't know them, and they looked like they were going to bother her. She was right. They tried to throw leaves all over her and block her way on the sidewalk. She started to panic. Then she took a breath and said, "Oh no! This is Tuesday, isn't it? I'm going to be late for my music lesson. My mom is going to kill me." And then she left, running toward home. The boys just stayed where they were.

Another option for dealing with bullying is making sure you are with friends. If there is no one you know nearby, just standing next to a group and pretending you are part of it can work. I have children practice turning to someone else in the class, asking if they want to play, and moving off with them as if the bully wasn't there. With this strategy, you are not being friendly to the bully. You are in essence, making the bully invisible.

In the same fourth grade class mentioned above, another girl was being harassed by some middle-schoolers. Seeing a classmate she knew across the street, she called to her starting with "Hey!" in a loud voice. "Hey, Mary! Wait up! I'll walk you home." (The 'Hey' suddenly changes the focus of the interaction happening with the bullies.) With a happy expression, she waved and walked across the street quickly.

When I was in college in New York, waiting for a train, a man kept following me, trying to bump into me. I was traveling by myself, but there were plenty of other people in the train station. I found a family group and stood next to them, trying to look as if I belonged with them. The man left after a short time.

Any intervention used needs to be convincing in order to work. This means that the facial expression, tone of voice, and body attitude all have to go together with what you say. All of the interventions described above need to create the emotion of surprise in the would-be attacker. Surprise creates a brief moment of disorientation that opens the door for a change to take place. To create surprise, the targeted person must use a higher voice than used in assertion while speaking loud enough to break into the bully's awareness. Abruptness in the first word is also important in surprising someone. To remain safe when attempting one of these interventions, the ideal distance to have the bully in relation to you is at least two arm lengths away, preferably three. Sometimes you get scared or surprised yourself, and by the time you organize and decide what to do, the bully moves into your personal space. You can still move out of range while doing many of these interventions without seeming to run away. The suddenness and surprise you create give you a moment to move.

There are times when bullying behavior does not pose a physical threat but rather an emotional one through teasing. Giving a compliment or changing the subject as discussed above work here too. A common theme brought up in prevention classes is that of siblings teasing each other. Children love the sense of power they get when they realize they can end most sibling teasing by acting "as if" it were not happening. If the child being teased can simply begin talking about something else such as school happenings or what's for supper or can compliment the teaser, the teaser will frequently get sidetracked to the new topic. However, this is not as easy as it sounds. When someone is teasing you, the usual response is hurt feelings and retaliation. It takes a conscious decision to let go of that response and pro-actively change the subject. The ability to ignore provocation is necessary for the above strategies to work. But ignoring direct provocation without taking pro-active steps is very difficult for children and adults. This chapter will elaborate on pro-active strategies. The ability to ignore as well as how to develop concentration and focus was covered in Chapter Three.

There are other strategies in addition to changing the subject and giving a compliment that can neutralize teasing. Making a joke out of teasing is another approach that children readily understand.

> In one first grade class, a child with the last name McDonald got teased about the restaurant by that name. Her class gave her the idea of responding with "Oh yes! My restaurant makes wonderful hamburgers." Prior to their suggestion, this child would come to the teacher whining and crying at least once a week. She had not been able to say "stop" assertively, but she was able to stop the teasing using this technique. Several children in this class felt that they would not be able to come up with their own reply to neutralize teasing while others felt they would have no problem. Since teasing is often repeated regularly, there are many opportunities to come up with a retort. In this class four children volunteered to be helpers for anyone needing to come up with a reply for the next time they were teased. This seemed to work well, and the upset around teasing decreased significantly in the class.

Some children like to act goofy and are able to deal with both a physical threat and teasing by doing something physically funny as opposed to telling a joke. They might start acting like a monkey or making silly sounds. They might simply start laughing and say what a good teaser the other child is.

Another approach to teasing is called the broken record technique (a name threatened with extinction by CDs, you may need to explain this analogy). In this technique, a child comes up with a neutralizing reply to teasing and repeats this response over and over.

> A first grade boy reported to me that three second graders that he did not know had come up to him during recess and called him an "a-hole." While the boy did not know what that phrase meant, it was clear from the second graders' body language and tone of voice that they were being anything but friendly. The boy decided to try the broken record technique. He turned to them and replied, "Oh yes, I get A's on almost all my tests." The second graders then said, "We're not talking about your tests, we're calling you an 'a-hole.'" The boy again repeated, "Oh yes, I'm a good student. I get A's on almost everything." The second graders got annoyed, and in an angry voice, they yelled that they were calling him a name, not talking about his work. The first grade boy again gave the same reply and quickly turned and walked away. These second graders never bothered him again, and he did not report them to a teacher. He felt that it was done. When asked how he felt about the situation, however, his response was not proud, as I

had anticipated, but hurt that these boys who did not even know him would say this hurtful thing to him.

This incident generated several discussion topics. The first was about how to tell when to walk away when using the broken record technique. Too many repetitions would have started a physical fight while saying it only once might have encouraged the second graders to persist in their teasing. Three times seemed optimum. We also discussed the importance of finding someone to share hurt feelings with after a harassing incident. This particular incident became a win-win situation; the first grade boy was never bothered again by the second graders, and the second graders did not get into trouble nor did their behavior escalate into something more serious. Lastly, this incident served as a lead-in to discussing when it is okay to handle a situation alone and when it is important to involve an adult.

Children can also use all the strategies discussed above when a friend or classmate is simply being a pest. In fact, it is wise to encourage children to practice these techniques in situations that are not dangerous. Once they get comfortable using them to handle minor conflicts, the probability of being pro-active in real danger is greatly increased.

Incidents involving real danger need to be reported to an adult, but a child must be able to get to the adult first. Pretending that you are going to vomit, that you are crazy, or that you have fainted may do the trick.

> *In one instance, a young man found himself alone while waiting for a subway. As a gang of youths entered the waiting area, the young man got the sense that he was in danger. The gang was approaching him, and he had no where to go and no one to call to for help. In desperation he began to act "as if" he were crazy. He began jumping up and down and screaming. He started drooling and ripping at his clothes. He must have been convincing because the gang left the station. Most people are very uncomfortable around someone who acts so "weird."*

> *The teacher of a first grade classroom shared the following story with the class. She was touring Egypt with a friend. One day as they were walking around, a soldier pointed his rifle at them and started shouting. They did not know what they had done wrong. The soldier or guard did not speak any English, and they couldn't understand him. It looked like he was going to hurt them, so they started to run away. He ran after them with his rifle still pointed at them. They were petrified, and finally, in desperation they fell on the ground as if they had fainted. Then they began to laugh hysterically. Upon seeing them on the ground, the guard walked away. They never learned what the incident was about.*

These techniques would not work if they were used over and over again on the playground. But used selectively, they may be exactly what is needed when someone's physical safety is at stake. Some approaches should be used only in imminent danger. In fact, some of them we only talk about and do not practice. Calling "FIRE" as loud as we can is one such tactic. Many adults, used to hearing children scream, may not come running. That actually happened to me with my own children. We were swimming in the ocean when two of my children got caught in a cross current and could not get to shore. My daughter started screaming for help, but I couldn't hear her words over the surf, and she screams so often in play that I had no idea she was in danger. Luckily, a lifeguard knew about the crosscurrents and came to the rescue. Sadly, not only do some people ignore the screams of children, but some also ignore the cry of "HELP." The cry of "FIRE," however, is almost never ignored. Because of the potential for real action to happen when loud cries of this word are heard, this strategy is not practiced, only discussed. To make sure children can muster the volume and strength needed to make this approach effective, we practice yelling other words such as "stop" or "help."

Another technique that we do not practice but is worth discussing with certain groups is actually wetting oneself. Again this is done only to ward off a violent attack. Vomiting or acting as if you are going to vomit can have the same effect. These can work just as effectively if someone is about to grab you or if someone is already touching you. Since people instinctively pull away from vomit and urine, either approach may give you a chance to get away from the attacker.

There are many more types of pro-active interventions possible. Among them, agreeing with a verbally hostile bully or talking nonstop with a bully to build a personal relationship are two. As the children explore the techniques listed above, they often generate ideas of their own. This is how several of the preceding ideas became part of this curriculum. It is important to allow for this exploration and to evaluate the safety of the children's choices. As stated earlier, I always begin teaching pro-active techniques with work on direct assertion. Lesson plans for teaching this and other strategies follow.

Activity 1, Pro-Active: Teaching Assertion

Overview: Children practice saying "Stop" in a serious and believable manner. All aspects from facial expression to tone of voice to body posture to proximity are discussed and demonstrated. Children practice acting assertive as adults approach them in a mock-threatening way. They receive feedback to improve their effectiveness with this intervention.

Children explore different ways to look strong and assertive.

Teaching Thoughts: When working with children who have physical disabilities that would limit or rule out practicing the front stance, creative adaptation is necessary. Find a way for them to look and feel as strong as possible. This may include sitting up tall and straight in a wheelchair. It could also mean angling the chair slightly sideways so that the approaching bully cannot push the chair over as easily. Each situation is different and will require experimentation to find the best solution.

Also, some children even with a lot of practice cannot effectively assert themselves. You need to make sure that these children learn several other interventions they can use while still practicing this skill. Even if they cannot master direct assertion at this age, the introduction to acting "as if" they are strong as well as seeing other children demonstrating the correct way will hopefully have an impact in the future.

When giving children feedback about what to work on, do not overwhelm them with too many things at once. Give them one or two things to try and then tell them how well they are doing when they master that, even if they are still not effectively assertive yet. The next time you practice, give them some other aspect of the technique. Children will work the hardest when they feel they are making progress, when they feel they have the possibility of mastery. Sometimes pairing two children who are both having difficulty looking and sounding strong (have them both say "stop" together as you approach) can help both children to become stronger.

Another problem that frequently occurs is that children have great difficulty saying "stop" seriously when they have been playing something exciting. A common occurrence happens when children play exciting games, involving chasing on the playground. Everyone starts out having fun, laughing, and shrieking. When one child wants to stop the game, however, they are too excited to use a serious voice. The same thing happens in rough-housing or tickling games. A successful solution is to have everyone pick a code word such as "really" or "code red." It does not matter what word is chosen as long as everyone involved knows the word and agrees to stop when this word is used. It is my experience that children need coaching to follow through on this successfully.

Activity 2, Pro-Active: "Hey! Look..."

Overview: Children are introduced to the concept of redirecting aggression without resorting to violence. The potential victim points to something diagonally behind the approaching bully and says, while walking toward it; "Hey! Look at _____." The diagonal line of walking keeps the child from passing too close to the bully. The change of subject introduces the emotion of surprise, which allows the emotions of the moment to change. Also addressed is how this strategy can be used in other situations such as teasing siblings or pestering friends.

A child walks past me on a diagonal continuing to point. I (the bully) am left wondering what happened.

Teaching Thoughts: For some children the whole idea of the "Hey! Look..." intervention is very empowering because it opens the door for them to handle danger in an entirely new way. It also leads into discussions of how changing

Child points while I approach roleplaying bully.

the subject could help them handle taunting from a sibling. If a sibling is trying to start a fight by teasing, the child can act "as if" the teasing isn't happening. Asking friendly questions about the school day or what they are going to eat for supper can redirect or change the mood of the interaction. While this is not exactly the same intervention as "Hey! Look...," it works on the same premise, and it gives children the chance to practice this skill in everyday situations. They love the feeling that they can handle taunting or teasing on their own. Children can be asked to try this out at home and report on their progress the following week.

Many children like to say "Hey! Look, there's Superman" or something else imaginary and then run away. This is an intervention used in cartoons. It does serve as a means of distraction, and in some circumstances such as a one-time encounter, it may work. But if the bully is someone you see regularly, running away this time means that the next time the bully will know you were scared.

The "Hey! Look..." in this intervention is different because it works on the premise of showing something interesting to the bully, of actually changing the interaction from a hostile one to a friendly one or at least to a puzzling one. This opens the possibility that the bully will think you are weird and stop bothering you or will actually become interested in what you are pointing out. Of course, the possibility of the bully still beating you up or threatening you remains no matter what intervention you use.

Activity 3, Pro-Active: Giving a Compliment

Overview: The children are taught to give a bully a compliment in response to teasing or threatening actions. Again, they have to act as if there is no threat. They have to get the bully's attention, and, looking friendly and interested, make some complimentary comment.

Angry child approaches and is given a compliment by his partner.

Teaching Thoughts: Once children have been taught assertiveness and redirection, the other interventions are taught in a similar way. Giving a compliment is usually the next pro-active strategy introduced. It is very similar to "Hey! Look..." in that you have to get the bullies attention first by saying "Oh!" or "Hey!" in a surprised voice, and you have to act "as if" there was no danger or meanness taking place. You have to find something about the bully to compliment and talk about it in a dynamic way, for example, "Oh! I love that shirt you're wearing. Where did you get it? I wish my mom would get me one like that." If their shirt doesn't appeal to you, you can discuss haircuts or shoes; you just have to choose something you can talk about positively. After you demonstrate this strategy, discuss it, and then have the children practice it.

Activity 4, Pro-Active: Acting Friendly to the Bully

Overview: Children are introduced to the concept of treating the bully "as if" s/he were really a friendly, kind person whom they would like to play with.

Teaching Thoughts: This intervention can be scary. Those who use it need to have the personality it takes to make it work. They have to be able to appear un-afraid and to genuinely seem to like the bully. They also have to give the impression that they really believe the bully is a good person who would not hurt them. The old woman with the grocery bags is a good example of this. She truly looked like she was thrilled that these two men had come along and was sure they had come to help her out. Most people are surprised by this response and, when treated with respect, will reciprocate.

Children practice acting friendly as partners approach in a mean way.

Activity 5, Pro-Active: Changing the Subject

Overview: The concept of changing the subject has already been used in several interventions, being friendly, giving a compliment, and saying, "Hey! Look..." These interventions were very specific. This intervention is more generic, changing the subject to anything else, acting "as if" no teasing was going on. This is almost the same as being friendly.

Child acts with animation as bully approaches.

Activity 6, Pro-Active: Asking for Help

Overview: The pro-active intervention, asking for help is introduced. Children again use some type of exclamation to get the bully's attention and then ask for help in a desperate or happy voice.

Teaching Thoughts: Now that several techniques have been practiced by everyone in the class, it is time to have the children approached randomly by an adult roleplaying a bully and have the children try to come up with a response. At this point in teaching it may be helpful for the adults to persist in their roleplay until the child's response is convincing. This has to be done carefully so no one feels traumatized. I learned this the hard way a few years ago.

I was working with a first grade class and had divided them into groups of about eight students and one adult. The kids stood in a circle, and the adult would approach them at random. I approached one girl who pulled back. I encouraged her to stand firmly and try a strategy, which she did. I pulled back a little but then approached her again. I encouraged her to stay with it and try again, and she was able to do a technique even better. I responded by backing off and praising her. She then started to cry. Everyone supported her and the class discussed how crying can be a normal reaction after a scary incident is over. The girl continued to cry on and off for the rest of the period, and nothing anyone said or did seemed to help. I, of course, was feeling very badly that I had intimidated her so much. When the class was over, she and I talked. She said that she was not scared of me, but she was afraid of being hurt in real life. With my therapy background, I immediately thought of abuse. I gently questioned her about her fear. There was nothing at home she was afraid of. No one had hurt her at home, in the community, or at school. But she was afraid of an unpredictable boy in her class. While he had never hurt her, she suddenly realized that he might someday, and she was panicked. I asked her to list some of the strategies she felt comfortable with from our class and then asked what she would do if he tried to bother her. After some hesitation, she readily came up with a plan of three things to try, including getting help from her teacher if the first two didn't work. After realizing that she was not powerless, she felt fine. I contacted her teachers and parents as a follow-up but there were no more problems.

After this incident, I was more careful to check-in with students before I persisted in the bullying roleplays. But the incident was not all negative. It led to further discussions about how it feels to be bullied and how one needs to take care of oneself after an upsetting incident. It also caused the teachers to reassure their class that they would be taken seriously if they shared their fears. The unpredictable child was not singled out. The discussion was for all the children, including him. However, since he had neurological problems, which were not going to go away, closer supervision during transitions and recess was instituted.

Activity 7, Pro-Active: Remembering an Appointment

Overview: The children are introduced to the idea of suddenly remembering what day it is and responding somewhat frantically by saying something like, "Oh No! It's Wednesday, isn't it? I've got a doctor appointment, and I'm going to be late. I'm in for it now." Then they leave abruptly. They act "as if" there is no threat worse than their parents' wrath.

Teaching Thoughts: This technique was developed for use on the way home from school. It could be adapted, however, to use on a school playground by having the children suddenly remember that they were supposed to meet their teacher to take a test or to complete work or have detention or whatever excuse they can come up with under pressure. The children are acting "as if" they just remembered they forgot an appointment and are frantic about getting to it. The frantic behavior is part of the intervention.

Activity 8, Pro-Active: Being with Others

Overview: Children are introduced to the pro-active intervention of being with other people and then practice it. They are shown three different ways of doing this.

Teaching Thoughts: Most bully prevention programs suggest being with other people as a protection against being bullied in the first place. Certainly walking to and from school and going around the neighborhood is safer with a sibling or friend. I wholeheartedly recommend this, but I also teach children alternative ways of turning to others when the need arises. Children can call to a friend and walk over to them as if no one were bothering them. They can also physically join a group of children or adults, even if they do not know them. By being in their proximity and looking like they are a part of the group, they can provide the illusion that they are safe with others and cannot be bothered.

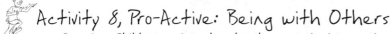

Activity 9, Pro-Active: Making a Joke out of Teasing

Overview: Students are introduced to another intervention that is specifically used for teasing or verbal harassment. Students must find a way to take the insult and neutralize it, taking the power away from the verbal bully.

Teaching Thoughts: This technique works well for people who are verbally adept at making jokes. These same children can help others who are being teased the same way on a regular basis by coming up with a response for them to use the next time they are teased that way. The idea suggested in the lesson plan of getting students in your class who feel they would be good at this type of technique to volunteer to help others being teased is a good one for creating a sense of unity against bullying. If the class can make a contract to support each other against bullying and to not behave in a bullying way themselves, you have come a long way in decreasing violence. See the role of the witness later in this chapter.

Activity 10, Pro-Active: The Broken Record Technique or Agreeing with the Teasing

Overview: The children are introduced to the idea of selecting a neutral response and repeating it in response to teasing without getting into a discussion or argument.

Teaching Thoughts: There is a tendency for children with poor social skills to use this technique as a way to get negative power. Instead of using this in response to bullying, they will use it as a way to annoy others by picking something at random to say and then say it over and over. Since, in these cases, this person is using the broken record technique in response to any verbal intervention, this might be the time to practice ignoring, leaving the child alone until s/he gets out of that mood. The wise versus obnoxious use of this technique can be discussed as a class.

In one situation, we had a child who was clinically depressed, who would hide under his desk when getting overwhelmed by social demands. He found a way to use this broken record technique as an alternative to hiding just by repeating, "I need to be alone" no matter what anyone said to him. While others found this obnoxious, it was actually better than hiding and crying.

Despite the fact that some people utilize this intervention negatively, it is a very powerful one for individuals who need to respond verbally and have a hard time coming up with what to say. Having a standard response such as "Thank you for sharing that" gives them a sense of security.

Activity 11, Pro-Active: Ignoring

Overview: Children review strategies for ignoring, revisit the ABC's of Safe Ignoring from the previous chapter, and explore the role of ignoring as a pro-active intervention.

Teaching Thoughts: Ignoring provocation is extremely hard. Students need to review and practice strategies that allow them to use this intervention without adding excess tension in their bodies. Review the techniques students used in the last unit and practice them again. Children usually love the "Don't laugh activity" (see Chapter Three).

Activity 12, Pro-Active: Being Funny or Goofy

Overview: Introduce the idea of being silly or funny as a way to change the subject.

Activity 13, Pro-Active: Emergency Interventions

Overview: There are several interventions that should not be used for teasing or playground fights. Students are taught a series of things they can do if they are being abducted, robbed, or threatened by an adult or a gang when the students' physical safety is at risk. Safety rules are then reviewed.

This is discussed earlier in this chapter. While it is not good to scare or traumatize students by graphically describing all the bad things that might happen to them, it is also important to give them tools to use just in case. Generally mentioning robbers or attackers without going into specifics of abduction or sexual abuse is important.

Going over safety rules and developing a list of them that children understand is important. We want them to know ways to avoid emergencies, not just know how to handle them. What follows is a preliminary list of safety rules.

> It is okay to lie (telling an attacker you promise never to tell anyone) in order to get away from a dangerous situation. When you do get away, you must tell someone even though you said you wouldn't.
> Always go to a grownup if you see weapons, hear threats of hurting someone with weapons, or feel that your safety or that of others is at risk.
> If one grownup does not believe you, then go to another one and another until someone does believe you.
> You have the right to feel safe.
> Always make sure the grownup in charge knows **who** you are with, **where** you are going, **how** you are getting there, and **when** you are coming back.
> It is not a child's job to help an unknown adult who asks for assistance. Adults should ask other adults for help. Even if it is a friend, children should not help without the knowledge of their parent, teacher, or whoever is in charge.

No one can know exactly how he or she is going to act in an emergency. The fight/flight response speeds up everything, and roleplays cannot simulate this response. But, practicing a number of different types of responses provides a ready vocabulary for your mind and body to race through should you ever need it. An emergency is not the time or place for relaxation nor is it the time to freeze in terror. Self-talk phrases such as "Breathing and thinking will get me through this" can be taught and practiced as a group. You could have your class pretend that something terribly frightening has just happened and quick action must be taken. The phrase reminding everyone to breathe and think is actually not said out loud but is said in a flash in one's mind as you try to cope. It is very reassuring to most children to know that they can use an intervention when scared or even if someone has abducted them. They feel empowered with the knowledge that they have things to try no matter at what point in a dangerous situation they might find themselves. It is very important to also emphasize that there is no guarantee of safety even if they know all this. The potential for safety by trying something is better then doing nothing at all.

Activity 14, Pro-Active: Role of the Witness

Overview: Introduce the role of the witness in preventing bullying. Discuss and practice various interventions through roleplaying.

Teaching Thoughts: Even if you do not have time to teach all the interventions described in the activities, exploring the role of the witness should not be overlooked. Helping children develop strategies for the role of the witness is essential for ending bullying. Whereas most bullying goes on out of the sight of adults, there are frequently audiences of children, many of whom do not know what to do. Some join in the bullying to avoid being targeted themselves. Some watch and egg the bully on, and some watch in silence, uncomfortable, but not sure what they can do to stop the situation. This topic is brought up for discussion. Questions such as "How does it feel to get bullied?" "How does it feel when no one helps?" "What might keep someone from helping?" are addressed. The story of the child who was blocked from getting off the bus each day until she kissed the boy who was blocking her (See Pro-Active Activity 14 in the Activity Book for this story) illustrates what a witness might have done and looks at what can happen when no one helps. The following is a list of interventions a witness can use:

> Stand up to the bully and say stop in an assertive manner.
> Change the mood of the interaction through humor.
> Support the target by disagreeing with the bully.
> Support the target later in private.
> Get help by gathering other peers in support or by getting an adult.
> Help the target ignore the bully by engaging the target in friendly conversation.
> Compliment the bully as a way to side-track the aggression.
> Yell "FIRE!" or "Help!"
> Call 911.

As you can see, many of these interventions are similar to strategies that the target uses; except this time, they are used to help someone else. It's important to emphasize that it is not the witness' responsibility to put him/herself in physical danger. That is the time to get help.

It was a late afternoon in the spring, and two second grade boys were playing at the playground. Another child (a first grader) came to the playground and, with no provocation, took out a knife and threatened one of the boys who was playing on the climbing structure. His friend decided that this was not the time to intervene. Instead, he ran as fast as he could to his house, which was less than a block away and got one of his parents to help. By the time the parent arrived, the knife had been put away, and no one was harmed. Social services was notified. This first grade boy was referred to my in-school therapy group to work on anger management, among other issues.

The quick action of the witness was exactly what was needed in this situation. There are so few bullies compared to the number of witnesses that if the witnesses stand together, the bullies do not stand a chance.

In one second grade class, there were three boys who were somewhat larger than the other students were, and they tended to hang out together at recess and torment their classmates. Without naming names, this issue was brought up by the children during my class. The majority of the children in the class reported not feeling safe at school. The teacher did not seem to know that this was going on nor did she take it very seriously. After emphasizing that everyone has the right to feel safe, it seemed important to work with the class on this issue. We discussed the role of the witness in ending or controlling bullying. Having observed the dynamics of the class, I had a sense of which boys were doing the bullying, and without letting on that I knew, I asked those boys if they would roleplay bullies. I asked another child to be the target of the bullying. Then I pulled aside the rest of the class and explained that they were going to be assertive witnesses. If the class as a whole really didn't want the bullying to happen, there was no reason eighteen students couldn't stand up to three. The witnesses were told that when the bullying roleplay began, they were to stand together as a group, surround the student being harassed, and tell the bullies to stop in a loud, strong voice. With twenty students standing together shouting "Stop!" in a controlled, strong way, the three boys who were acting as bullies stopped in their tracks. It was a very powerful moment. The class could readily see that if they worked together, they could stop this group of boys from bothering them.

In most classes, witness interventions are taught the same way as the target ones. Students are introduced to an intervention, it is demonstrated and discussed, and then the students practice it. As soon as the idea of helping the target through group assertion is practiced, it is almost impossible to bother one student in a roleplay without three or four other students milling together and uniting against the adult roleplaying the bully. While this is a very powerful tool, it requires follow through by the classroom teachers to ensure that students are able to use this outside of class. I have had only one or two students report back to me that classmates had protected them during a bullying situation. I believe this is a crucial aspect of controlling aggression, which needs special attention in prevention programs.

Activity 15, Pro-Active: Keeping Track of Interventions

Overview: Students are introduced to rhyming verses to help them remember interventions. Each individual student fills out a worksheet elaborating his/her most comfortable strategies. Students are given a chance to roleplay bullying or confrontational situations they are currently encountering to see these interventions put into practice.

Teaching Thoughts: I do not usually go through these interventions in the order that they are presented here. I usually teach the first four and then brainstorm with the children to get a sense of what they are dealing with and to elicit new ideas for interventions. Sometimes we have time for only four to six interventions, so I try to choose the ones I think will work the best for each particular group. I may demonstrate and discuss several of them and have the children pick the ones they want to try. Use the handouts as pictorial reminders of their choices. I have a list of twenty possible interventions that I have used with children.

1. Say "stop" assertively.
2. Say "Hey! Look...," and walk toward a point of interest.
3. Compliment the bully.
4. Agree with the bully.
5. Say you are late for an appointment, and run off.
6. Ask the bully to help you carry something or find something, etc.
7. Make a joke out of teasing that neutralizes the insult.
8. Repeat a response and limit your conversation to only that response (the broken record technique).
9. Be with other people (friends preferably, but pretending that someone is your friend or family can work too).
10. Act as if you are insane.
11. Act goofy or silly to break the tension.
12. Yell "FIRE" or "Help."
13. Act friendly to the bully (invite the bully to play with you).
14. Ignore the person who is provoking you
15. Distract the person who is provoking you.
16. Run away.
17. Change the subject.

18. Wet your pants.
19. Pretend to vomit.
20. Surrender or do what the attacker demands until you can escape.
21. Get a grownup to help.

There are countless other possibilities of interventions, but twenty is quite a few to keep in mind. To help remind children what they can try, the following verses can be used. The order of the verses is not important nor do they all have to be learned. The children can pick a verse relating to the interventions they are currently working on, or they can make up their own. My goal in the prevention program is for all students to become competent and comfortable with three to five strategies. These strategies will differ from student to student depending on their personality and strengths. Have each child fill out the worksheet on choosing interventions when this unit is complete.

Children have shared how difficult it is to remember the interventions when they are in the middle of a conflict or crisis. The worksheet will help each child pick the interventions s/he feels most comfortable with and commit them to memory.
Pro-Active Strategy Verses:

Just say, "Stop" while standing strong.
Say "Hey look!" and walk along.

Compliment or ask the time
Make a joke, repeat a line.

Stay with others to stay secure
A friendly word might be the cure.

Ignore provoking, just stay calm
Distract or run, avoid the harm.

Ask the bully to help you out
Act sick or crazy to chill them out.

Goofiness, a funny joke
Could keep your nose from getting broke.

Emergencies need voices higher
Calling 'Help" or yelling 'Fire'

Wet your pants or "lose your lunch"
Surrender so you don't get punched.

Create surprise to change the mind
It could make mean turn into kind.

Agree with what the bullies say,
Pretend that you are late today.

When in danger, stay alive
Then tell a grownup. That's no jive.

When students share particular problems that are current, it is sometimes helpful
to have them roleplay the part of the bully while you try out different interventions.
This allows you, the instructor, a chance to experience exactly what the targets are
experiencing and a chance for the targets to experience what some of these interventions might feel like to the bully. If I am taller than the students are, I do as
much of the intervention as I can while kneeling. Since most bullying incidents
happen to someone who is smaller than the aggressor, it puts the power issue
into better perspective. Sometimes it takes more than one intervention to change
the behavior.

*In one first grade class, several students brought up the issue of being chased on
the playground. Some of them didn't like it and did not know how to get it to
stop. They had tried saying "stop," but when that did not work, they felt they
had to run or be pushed down. Some of the children doing the chasing were
students in that class. I tried having the students work in small groups with one
being the bully, one being the target, and one standing to the side to give the
target some ideas, but this particular class was extremely distractible, and solutions were hard to develop. Eventually, I asked one of the boys, who was persis-
tently ignoring interventions from his fellow classmates, to roleplay with me,
attempting to get me to run. I got down on my knees so he could approach me
on an equal, or dominant level. He came up and said, "Start running, I'm going
to chase you." I told him that I did not want to run, but he did not listen to that.
I said "stop" assertively but he didn't listen and continued to come into my space.
(I had told him he could pretend to do what might actually be done on the
playground.) Being on my knees made it hard to do the "Hey! Look..." intervention, so I tried complimenting him instead. When that didn't work, he still wanted
to chase me. Finally, I asked him if he wanted some candy. "Yes," he replied and
put out his hand. "Come with me," I said, "it's in the principal's office." He got
a shocked look on his face and walked away from me. I had many options I
could have tried; verbally tricking him was not the only one. I later roleplayed
with a few more students. After saying "No" and having that ignored, I changed
the subject by seeing if the chasers wanted to race together. I also tried persistent
assertion by standing there and saying, "If you're going to push me over, do it,*

but I just won't run" and by saying "What part of the word 'NO' don't you understand? The 'N' or the 'O'?" My role-plays and the discussions following them gave the students more ideas. The concept of persisting until something worked and the need for being willing to use three or four strategies to accomplish that allowed the small groups to work more successfully when they tried again. I also helped the class develop a list of activities for the children who were instigating the chasing games, activities that would be exciting without upsetting anyone. I felt that as a group leader, this was another way to redirect an upsetting dynamic on the playground. Tag, fantasy games, and challenges on the climbing frame were all felt to be good alternatives by the students in this particular classroom.

While chasing games on the playground are often not serious compared to some of the more aggressive and demeaning bullying tactics, the tension and frustration for those who are being pressured into running away everyday can be great. Some of these students do not want to come to school, they may not feel safe there. Teachers need to take this complaint seriously and help their students persist in finding a way to handle the situation. Getting students to develop the ability to persist in standing up for themselves while they are young (even if it means having to try several different strategies, sometimes over several days) should mean increased safety from peer pressure involving drugs, guns, alcohol, and sex when they are older.

As you teach and practice these interventions, it helps to have real stories to demonstrate their use. You don't need to have one for every intervention. Sometimes it's fun to ask the kids to try an intervention during the week and use their reports as your examples in other classrooms. I have included true stories in the lesson plans for most of the interventions.

CHAPTER SUMMARY

This chapter has dealt with ways to diffuse aggression. It is always amazing how empowering it is to learn that you have the potential to take care of yourself nonviolently in a dangerous situation. It is important to remember that these techniques are not a guarantee of safety. It is also important to remember how hard it is to change a habit. If you, or the children you work with, habitually retreat from hostility, it is hard to get yourself used to a new coping strategy. Be patient with the children you teach and with yourself.

The techniques described in this chapter are not all-inclusive. Some of the more sophisticated verbal techniques such as agreeing with what a tormenter says, asking the bully questions about prejudicial or hurtful statements in an open-minded way, expressing your feelings without allowing yourself to be too vulnerable, making statements that imply the support of authority ("Sure you can have my lunch, my brother made it. He's a police officer.") and other statements that trick an attacker such as implying that you or a family member have AIDS have not been covered in detail. The book *How to Handle Bullies, Teasers and Other Meanies* by K. Cohen-Posey is an excellent source for many of these. Keep an open mind for developing new ideas of your own. Things you see in the environment and comments from other people about how they handled crises can give you fresh ideas. Practice these strategies to diffuse tension during everyday situations, at work, and at home. Finally, this chapter explored pro-active responses to stress and danger. Activities were presented to teach children how to use facial expressions, tone of voice, and body language to assert themselves appropriately; how to clearly implement a range of other strategies for diffusing aggression; how to be a pro-active witness; and when to seek help from an adult. To move on to another skill, measure class readiness by assessing the following:

> Children can assert themselves by saying "No!" or "Stop!" effectively and appropriately.
> Children attempt to use the pro-active strategies from prevention classes in other environments.
> Children can handle minor conflicts effectively using their own strategies with or without teacher cueing.
> Children attempt to use pro-active witness strategies, resulting in less need to come to the teacher for help.

Once the children have begun to master the strategies from this chapter, we can introduce techniques to learn how to manage anger and build empathy. Children are taught how to express and interpret a range of emotions accurately and safely. Most people think of anger management as the first skill to be taught in a violence prevention program. The truth is that successful anger management requires several building blocks. The self-control unit that introduces modulation of arousal without complicating it with anger is one of these. Learning to ignore provocation and developing a repertoire of pro-active strategies for dealing with people is another. Becoming more aware of spatial boundaries and learning to respect others' spatial needs is also significant.

One more building block, the development of empathy, is also necessary. Learning how to read others emotions and how to express one's own emotions in safe ways has been shown to increase behavior control in children. Social emotional education is essential for violence prevention. This chapter introduces activities that teach children to express a range of feelings accurately with their face and body as well as to interpret a range of feeling expressions in others. Strategies for working with children on developing and increasing their empathy toward others are presented.

Only after all of these building blocks are in place is anger management taught. Since increasing empathy and anger management are two of the three skills bullies must learn for controlling their behavior (impulse control being the third) the next chapter will help your group make great strides toward that goal.

CHAPTER SIX

Managing Anger & Building Empathy
Expressing & Interpreting a Range of Emotions
Accurately & Safely

During the 1999-2000 school year one of my therapy groups consisted of five girls who had all witnessed and experienced some form of violence and abuse. One of the girls, Kim, a dramatic, intelligent, second-grader, frequently expressed anger in the form of bullying others, having tantrums, or storming off to pout loudly and ferociously. One day, while we were making up a story about baby animals hatching, Kim withdrew from the big nest with another girl, and the two started to make up their own subplot. Kim decided she wanted the large cloth that was being used as the nest. She tried grabbing it away from the others and shoving them. When I stepped in to help them settle things nonviolently, Kim and the other girl began name-calling and other provoking behavior. Any attempts at help were met with more displays of anger. I moved away, saying that there were positive ways to get a turn with the cloth, and, if they wanted, I would tell them what they were. I then proceeded to help the other girls remember their ignoring strategies.

Apparently Kim heard me because even though Kim's partner continued her harassment, Kim asked me to show her the positive strategies, which we called "positive problem-solving strategies." I introduced the idea of compromise. She could either ask to split the time each girl spent with the cloth that period, or she could claim the right to it for the next week. Kim loved the idea of reserving something she did not get at the moment, for use the next time. She used this technique for the rest of the year even when she had to wait several weeks until everyone else had a turn. She took great pleasure in having a tool that gave her some positive control in working things out. Her pleasure was contagious, and before long, the rest of the group began using compromises too.

The need for bullies to learn how to manage their anger as part of a violence prevention program is obvious to everyone. However, the importance of learning to express and interpret feelings and to feel empathy for others is not. Fights, which seem to erupt for no apparent reason, often start because nonverbal cues are misunderstood. And the ability to imagine the pain you might cause others makes it more difficult to cause it in the first place.

This chapter includes four sections. An outline of what is covered follows.

Feelings: Expressing and Interpreting Feelings Accurately

> Learn facial and body cues that signal basic feelings.

> Explore cues for more complex feelings.

> Learn to verbally express body cues connected to feeling expression.

> Explore the concept of having more than one feeling simultaneously.

Empathy: Developing Empathy, Attunement, & Group Cooperation

> Gain awareness of and connection with others.

> Experience acceptance and respect.

> Expand acceptance and respect of others.

> Learn techniques for showing that you care.

Anger Management: Learning Anger Management Skills

> Identify anger triggers.

> Develop a list of anger-release activities for different situations.

> Learn body cues related to anger-building.

> Learn techniques to help settle anger before burning hot.

> Practice showing frustration and anger in safe ways.

Empowerment: Gaining Empowerment through Positive Problem-Solving

> Practice handling minor conflicts utilizing pro-active strategies and self-control techniques taught in the previous sections.

> Learn and practice how to join a group, how to compromise, how to experience frustration and still cope, etc. (basic social skills with added self-calming strategies)

SPECIFIC MOVEMENT SKILLS TAUGHT:
> How to express feelings accurately in our face and body.
> How to feel what others are feeling to become better at interpreting others' feelings.
> Learn to move with others, matching their intensity or style as a way to make a connection.
> How to show that you care.
> How to join a group of children that are playing together.
> What body sensations signals anger building in your body.
> Learn what physical activities help to release anger.
> Connect calming strategies to anger release.
> Learn concrete strategies for staying calm when things do not go your way.

DISCUSSION TOPICS:
> Explore how it feels to be closely connected with someone.
> Discuss any feelings that arise if a partner does not imitate or match someone. Explore what someone can do when they feel that way such as using words, getting help, or trying to join a different grouping next time.
> What things make you angry? How do you express that anger?
> How does the angry formula or "I" statement help solve problems safely?
> When do you think anger can be good? What is anger's job in our life?
> How can we use anger to get our needs met? What are safe ways of expressing anger?
> What body cues signal that you are starting to get angry?
> Why do we need to control our anger? How do the self-settling techniques we learned relate to anger control?
> What is the difference between a right and a responsibility? Include the idea that others have a right to feel safe with us (Protective Behaviors, West, 1989).

> How can you remember that you have responsibilities as well as rights when you're upset?
> What are some safe activities you can do that help release anger? List some physical things and some quiet things.
> What are strategies you can use to work out problems safely and fairly? Help children remember pro-active interventions as well as positive problem-solving techniques such as compromising.
> What can you say to yourself when things are not going your way? How does self-talk relate to anger management?

EXPRESSING AND INTERPRETING FEELING ACCURATELY

This unit includes linking actions and words to feeling states. It works on understanding that sometimes one feeling covers up another feeling such as feeling angry when the person is actually sad. It evaluates clues for interpreting the feelings of others and demonstrates how there can be more than one feeling expressed at a time. Lastly, it looks at how some people send mixed messages, which can create feelings of mistrust.

One common cause of aggression is misinterpreting other people or having them misinterpret you. Therefore, one of the core skills taught in this unit is the ability to recognize and express emotions accurately. This includes learning how to coordinate one's body, face, and words to express the feelings you want to communicate. It is important to begin with the basic feelings: happy, sad, angry, afraid, surprised, disgusted, ashamed or embarrassed, proud, frustrated, and bored. Research by Ekman on emotions shows that the first six emotions listed above have universal characteristics (Goleman, 1995, p. 290). Many of the more sophisticated feelings are combinations of two or more feelings. For example, shyness is a combination of fear and sadness.

Another area of interpreting emotions accurately is the ability to recognize when there is a mixed message. I have worked with several children who felt that when a person who was not well known to them smiled at them, that person was trying to be sneaky or was looking for a fight.

A first grade class was working on saying "stop" as a partner approached in different ways. One girl approached her partner smiling. The partner stopped her after she had taken only three or four steps toward him. She became upset, feeling that she had been very friendly in her approach. Her partner was afraid that her smile meant she was trying to trick him and that she was actually approaching him in a hostile way.

We try to examine the signs that someone is giving a mixed message. When a person expresses two contradictory feelings with words or his/her body, there is a sense that something is not quite right such as a smile that does not include the eyes. Truly happy feelings are expressed by the eyes crinkling in the corners, not just the mouth smiling (Ekman, Friesen, 1975). Another example might be hands clenched or the shoulders held and raised while the person is smiling. These are fairly difficult observations to make but essential for avoiding the kind of misunderstanding described above.

It is not only children that have trouble reading mixed messages. Parents and teachers misinterpret them too.

> *A first grade teacher failed to recognize depression in her students as long as they were smiling. She had a seriously disturbed youngster who tended to smile to hide his depressed and angry feelings. There were body indicators of depression such as his concave chest and fleeting eye contact. Other people in the school could see that all was not right and provided extra attention, but this teacher could see only the smile. For the entire year, she was unable to recognize that this child needed emotional support from her.*

While the above situation was difficult, at least the family and other key members of the school staff were willing to acknowledge that there were problems and work with this child. When even the parents are not aware of mixed messages, it is all the more distressing. Children expect their parents to understand. Home is where you are supposed to be "known" for who you really are. Sometimes, however, it is very difficult to interpret the messages being conveyed by certain children.

> *I worked with a family who had adopted two sisters, seven and nine years of age, who were victims of physical neglect and sexual abuse. When the older one was denied something she asked for, she did not throw a tantrum, she quietly left the room and did some type of physical damage to the house. Because she did not display her anger in the typical way, the adopted mother had a very difficult time recognizing the danger signs. This child smiled, but her smile was not a full smile. She also had a certain body posture that she actually demonstrated in therapy, but the adopted mother had trouble remembering to watch for this. Clearly, this girl was very disturbed, and even if the adopted mother had recognized the anger signs, this child may still have acted it out in destructive ways. However, by not recognizing them and using those moments to teach this child appropriate ways to get her needs met, it was all the more difficult to gain control.*

Learning about emotions starts in infancy. Children learn words for feelings when their parents describe their behaviors and label them. Consider a baby who is not yet able to crawl, trying to get something out of reach. The baby rocks back and forth on his/her knees and finally cries. The parent can comfort and educate at the same time. "Oh, you really want that toy don't you? It's frustrating when you can't reach it." Now, depending on the age of the child, the parent might get the toy for the child, move it a little closer so that a big stretch would still reach it, or ask the baby what s/he might do, for example, wiggle toward it or roll. In the latter two choices, the parent is not only teaching the word "frustration" and linking it with that body sensation, but is also teaching the baby problem-solving and perseverance.

Teachable moments like this happen all through early childhood. They supply the foundation of emotional and social intelligence (Stern, 1987). Children may miss out on these early experiences due to neglect, trauma, serious illness, or inexperienced parenting. These children are much more likely to have problems interpreting the feelings of others accurately and having the skill to deal with them appropriately. It is never too late to teach and learn, however. Parents and teachers can acknowledge feelings at any age.

> I remember a fourth grade teacher of one of my children. All the kids in the class loved her even though she sometimes got irrationally angry and yelled at the class. While this made many parents uncomfortable, the children were not fazed. After observing frequently in the class, I finally decided that the children were so wild about her because she listened to their feelings and responded with respect. Each day was started with a sharing time, a time to talk about anything at all the children wished to share. This teacher would acknowledge the feelings that were related or evoked by the sharing. She was never too rushed by academics to fit this in. She would also remember what was shared and inquire about it the next day or week when it was appropriate to do so. All the children in that class felt acknowledged and respected.

Different cultures have idiosyncratic ways to express certain feelings, but research by Desmond Morris identified over sixty gestures that mean the same thing worldwide and many more that cover most of the world. Many of these gestures, which include arm, body, leg and facial movements, are related to emotional expression. It is the commonality of many of these expressions that allows us to put ourselves in another person's shoes and interpret how he/she might be feeling. While none of us will understand what every nonverbal gesture means for each person, I have found that these activities do make children more sensitive and aware. Clearly, the first step in handling our own emotions is learning to identify them in ourselves and in others. Therefore, the activities in the first section of this chapter involve examining the facial and bodily expressions that indicate certain feelings. They all involve some form of a guessing game, like charades, or they challenge children to express a specific emotion.

For the purposes of teaching this curriculum, I have included some facial and body cues for basic feelings. True happiness, for example, is not just an upturned mouth but also includes crinkles at the corners of the eyes. Teeth may or may not be showing. The body is usually wide and open. A smile without crinkles, or with a closed body, could indicate that someone is hiding their feelings by pretending to be happy. Sadness is seen with a down-turned mouth, eyes usually looking downward, and movement that is usually slow or heavy. You can be sad without crying. Your body is usually concave. You might be curled inward, without your face showing. When someone is angry, the eyebrows are usually pushed down in the middle, the mouth is tight, straight across, and sometimes the teeth are showing. The body has tension, and movements are strong like stamping or slashing or held in, as when gripping something. You may see fists even if there is no violence intended. Surprise is always shown with eyebrows going up, eyes getting bigger and often an open mouth. The head typically pulls back for protection in case the surprise is not a good one. When someone is scared, the pupils enlarge to see the danger. There is a lot of tension in the mouth and hands. Sometimes the hands are even shaking. Eyebrows may go down on the outside edges with just the middle going up. There is also a lack of direct eye contact. Quick and fleeting glances are most typical with the face hidden in between glances. Disgust is almost always seen with the tongue sticking out and the nose wrinkled. This is a universal expression used worldwide.

There are seven feeling activities. They take between ten to twenty minutes, including the discussions that go along with them. Most of the activities involve dividing the class into smaller groupings. An extra adult or two can be very helpful. If there are no extra adults and your children have a hard time working independently, you may want to do the activities as a whole class. This doesn't give each child as much practice time, but you know that what they are learning is accurate. The activity descriptions and worksheets are in the activity book, but I have included an overview of each activity and any teaching pointers that might be helpful.

 Feelings: Activities for Expressing and Interpreting Feeling Accurately

Purpose:
> To help children link body and facial expressions to feeling states.
> To increase accurate communication.

> To decrease misunderstandings due to inaccurate interpretation of nonverbal cues.
> To increase children's repertoire of expressive behavior.
> To increase understanding of complex feeling states such as "double dip" feelings (having more than one feeling at the same time).
> To increase the ability to recognize and understand mixed messages.
> To integrate use of early warning signs with increased understanding of feelings.

Activity 1, Feelings: Guessing Games

Overview: A child in each small group makes a facial expression to illustrate a feeling chosen from a list that everyone can see. Group members try to guess what feeling is being expressed and why. Everyone gets a turn to make a facial expression and to guess the meaning of someone else's expression. When the children are accurate at the basic feelings, more difficult ones can be added to the list.

Children in small groups take turns guessing the feeling expressed by group members.

Teaching Thoughts: This activity is fairly straightforward. Remember to discuss the feeling expressions and demonstrate them before starting the activity. I usually combine this activity with the next one, having the discussion cover both.

Activity 2, Feelings: What is My Body Showing?

Overview: This activity is similar to the one described above, but instead of guessing feelings from someone's facial expression, children try to guess a feeling from someone's body posture.

Children express feelings using body posture.

Activity 3, Feelings: Moving our Feelings

Overview: This activity is similar to the one described above, but now, instead of guessing feelings from someone's still body posture, the children try to guess a feeling from a movement phrase.

Teaching Thoughts: While this activity is similar to Activity 1 and 2 above, I would not teach them in the same day. Children need to experiment with this material more than one time. This advanced activity would require reviewing the other two activities first and, thus, would provide more feeling expression and interpretation experiences.

Activity 4, Feelings: Individual Feeling Shapes

The children are making shapes to illustrate the feeling of joy or happiness.

Overview: Children take turns representing a specific feeling with a body shape held like a statue. Others in the group take turns verbally describing how this shape does or does not accurately represent the feeling. This activity helps children to become more accurate in expressing feelings and to become more articulate about describing what they see.

Teaching Thoughts: I look at statues as different from Activity 2 because the statues can be more abstract representations. This may not work well with children too young to understand this concept.

Activity 5, Feelings: Group Feeling Shapes

The children work together to make a shape showing anger.

Overview: Children work on forming a group shape to represent a feeling. This activity works on cooperation as well as feeling awareness.

The children make a group shape illustrating happiness.

Activity 6, Feelings: "Double Dip" Feelings

Overview: This activity explores the idea that you can have more than one feeling at a time such as sad and mad or excited and anxious.

Children attempt to show mixed feelings in body and face. i.e. The blond headed girl is showing excitement and worry.

Activity 7, Feelings: Feeling Approaches

Overview: This activity is similar to the activity described in the Chapter Three, called "Approach and Stop." Children are paired and take turns approaching each other while expressing a variety of feelings. The children being approached try to interpret these feelings and decide a safe distance to stop their partner.

Teaching Thoughts: Since all the activities in this section have to do with identification of feelings, discussions concerning situations in which various feelings might occur can be helpful. Personal stories help to make the discussions more exciting. Some children, however, may share personal information not appropriate for the class to hear. You should be prepared to limit such information. One rule I use is that children may not name other people when telling about something that happened to them. They have to refer to others as a boy or girl or a friend, etc. If a story seems to be getting into touchy areas such as violence in the home, children should be instructed to structure their comments in the third person by saying "someone might feel this way in this type of situation" as opposed to "I felt this way in this situation." You need to feel this out carefully.

In some classes, I let the children divide into small groups themselves. In other classes with more behavioral issues, I decide the groupings to balance the strengths in each group. Other classes, I do not divide up at all.

Children who regularly practice recognizing feelings in others and have their own feelings recognized, are more socially adept at school (Goleman, 1995). They have more confidence in their ability to understand the people around them. I cannot emphasize enough the value of emotional education. While the rules for grammar, spelling, and writing are laid out concretely for children, the nonverbal arena is not. Children who are not able to pick up the rules on their own and do not get help, often end up isolated and angry. Schools and families that are willing to teach nonverbal communication open the doors to mutual understanding. (See appendix for suggested readings to supplement the movement activities.)

Since many of the activities suggested here actually work best in small groups, these are all activities that a family could do at home. Feel free to pass these ideas on to families and daycare providers.

An additional activity, which works better in families and therapy sessions than in classrooms, involves guessing feelings from actual situations. Each person thinks about their week and picks an incident that evoked a strong feeling. Taking turns, each person acts out the feeling (not the incident) surrounding that situation. Everyone in the family tries out the movement used in the mime and then guesses the feeling. Participants may or may not be willing to talk about the incident, which evoked the feeling.

DEVELOPING EMPATHY, ATTUNEMENT, AND GROUP COOPERATION

Empathy includes not only understanding and experiencing what someone else might feel in a particular situation but also the ability to show someone that you understand and care. Empathy plays an important role in ending bullying and other violence. When someone is able to feel the impact his or her behavior is going to have on another, it acts as a powerful controlling mechanism in the same way that a strong sense of values acts as a guiding force in the choices a person makes.

In normal development, empathy emerges as part of the process of bonding. First, a child receives empathy. On a nonverbal level, this takes place when a parent matches the energy level and quality of the movement that a baby makes. When you watch an adult with a baby, you should see a lot of adult imitation of the baby's behavior. This imitation, or matching, creates a feeling of attunement with the baby (Stern, 1987). The parent and the baby are one. The baby feels recognized and acknowledged. From this state, the baby begins to imitate the parent and others. As a parent meets the baby's needs, the baby feels soothed and begins to trust that the world is a safe place.

Empathy continues to develop as parents teach a child about his or her feelings and about the feelings of others. "When you grabbed Suzy's toy, her feelings got hurt. No grabbing, ask first." "Remember when Allan hit you yesterday and you cried because it hurt? Suzy is crying now because she got hurt when you hit her." Or, "You feel sad that Suzy had to go home. You wish she could stay and play longer, don't you?" These are some examples of daily interactions that go into the development of this skill.

When children do not experience this reflection and teaching early in life, they lack an understanding of their own and others' feelings. They do not develop a sense of being seen and understood by the people most important to them in their early life. This leaves them vulnerable to either victimizing others or being victimized. Having a positive relationship with at least one person who believed in them and acknowledged their feelings is the one thing that successful adults who came from violent or abusive pasts have in common with each other (Frederich, 1990). The intensity of the abuse, the age of occurrence, the number of years it happened, the amount of chaos in the family, none of these factors show significant correlation with adult success. In the end, it was empathy, being acknowledged and accepted by at least one person, that had the most impact.

Being acknowledged and accepted feels good at any age and can allow more socially appropriate behavior. The exercises in the section on empathy work to allow a child to experience these early feelings.

In the girls group cited at the beginning of this chapter, there was another second grade child named Felicity. Her father had sexually abused Felicity at an early age. Her mother had been physically abused for years but had finally left her husband because of her fear for her children's safety. Now remarried to a man who did not physically abuse her or the children, but who was very demanding and emotionally abusive, Felicity's mother did not have a lot of energy left to nurture her three young children. In our therapy group, Felicity had a very hard time connecting to the other girls. She wanted to have friends but had no idea what appropriate behavior was. She had terrible hygiene, looking dirty and unkept as well as smelling unwashed.

During the group, the children loved to become baby animals and make up stories. Part way through the year, Felicity regularly became a monkey in the story, who got into mischief and wanted to be comforted by her "mother." Fortunately, I had enough aides in this group that one was able to focus on Felicity and truly mother her. She was held, mirrored, fed a bottle, etc. just as if she were an infant. This went on for weeks. She showed no desire to relate to the other animals; she just wanted to be held and nurtured.

Toward the end of the year, another girl in the group came to visit Felicity in the story. This girl was pretending to be a baby cheetah. Over a few weeks the two animals did some visiting back and forth. One day, Felicity and the cheetah *asked for an imaginary sleepover as part of the plan. As a monkey, all Felicity ever wanted to eat was bananas. Now, she looked at her visitor and decided she had to go get some meat for the cheetah. For the first time, Felicity had thought about someone else's needs. The other children in the group began to tell us that Felicity was playing with them at recess. After receiving nurturing and empathy for several months, Felicity was able to begin reaching out to others with the same approach. Her hygiene improved significantly. She was less sneaky in class, and her behaviors were more appropriate.*

It is important to realize that when a child has as many issues as Felicity did, the prevention program alone is not going meet all her needs. In Lapham Elementary School, we are fortunate to have in place prevention classes for everyone and dance/movement therapy for those children whose needs are more involved than prevention classes alone can handle. Even when there is no therapy, helping the class as a whole to learn to better deal with inappropriate behavior can still have a major impact.

I worked with a boy, whom I'll call Brent, who had neurological problems that made him very excitable. When Brent entered middle school, The Madison school system was attempting complete mainstreaming. Brent had always had a special education room as his primary space with mainstreaming happening as a reward on good days. Now, he was in regular classes all day long. To make matters worse, special education students were sent to the nearest school that had a program meeting their educational diagnosis. Consequently, Brent was sent to a middle school that had no students from his elementary school. His acting out behavior increased dramatically. There was sexualized talk, grabbing at both girls' and boys' genitalia, storming around the room, etc. To make matters worse, when Brent would act out, the other students who were rather shocked by his behavior would laugh.

At my suggestion, the teachers held a meeting with the whole class minus Brent. They decided to approach Brent's behavioral issues as a community problem that effected everyone's ability to learn as opposed to Brent's individual problem that did not concern them. While this meeting was my idea, the follow through was theirs. I'm still not sure how, but they managed to get all of the students to agree to completely ignore any inappropriate behavior that Brent exhibited. Within two weeks, difficult behaviors had decreased considerably. When Brent used inappropriate language in the middle of class time, the students just looked at the teacher and let an aide work with Brent. When he tried talking about someone's mother in the lunchroom (he, of course, picked someone who would normally start a fight over nothing), Brent was again ignored.

By the end of the first semester, Brent no longer stood out like a sore thumb. He still acted out occasionally, but students continued to ignore that. What seems even more remarkable, however, was that at an age when teasing and cruelty are at a peak, Brent was never ostracized. With better discipline in the classroom, students became aware that Brent had original and interesting contributions to make during class discussions.

Note that the peer attention to negative behaviors was more of a reward than any behavior program set up for eliminating those behaviors could have been. Reducing the negative attention as a class group created more positive change than any one of us could have ever predicted. Ignoring the inappropriate behavior was one of the main goals fo the first classroom I worked with. I wanted the class to be able to ignore the inappropriate behavior of the two children who were very disturbed in an attempt to get the class to function better.

The empathy activities take intense concentration for children, but it's the kind of concentration that even children with attention problems can generally handle. I've done mirroring (See below) with some of my most behaviorally troubled classes and found that it soothes them. Teachers have been astonished to see their class so focused. A second grade teacher last year decided to do brief interludes of mirroring to settle his class down before a work time or when they were restless. This became a helpful strategy for him. The empathy activities develop a sense of group cohesion. For that reason, not only do I teach a unit on empathy, I usually teach some of the empathy activities while working on other units.

 Empathy: Activities for Developing Empathy, Attunement and Group Cooperation

Purpose:
> To increase children's awareness of each other.
> To experience being accepted and moved with in synchrony (attunement).
> To experience following and matching someone else.
> To increase trust in others.
> To experience joy in moving together, feeling accepted, accepting others.
> To increase awareness of other people's feelings.
> To allow the increased awareness of others to effect behavior in a positive way.
> To increase children's understanding of their responsibilities to others as well as their own rights and needs.

Activity 8, Empathy: We all Stop Together

Overview: The children walk around the room. Anytime one person stops, the whole group stops. This requires focus and the ability to scan the whole group. When walking is mastered, other motor skills can be added.

Activity 9, Empathy: Matching Intensity

Overview: Children try to make their hands have the same intensity or tension level as their partner's. Everyone gets a turn to lead and follow.

Teaching Thoughts: Matching the intensity of hand tension is good for learning to read cues in the body. This matching of intensity is called attunement. When a baby cries and a parent comes to offer comfort, the parent often, without realizing it, matches the baby's intensity by bouncing or rocking at that energy level or rhythm. Attunement gets the baby aware of the parent, a connection that allows the child to settle down. A connected parent will then also calm down the bouncing. As a child gets older and has a strong, intense feeling, having someone match the intensity of the feeling in a positive way, either with movement or a strong voice acknowledging the feeling, helps the child to feel understood. This connected or accepted feeling then allows the child to calm down.

Matching or attunement, however, does not necessarily mean imitating. When an older child is angry, imitating them may be interpreted as mocking behavior and will only escalate the anger. Matching the intensity with a different part of the body, or with the voice, is more likely to be accepted.

Activity 10, Empathy: Who is the Mirror?

Overview: Sitting in pairs, facing each other, children mirror each other, first with a designated leader and then with no set leader. When done right you cannot tell who is leading and who is following. This works on developing the kind of synchrony parents ideally develop with their babies; it promotes a sense of self and of a sense of relatedness to others.

Two children mirror each other, trying to move exactly the same as the other. This takes a lot of consideration.

Teaching Thoughts: Mirroring activities are very powerful. They can evoke a sense of closeness. Children thrive on the times that someone is completely focused on them, which is what happens when a child leads in the mirroring activities. Children also thrive on being able to connect with others by moving exactly like them. This is how babies learn and form attachments, by being mirrored and mirroring others. When you can move so that you do not know who is leading, you are deeply connected to your partner.

When I introduce the mirroring activities, I always try to challenge the pairs of kids to try to move so well together that an observer would not know who is leading and who is following. Challenges hook in kids. This has never been a challenge with an external reward, just a challenge to see if they can trick me.

There is a progression to mirroring, which helps children master the skills. Children must be able to mirror hand tension before moving on to arm movements. They must do arm movements well before I let them stand and move around in space while mirroring. And, they need to be able to do mirroring while moving in space before I move on to the baby animal activity. (See Empathy Activity 10: Animal Babies.)

Activity 11, Empathy: Group Mirroring

Overview: Divide the class into groups of four. Have one person in each group start a movement that the rest of the group imitates. At any time, anyone may change the movement, and the group must change too.

Teaching Thoughts: I do not recommend using music with this activity. In the silence, the children's own rhythm will be able to emerge. However, if rhythmic music makes you and the class more comfortable, there is nothing wrong with it.

Tell the children that several people may try to initiate a new movement at the same time. They have to watch and be willing to drop their movement idea if the class picks up on someone else's movement. This can be hard for some children. Be prepared to repeat the activity so that most children get a turn to introduce a movement. Reiterate the idea that each child may introduce a movement only once. Refer to making it fair for everyone since fairness is also part of empathy.

Small groups of children try to move together without a designated leader.

Activity 12, Empathy: Group Rhythm

Overview: Children are asked to find their own tempo for walking, then to join others in the class that are moving in a similar tempo and then for each group to watch all the other groups and see if everyone can find a class rhythm by each group changing slightly. (DO NOT use music during this activity since the tempo has to come from the students.)

Teaching Thoughts: Finding a group rhythm, which may vary from day to day, increases the sense of connection in a group. You may discover that the individuals in your group have very divergent rhythms. Instead of worrying about the difficulty of coming together, try having everyone take turns moving with each person's rhythm, either all on the same day or on different days. The important thing is for each person in the group to feel that the rest of group is willing to join in at his/her pace. Everyone needs to feel accepted as they are. If you repeat this activity over time, eventually there will be days when the whole group is in synchrony. In the meantime, your class creates an atmosphere of acceptance and respect for each other. Since violence in our society will not stop until people feel accepted and valued, developing these feelings at school and in the home is an important part of the solution.

Activity 13, Empathy: Paired Pushing

Overview: Students are paired and stand facing each other, palm to palm. Both partners are instructed to push hard against the other, at first equally, and then with the designated leader pushing just a little bit harder. This results in the pair slowly moving across the room in the direction the leader is facing. When they have slowly, and with much effort, made their way across the room, leadership switches and the pair moves in the other direction.

Children are in a front stance pushing equally so that neither one overpowers the other.

Teaching Thoughts: The first part of this activity, pushing equally and then breathing, balances strength and release. It also allows you to see if the pairings are able to balance their strength before trying to move across the floor. The breathing together enhances the sense of connection between partners. The use of connected pushing allows children to focus and feel settled.

Children push for a count of four and then breath together keeping hand contact.

One partner is designated to push a little harder, pushing their partner across the room, step by step.

This pushing activity can be done with an adult and child as long as the adult can modulate his/her strength. Make the child work hard to push you across the floor. Comment on how strong s/he is. Don't forget to have the children allow you to push them too. It's the give and take in this exercise that is important. If you are not pushing, but are circulating among the children, watch for pairs that are really connected to their strength and compliment them. It is not how strong they are but rather how they are offering resistance to each other.

Activity 14, Empathy: Circular Pushing

Overview: Students are paired and stand facing each other palm to palm as in the previous activity, "Paired Pushing." This time, instead of pushing each other across the room, partners stand in place, first one person pushing harder and then the other. This results in a circular motion like a train piston and requires constant give and take.

Teaching Thoughts: I used this activity in a therapy group of children that had ADHD. We started each period with it. It provided good resistance in the shoulder and hip joints, which has been found to be helpful for settling down some children with minor neurological involvement. It also provided focus and connection with others. Before instituting this as a starting activity, it would take about half an hour before all the boys became focused. After we began using this, it took less than ten minutes to get going. Although it is hard for the children to do at first, it is a quick focusing and grounding activity once they learn it.

The instructor is offering resistance but allowing the child to push harder. The child then offers resistance while the instructor pushes harder, making a circular path with their hands.

Activity 15, Empathy: Group Pushing

Overview: This is a group connecting activity that requires balancing strength and letting go. The group stands in a circle, hands against their neighbors on either side. The group takes a breath in together, then as they slowly breathe out, they push against each other on both sides, not pushing harder than their neighbors do. As they breathe in again, they let their hands drift up toward the ceiling. This whole action gets repeated several times.

Everyone pushes with the same strength but not more than his/her neighbor.

Activity 16, Empathy: Group Sculptures

Overview: This is similar to the Feeling Activity 5, "Group Feeling Shapes" described in the feeling expression section above. The class is divided into small groups (two to five students in a group). Each group is asked to make a group shape that expresses something about peace or violence prevention. Other groups can try to guess what the shape means, or each group can explain what they were trying to express.

Teaching Thoughts: With group sculptures, it is fun to see what messages your class can come up with. There may be many messages. The important part, again, is to accept each person's input and work together as a group to value it.

Activity 17, Empathy: Animal Babies

Overview: This activity is a special treat for the children, usually reserved for the final session. The children apply their empathy skills in an imaginary situation, which involves mirroring movement and attachment of baby animals to their parents. The "parents" must teach their babies how to travel, get food, and survive danger. There are two variations of this activity. One emphasizes energy modulation along with empathy. The other emphasizes the application of several safety skills in addition to empathy. The second variation requires more self-control. The activity ends after the teacher acts out some danger, a tornado or a wild animal, for example and the parents bring their babies back to the nest, safe and sound.

Child guarding her egg.

Teaching Thoughts: Some babies do not want to hatch. This is a tricky situation. It can be very therapeutic to be allowed to stay in the egg the whole time, but it can be very frustrating for the child in the parent role. I tend to compromise. I will allow a child to stay in the egg a little longer than everyone else, but I will set a limit on how long. This can also become part of the discussion.

Baby hatching, meeting it's parent.

Some babies will not mirror or tend to run away. And some parents do not keep a watch over their children. Use this as a springboard to discuss how, among real animals, there are some babies that do not stay in the nest when their parents

Parent mirroring baby.

Baby mirroring parent.

leave and sometimes get hurt. There are also some children who do not listen to safety rules or parents who do not watch over their children as closely as others do.

Many feelings are evoked during this activity. There can be frustration, and there can be very close connections. Again, a discussion should follow the activity. Begin by asking children how they think others in the class or in their family grouping felt. We are trying to train the children to be aware of how others feel. This is empathy.

Variation B is less structured in its use of space and energy zones, and therefore, more difficulties may arise with wandering babies and parents. This opens up the possibility of more indepth discussion. Part of the discussion can also include how this relates to human families, how parents feel when their children will not listen, and how children feel when their parents do not pay attention to them. This discussion needs to be one step

Parent and baby leave the nest.

removed from reality, however. In other words, this is not a time for children to reveal neglect. Sharing is on as "as if" level. If there are personal things that someone seems to need to share, invite them to do so with you at a private time.

Parent teaches child how to travel.

Teaching Thoughts: Stretch sacks give added tactile feedback, which is very helpful with children having ADD or ADHD or other neurological issues. Animal mirroring can be lots of fun even if you do not have stretch sacks. Parents can play this at home too. Kids get a kick out of seeing their parents in the role of babies. Role reversal is fun. The baby can hatch from an imaginary egg or from a piece of material covering them. For families, the danger that comes at the end of the story may need to be revised. Talk about a tornado or a wild animal coming and act "as if" it were happening. Or, if the danger component is too stimulating at home or in the classroom, the baby part is fun even without the element of danger.

Parent helps child make friends.

Activity 18, Empathy: Making Waves

Overview: In circle formation, a child makes up a two-part movement that the whole group does in a wave or ripple.

Activity 19, Empathy: Follow the Stretch Cloth Leader

Overview: This is similar to group mirroring but uses a stretch cloth.

Teaching Thoughts: This activity can take a long time.

Activity 20, Empathy: Giving Our Weight to the Stretch Cloth

Overview: This activity is the same as Chapter Three, Activity 11, "Grounding While Standing in a Stretch Cloth" with added emphasis on empathy. For this activity, the children will stand in a circle inside of the stretch cloth. With knees bent and hips back, children are told to lean back together letting the cloth support the class. When this is accomplished, add a gentle side-to-side rock, feeling connected by the cloth and affected by their neighbors' movements. You can add a pulling and resistance component if your class is cooperative. Children gently pull side to side and then gently twist and move forward and backward, paying attention to how everyone keeps their balance.

Teaching Thoughts: If your class can barely lean back without arguments developing, you may not be able to do more than the leaning in one session. Try it again another day to see if your class has made any progress.

Activity 21, Empathy: See Saw

Overview: Children will act out a see saw, one going up while the other goes down. This happens while they support each other's weight.

Teaching Thoughts: Trust exercises are a lot of fun, but you have to make sure no one in the class is going to drop their partner. If you have concerns about one child, just make sure you are working with the pairing s/he is in. If you have concerns about several children, this may not be a suitable activity for your class.

Children lean back and support each other's weight while they go up and down.

Activity 22, Empathy: Showing That You Care

Overview: Children are taught a variety of ways to show someone they care. Then they break into small groups and practice these skills in roleplay situations.

Teaching Thoughts: The activity, "Showing that You Care," is the culmination of the empathy unit. For this to work, you must have already developed a sense of group unity and trust. Unless you have extra adults to help, you may need to do the activity the first time as a class instead of breaking up into small groups. Have a few students at a time go into the middle of the circle to act out a situa-

Child comforts upset classmate.

tion, while the rest of the class acts as observers, offering suggestions to help when asked and discussing their observations at the end.

To help or not to help is a delicate balance and one that adult's struggle with too. I use myself as an example. After yelling at my son one day for jumping in and taking over the computer when his sister was having a problem that she was trying to work out herself, I later found myself doing the same thing to him. It was very hard to control the urge to step in and end his struggle. But, if you really want to show that you care about someone, you can only help when help is wanted. Otherwise, it is perceived as intrusive.

There are many times when someone is upset and help is called for. Children can use some examples to start them thinking creatively about this. If someone has lost something, for example, you can help by: helping them look for it, brainstorming with them about where they might have put it, lending them yours if you have one, or distracting them from their worry by changing the subject to something else. Once children get the idea that there can be creative ways to help, they enjoy brainstorming themselves. Get them to ask themselves how they would feel in different situations and what things would help them feel better. Try to get them to put themselves in someone else's shoes. This, after all, is what empathy is all about.

Comments on the Empathy, Attunement, and Group Cooperation Activities:
The activities described above help to develop a group sense, a feeling of trust, cooperation, and sensitivity to others. They impart a sense of competency in connecting to others, and provide a chance to feel what it is like to have others connected to you. They also help to develop an understanding of how others might feel in different situations and the feeling that each person's needs are recognized and accepted. Building on this experience, we hope that students who have difficulty with bullying will begin to care about how others feel and to understand the impact of their behavior on others. This is a very important unit, with many activities. You do not have to do all of them to complete it successfully. Choose the ones that work best for you. When children in your class are able to talk about the feelings of others and seem connected to others in a caring way, then you have met the goal for this section.

LEARNING ANGER MANAGEMENT SKILLS

Learning anger management skills involves helping children become aware of what anger feels like in their bodies, learning to recognize it before it is out of control, and finding ways to express it safely. The earlier in the anger cycle one intervenes with a strategy, the more likely it will be successful (Goleman, 1994). This topic introduces the concept that while all feelings are okay, the behavior used to express these feelings must not impinge another person's right to feel safe.

Once children are able to identify feelings in themselves and in others, it is time to begin controlling the behavior that expresses them. If you have been following the curriculum up to this point, several of the skills necessary for anger management have been taught. For many children, anger management improves all by itself once they have developed the skills involved in impulse control, empathy, and in identifying and settling arousal in its early stages.

Other children need additional education about anger. Since many of these children do not have much time between encountering an anger stimulus and being fully aroused and ready to act, learning what their personal anger triggers are may enable them to avoid many of them. They may also need to develop a repertoire of behaviors that allow safe expression or distraction from these intense feelings. And they need to learn a movement phrase that releases the anger urge without aggression.

> Brent, whose middle school experience was discussed earlier, was also very excitable at home. He would get violent if the doorbell rang and one of his siblings went to answer it instead of him. This would also happen around turning off the television or getting to sit in the front seat of the car. His family decided to try to help him control his outbursts by having these events take place in a predictable fashion. When the television was going to be turned on, it was decided ahead of time which child would turn it off. There was a rotating door-answering assignment. These types of rituals helped him to avoid getting aroused and losing control. At the same time, he was taught a movement phrase to replace hitting when he encountered a trigger that he couldn't avoid. He would push a button on his watch, causing it to beep, then declare "hard time" and squeeze his hands together. This approach brought most of Brent's aggression under control.

The gesture of bringing an arm up abruptly and clasping the back of the neck hard is used worldwide to indicate anger (Morris, 1994). This gesture allows for safe expression of arousal. The clamping onto the neck keeps the hand from hurting someone while allowing some release through a strong abrupt movement. The movement sequence involved in the "4 B's of Self-Control" does something similar. You clasp your hands abruptly together and squeeze hard. It is the breathing and settling that follows that helps the person calm down afterwards. Any similar sequence can be used to help a person who has aggressive impulses that are difficult to control.

In the anger management section of this chapter, the difference between feelings and behavior is emphasized. All feelings are okay. It is the behavior that we use to express them that needs to be monitored. Children need to be taught that they not only have the right to feel safe all the time but that others also have the right to feel safe with them. This statement implies that there are responsibilities involved in being a safe person.

Anger Management: Activities for Learning Anger Management Skills

Purpose:
> To increase awareness of anger triggers.
> To increase awareness of early anger cues in the body.
> To integrate the use of self-settling strategies when aroused emotionally.
> To develop safe physical releases for angry feelings.
> To teach the anger formula and develop rules for being angry safely.
> To develop anger management workbooks for each child.
> To develop the understanding that all feelings are okay but that all behaviors are not.
> To teach the concept that everyone has a right to feel safe all the time, which includes the right for others to feel safe around us.

Activity 23, Anger Management: Anger Cues

Overview: After making a list in writing or pictures of things that trigger anger, each child will have a chance to move from calm to angry, paying attention to body cues as he or she goes along. These cues will then be discussed and added to the anger trigger sheet. By the end of the activity, all the children should have an individual list of their own anger triggers and body cues that signal anger.

Activity 24, Anger Management: Connecting Self-Settling to Anger Control

Overview: After reviewing at least four self-settling techniques (abdominal breathing, the 4 B's, tension release, and guided imagery), children will have a chance to practice these in anger roleplays and learn their importance as an anger management tool.

Activity 25, Anger Management: Practicing Self-Settling in Anger Release

Overview: After reviewing the self-settling choices children made in the previous activity, they are given a chance to try these techniques in structured and then less structured roleplays. They are then challenged to use these outside the movement class and keep a journal of their progress.

Activity 26, Anger Management: The Anger Formula

Overview: The children are taught a verbal formula for communicating their anger, and they develop a set of rules for expressing their anger safely.

Activity 27, Anger Management: Mad Roleplays

Overview: Students develop a class list of things they can do in addition to self-settling to help them cool down when angry. The students then roleplay actual incidents that make them angry and try implementing some of these strategies. Finally, each child develops his or her own list of things that he/she might actually do in different types of situations to diffuse anger.

Teaching Thoughts: Some children, by virtue of their individual temperaments, have an easier time with anger management than others. Some children are naturally easy going, slow to arouse and quick to settle down. Others, however, have trouble with their temper. Children's behavior in response to anger is often modeled after the people they live with. If there is violence in the home, children learn violence as a valid way to express anger. These exercises can be useful for adults as well as children—something to bear in mind throughout the program. I have used the self-settling and ignoring strategies often myself.

If anger is an issue in your class, you may want to develop an anger challenge sheet once the skills have been learned. (See the challenge sheets in the Activity Book.) Challenges help people practice new behaviors. They provide a structured reward of some type for a given number of days of recognizing anger warning signs and doing something positive about them. Anything that motivates your group is a good reward. Successfully completing the challenge does not change anyone's temperament, only the behavioral responses to it. Once the challenge is complete, your class may still have to work at practicing the behaviors from the challenge. When ready, you can set a new challenge to develop and reinforce additional positive behaviors.

Some individuals, because of neurological issues or issues of temperament, have a difficult time sensing the build up of arousal. Either their arousal level rises very quickly, or they do not sense their anger until it is ready to explode. These individuals need to learn what their anger triggers are and use distracting or relaxing techniques as prevention before they sense arousal. They may also need to learn to avoid certain situations. This is similar to what I have to do to manage my migraine headaches. I know they are triggered by cigarette smoke, so I avoid places where smoking is allowed. I also know that red wine can trigger a headache within minutes, so I do not drink it. If you know that certain types of situations such as tests, math assignments, crowded places like the auditorium or fairs, etc., or other specific situations are going to trigger anger in a child, teach him/her how to deal with these. They can't escape taking tests, but they can learn relaxation techniques or have a soothing object such as a Koosh ball to hold onto while doing one. They could have a special place to sit during a school function where they won't be surrounded by as many stimuli. Brainstorming with a particular child can help them feel in control and that, in and of itself, may help.

One child I worked with in therapy had a very difficult time controlling himself. He would have violent temper tantrums at school, knocking things off children's desks, hitting, etc. They tended to escalate as the day went on and were particularly bad after lunch. In therapy, the child was able to share that the noise and confusion over lunch made him feel "all wiggly" and out of control. It was arranged for him to go the nurse's office for ten minutes after lunch to play quietly with some toy cars. The tantrums decreased significantly. Looking creatively at how to give him some "unwind" time made the rest of this child's school year successful. By the following year, he no longer needed this break.

Teaching Positive Problem-Solving or Empowerment

Thus far in the chapter, we have examined identification of feelings, the development of empathy, and anger management. The last section concerns the social skills necessary to get one's needs met without hurting others. I call it positive problem-solving, and I think it is an essential piece of the formula for ending violence. If I know that I have the resources it takes to cope with my needs, I do not continually need to be anxious about getting them met. If I feel that I have some power, I do not need to take it from others. The activities in this section cover several social skills. The children are taught how to meet and join new groups of people. They also learn strategies for handling their feelings when things do not go their way. Negotiating and compromising are introduced so that children learn how to gain some power in frustrating situations. Once these skills are learned, the children practice using them to express anger safely.

Positive problem-solving or empowerment addresses the issue of how to get one's needs met while keeping one's self and others safe. What are some empowering techniques? How do we teach children that everything will not go their way all of the time? How do we develop delayed gratification in our children? In the story that begins this chapter, Kim learned a technique that would get her needs met but only if she was willing to compromise to accept that they might not get met right away. For Kim, using the technique gave her gratification.

Empowerment: Activities for Teaching Positive Problem-Solving or Empowerment

Purpose:
> To teach children strategies for getting their needs met appropriately, including compromising, taking turns, negotiating, calling "dibs," sharing feelings, suggesting new ideas, being open to other's ideas, sharing.
> To reinforce the use of the anger formula as a safe and effective strategy to express angry feelings.
> To help children think about other people's feelings as they problem solve.
> To help children realize that things do not always go their way.
> To teach children how to settle themselves when things do not go their way.
> To explore ways to join others who are playing.
> To explore ways to play with more than one person at a time.
> To explore what goes into being a good friend.

Activity 28A, Empowerment: I Didn't Get My Way
Variation A: Structured Problem-Solving
Overview: The class is divided into small groups. Everyone is told how wonderful it is to be first in line because that person is in charge. The children are also told that only one child will get a chance to be first. The other children must then act out how they will settle themselves despite being disappointed.

Activity 28B, Empowerment: I Didn't Get My Way
Variation B: Open-Ended Problem-Solving
Overview: This variation is less structured and entails fantasy play. It allows children to apply problem-solving skills in interactive situations.

Teaching Thoughts: If you have an impulsive class and there is only one adult, have one group at a time do a roleplay in the center of the circle. The whole class can brainstorm possible solutions to the problem.

Activity 29, Empowerment: I Can Be Mad Safely

Overview: This is a variation on the activity "Feelings Shapes" (See Feelings Activity 5) with the emphasis on positive problem-solving and group cooperation. Many children are expected to complete assignments in cooperative groups. When there is an uncooperative member in the group, children frequently do not have the skills to resolve this conflict on their own.

Teaching Thoughts for Empowerment Section: An important part of anger management is having the skills to get one's needs met nonviolently and having the knowledge and expectation that you can't have your way all the time. Roleplays are very helpful for practicing and integrating social skills. As a teacher, you can be specific about areas in which your class needs help. Different issues surface at different ages. Second and third graders often deal with being left out, for example. Talk to your children and watch them when they play with each other and with friends. Do you notice any problems such as being too bossy or too compliant, having difficulty sharing, always needing to go first, teasing other children? You can work these issues into your roleplays without singling out the child having the problem. Talking directly about the problem(s) can sometimes cause a child to become defensive. Working on it in an "as if" basis allows for more openness. If the child you have in mind does not generalize the problem-solving strategies from the roleplays, then you can always discuss the issue later on, reminding them of how they solved similar situations during the roleplays.

At this point, you may understand better why I labeled the above activities as "Empowerment Activities." One approach to stop bullying is to teach other ways of feeling powerful. And one way to make yourself less likely to be a victim is to feel empowered. Positive problem-solving skills allow children to feel competent socially and, therefore, empowered.

CHAPTER SUMMARY

This chapter covered four topics: 1) accurately expressing and interpreting feelings, 2) developing empathy, experiencing attunement and group cooperation, 3) learning anger management skills, and 4) gaining empowerment through practicing positive-problem solving. Children completing this unit should be able to show a range of feelings accurately with their body and face, interpret a wide range of feeling expressions, and demonstrate a repertoire of movement and verbal responses for safely expressing feelings. They should have built an awareness of early anger signs in their body, learned to recognize many of their anger triggers and how to avoid them, developed strategies to cool down their anger, and learned when and how to use the anger formula. They should also have acquired a range of positive-problem solving skills that work for them. Teachers or parents should see a decrease in angry outbursts, an increase in appropriate responses to others, and more appropriate expressions of feelings as a result of obtaining these skills.

The next chapter deals with a variety of issues that have a major impact on violence. Prejudice, isolation, peer pressure, and weapon use are some of these issues. Unfortunately, in our society these are issues that must be dealt with even at an elementary school level if a violence prevention program is to be successful.

CHAPTER SEVEN

Additional Issues:
Guns & Other Weapons, Alienation, Prejudice, Media, & Cultural Influences

A fellow dance/movement therapist and I were talking about weapons and violence the other day. She began to reminisce about her childhood in the seventies. Her father had been a police officer, so she thought there surely must have been a gun in her house, but she never saw one, and none was ever mentioned. Since no one had taught her about gun safety, it was lucky that she never found the gun by accident. A classmate of hers also was the child of a police officer. This father decided to make sure his son understood about gun safety, so he educated him about how to handle and clean weapons. One day, when his father was not home, the boy, then a seventh-grader, decided to clean the gun himself. It accidentally went off and killed him.

The above story happened long before school shootings became so prevalent. But even when rage is not the issue, there is no real way to ensure the safety of children with guns. Accidents can easily end up fatal, and children are persistent and unstoppable when they are curious about something. There are stories of children whose parents kept unloaded guns locked in one place and ammunition locked somewhere else, and still children were able to put the two together in a fatal combination.

I have not personally had many experiences with weapons affecting my life. Within the last three years, however, two classmates of my daughter have been shot to death, with one incident taking place a block from our home.

The first incident, the one near our home, was particularly senseless. A twelve-year-old boy, James, who attended elementary school in our neighborhood, was remembered as a friendly, sweet, affectionate kid, but he had not had an easy life. He had moved several times in his school career (a problem for many students), the last move and the hardest being Chicago. There James began to change, becoming angry and more difficult to control. His uncle had recently gone to prison, and James bragged about going there himself.

Just before the shooting incident, James returned to our neighborhood to stay with relatives, hoping to escape gangs and violence. He had enrolled in the local middle school but was not attending on the day of the shooting. He reportedly had been talking to friends about shooting someone, but no one took him seriously. Even when James was seen by two older teenagers, displaying two handguns and threatening to rob a gas station or kill someone, nothing was done to stop him. He had been able to steal the guns easily from a local shopkeeper who kept them unlocked and had even shown the boy where they were kept. No one knows what really happened next except for James, and I'm not even sure he understands it. On a Friday in January, 1999, he and a girl, Misty (a classmate of my daughter in elementary school), were hanging out together in the front hallway of her home. It was during the school day, and neither of them was in school. They were friends, and as far as anyone knows, there was no anger between them. Nonetheless, at some point while they were sitting there, James shot Misty, ran away and left her bleeding. Misty died less than a month later in the hospital.

There are so many questions in this situation, as in any senseless crime. Shaina had been having problems. She was getting special help in school and was trying to turn her behavior around. People were trying to help her, but she had many unsupervised hours in the day because her mother worked long hours and because she sometimes skipped school. Why was no one following up on her truancy problem? One of the biggest risk factors for problems with violence, drugs, etc., is long hours of unsupervised time. Daycare ends when a child starts middle school, but the need for supervision doesn't. "...About half of America's adolescents have too little to do after school and are in danger of falling victim to gangs, drugs, violence, sex, or other activities that could limit their potential as adults" (Mayer, 1995).

And what about Louis? He had three school changes in the two years of attending school in Madison. Multiple school changes is also a risk factor for problems. Louis was both unsupervised and had multiple school moves. He associated with delinquent or negative peers after his move to Chicago, which has also been shown to increase tendencies toward anti-social behavior (Mayer, 1995). His family tried to help by enrolling him in school back in Madison. I presume they also tried other interventions, but somehow, the help was either too little or too late.

In response to this incident, the city of Madison took some action to try to prevent things like this from happening again. Stricter gun control ordinances were proposed by the city but were then overridden by State Law. The truancy law was revised to deter skipping class. Law enforcement officials were hopeful, but the students were skeptical about the new law's potential to change anything. The students felt that the law did not "address the root causes of the problems—a pervasive sense that school is pointless and nobody cares about them" (Erickson & Brinkman, 2000). My own experience with the new truancy law would verify the students' opinion.

> Last year, for the first time in her life, my daughter skipped part of a school day. She was in ninth grade, the first year of high school. Because the school gets so many cuts or unexcused absences everyday, my daughter's cutting of one class, as a first-time offender, was seen as a minor infraction. We got a phone call from the school, but our daughter told us it was a mistake and that she would clear it up the next day. At first we believed her. There had been several such mistakes at the beginning of the year that we had investigated and found to be false. Then we discovered she really had cut. A call to the office let us know that an unexcused absence would be noted on her report card and school record. I was incredulous that this was all that would happen. I demanded that the school act promptly to give my child the message that cutting would not be tolerated. I felt that the school had an opportunity to keep my daughter from repeating this behavior but that they were not going to do so without prodding from my husband and me. After some discussion, we worked out a reasonable consequence that the school would administer as a deterrent. I was pleased that they cooperated but was surprised that they hadn't thought of doing this themselves. The person she cut with apparently cut regularly, but since the parents worked, the child was able to erase any phone messages from the school about the incidents. Since there were no other consequences, the family had no idea it was going on.

Although this may seem to be a sidetrack, I included this incident because it shows some of the problems that occur with a lack of adequate supervision and logical, immediate consequences for deviant behavior. One year, almost to the day, from Misty's shooting there was another fatal shooting of a middle school child in Madison.

> This incident happened at night. Three young men entered a house where there were numerous children present but no adults. The family itself consisted of five children and their mother. On the night in question, the five children were home with some friends while their mother was at work. The child who opened the door did not know the three men but let them in anyway. The men went upstairs

and a shooting occurred in which the oldest child, a fifteen-year-old boy, was injured and his thirteen-year-old brother was killed apparently trying to protect the older boy. Not all of the details in this shooting are clear, but the key issue of course was that the mother had to work so many hours to support her children as a single parent. She attempted to keep close tabs on them as well as she could from work with phone calls required before any outings and regular phone check-ins. Even with the best intentions, this mother was not able to keep her family safe. What does one do?

Unfortunately, in our current cultural climate, any violence prevention program would be incomplete without a section on guns and other weapons. It would be easy, but pointless, to blame society as a whole for the easy accessibility to guns, for the culture's glorification of violence, and for the use of weapons as an acceptable strategy for dealing with frustration, anger, or conflict. However, there are no single causes or simple explanations for our current predicament regarding the use, and misuse, of weapons. Within the scope of this book's parameters, this chapter will look at four topics: 1) teaching children to resist the pressure to resort to violence and the use of weapons, 2) decreasing alienation, 3) decreasing prejudice, and 4) examining the role that institutions in our community have in maintaining the status quo of living with violence and fear. The activities work toward giving each individual the skills necessary to take a responsible role in making our society a safe place.

An overview of the contents of each section follows.

Resisting Peer Pressure: Developing an Ability to Resist the Pressure to Resort to Violence and the Use of Weapons

> Experience a number of strategies for resisting pressure.

> Gain an understanding of the feelings involved with these approaches.

> Experience the strength needed to resist pressure effectively.

> Experience inner strength on a physical level.

> Connect physical strength to inner emotional strength.

> Develop a safety plan for dealing with a weapon at someone's house.

> Connect resisting peer pressure to use of drugs or alcohol with resisting the pressure to use violence and weapons.

Decreasing Alienation: Skills for Dealing with Isolation and Alienation

> Experience how it feels to stand alone, apart from the group.

> Learn a repertoire of positive activities that can be done alone, and connect positive feelings with these activities.

> Learn strategies for joining groups of children.

> Explore what it feels like to be turned down by the group.

> Build awareness of and empathy for the person in the role of the joiner or outsider.

> Develop strategies to cope with being excluded, for example, finding another group to join, playing alone, asking a teacher to help you become included in a group.

> Learn how to respectfully assert your right to play with a specific group of friends without making others feel rejected.

> Discuss how to cope with the feeling of loneliness.

Decreasing Prejudice: Dealing with Prejudice

> Share experiences of prejudice and the feelings that it evokes.

> Explore ways to reach out to others who are different.

> Explore the connection between prejudice and isolation and between isolation and violence.

> Develop respect and understanding of cultural and racial heritages.

> Explore the fear that can accompany reaching out to people who are different.

> Explore the joy and energy that can develop from acceptance and friendship with others.

> Develop an appreciation of our differences as well as the commonalities that unite us.

> Emphasize the responsibility of each individual to take a role in making our society a safe place where people do not experience isolation and prejudice.

The Role of Cultural Influences on Violence in Our Society

> Explore the role of television and video games on our attitudes toward violence.

> Explore media such as magazines and newspapers and their role in glorifying violence.

SPECIFIC MOVEMENT SKILLS TAUGHT:

> How to use strength, both physical and emotional, to aid in resisting temptation.
> How to maintain an inner focus to aid in resisting temptation.
> Experience on a body level what it feels like to stand alone, to play alone, to be alone.
> Develop a repertoire of physical skills to use in playing alone and with others.
> Steps involved in joining a group without being intrusive.
> Ability to observe others and to maintain space.
> Ability to wait before making advances or before closing off to someone.
> Ability to move with others in their rhythm or style and allow them to join you in your style.
> Experience on a body level how it feels to be isolated or rejected and use that to develop empathy towards others who experience that.
> Develop strategies for reaching out to others who seem different or isolated.
> Use such strategies to work toward ending prejudice and isolation in your community or class.

DISCUSSION TOPICS:

> What are different ways to resist peer pressure? What are some of the pressures you encounter?
> How does it feel to stand alone, apart from the group? What can you do to tolerate the lonely feelings that may develop?
> How do you think others feel when you choose something different from them? How can we accept people who have different beliefs or preferences than ours? How does this respect and acceptance relate to violence prevention?

- Are there differences in beliefs that you would not accept? How would you handle this?
- Have a discussion about resisting peer pressure, relating it specifically to guns, other weapons, and violence. (Children need to discuss the topic of guns, their potential dangers, and the need to resist them concretely with real life situations and consequences as examples.)
- What does it feel like to be turned down by a group you want to join?
- What options are available for dealing with that situation?
- What if you are part of a group and you do not want anyone else to join?
- How do you protect your boundaries in a respectful manner?
- How does it feel to reach out to someone who is not your friend or someone who may not play safely.
- What are things you can do about being left out? What do you think would work for you?
- How does it feel to be alone? Why do people in general have a negative feeling about being alone? Brainstorm about fun things that can be done alone.
- Fearing the unknown is common. How do we keep ourselves safe without cutting off the unknown? How does this relate to prejudice, both racial and of people with different needs?
- Discuss how we decide if others are friendly or not. How should we approach them? How does it feel to be approached by strangers? How does it feel to approach someone or something strange or unknown to you? When others are approached by or approaching a stranger, what do you notice?
- Discuss how it feels to move with someone you don't know well. How does this relate to prejudice?
- Were there any similarities in the types of movement, any familiarity?
- Discuss stories from other cultures. Discuss how we can better understand and respect people of other cultures.

SKILLS NEEDED FOR RESISTING THE USE OF WEAPONS

SAFETY RULES

Children need to talk about guns, their potential dangers, and the need to resist them, using real life situations and consequences as examples. This does not mean overwhelming a child with horror stories. I ask the children to bring up fears and concerns about weapons. We discuss these concerns and develop a set of safety rules. I try to elicit these rules from the children, but if they do not bring up the following key points, I make sure they are included:

1) If you see a gun or weapon at someone's house, leave immediately. This, of course, may be difficult in some situations, for example, if your mother has dropped you off and you do not live within walking distance of home. In this situation, if you cannot reach a parent by phone, you may have to stay where you are.

2) If you must stay, go to a room away from the weapon, preferably on a different floor. It's even all right to call 911 if another child or an adult is brandishing a weapon in your presence if you can do so safely without alerting or agitating the person with the weapon. If someone is walking around with the weapon, you may even want to leave the house and go to another house or to a store and call for help from there.

3) If you hear someone talking about carrying a gun or weapon at school, consider it an emergency and tell a teacher immediately.

4) If you are asked to hold a gun or knife for someone, either refuse firmly and then tell an adult, or if you think you would be in danger if you refused, take it from them, and when they leave, get an adult.

IMPORTANCE OF ANONYMOUS REPORTING PROCEDURES

It is important not to ignore the possibility that a child might be threatened with injury or even death for telling anyone about weapons or other safety violations. For these situations, there are no easy answers. It would be nice to be able to say that if you tell an adult in charge about a gun, something will be done, and you won't get hurt. But real life situations are rarely so straightforward. So much depends on your community and the chance you have of remaining anonymous and safe from retaliation. It is important for each school to find a way to allow anonymous reports and to make sure children know and understand the procedure.

One crucial piece of violence prevention, which bears repeating here and in your prevention groups is that there is no guarantee of safety in life no matter what skills you have. You simply have to try your best to develop a variety of strategies to use if you do run into danger. Sometimes convincing the owner of the weapon to turn him/herself in may be a better strategy. These subtleties are too confusing for young elementary school students. For them, a simple "keep away from guns, tell a teacher or parent if you see one, and never touch a weapon" may be the most useful message.

Parental Roles and Family Rules

Each parent has a set of personal beliefs about the use of weapons and whether guns should or should not be in the home. Regardless of whether or not a parent owns or uses firearms, all families should clearly communicate their feelings and rules regarding weapons, especially in regard to gun safety. It may also be helpful to differentiate the way guns are used legally to promote safety, for example, a police officer in the line of duty versus illegal and unsafe ways to use a gun, for example, a child picking up a loaded gun (Capello, 2000). In families where there are no guns and the children do not play with toy guns, it is still imperative to discuss safety rules concerning weapons. There is no way to know whether your child might encounter a gun or another dangerous weapon at a friend's home, at school, in the hands of a police officer, in the hands of a criminal, or in other situations outside of your home. "Many people, young and old, don't realize how accessible guns and rifles are. The equivalent of swap meets for guns and rifles allows people in almost every city to buy, trade, and sell guns as easily as you would a used sweater" (Capello, 2000).

In addition to access to weapons, children are exposed to thousands of violent incidents depicted on television dramas, on news shows, and in computer games. Frank conversations initiated by parents can help children recognize the difference between TV and video characters and reality, for example, in real life, people do not pop back to life after they have been killed. Parents can also help children think about the feelings of the characters depicted on the shows (connecting to empathy) as a way to counteract the effects of witnessing the violence. Connecting to an empathetic response is one way to help people use nonviolent approaches. **Children need to understand that guns are intended to be deadly and that there are legal and emotional ramifications from their use and misuse.**

Children also observe many acts of violence in day to day living. Examples of these range from fighting with siblings, to having their feelings hurt by an adult in an irritated mood, or developing road rage. Parents can assist children in acquiring productive ways to manage their frustration, anger, stress, or other strong emotions by acknowledging and discussing their child's feelings (see Chapter Six) and modeling productive ways to deal with stressful situations (refer to various activities in the curriculum).

Resisting Temptation

In order to resist using weapons, children must be able to resist temptation in general. In Chapter Four, the Ignoring section elaborates on activities that work on this skill. Of particular note is the activity, Resisting Temptation, in which bubbles are blown around the children who are instructed to sit still without touching or popping them. While bubbles may seem far removed from weapons, the ability to see something appealing and resist touching it is the common goal. Another way to work toward this goal could include not touching candy that is placed on each child's desk until snack time or the end of the day. Resisting the temptation to take someone else's candy could also be incorporated in that goal. Walking down a hallway at school or in a store with the challenge not to touch anything is yet another way to practice self-control. One of the key ingredients in each of these activities is a discussion linking the ability to resist temptation during these practice challenges with the ability to resist weapons, drugs, and other inappropriate temptations.

PEER PRESSURE

While the ability to resist peer pressure is clearly connected with resisting temptation, it has the added complication of friendship alliances. It is one thing to resist the passive candy on your desk, although that can be pretty difficult for some, but is quite another to resist the ongoing pleas of peers whose acceptance or respect you seek. Telling kids to "Just say NO" is not enough. The following activity is not described in the main curriculum because I usually use it with older children. It is called "resisting the pull" and is done with a stretch cloth.

 Resisting Peer Pressure: Developing an Ability to Resist the Pressure to Resort to Violence and the Use of Weapons

Purpose:
> To help children feel how hard it is to resist pressure.
> To experience a number of strategies for resisting and to understand some of the feelings involved with each approach.
> To help children experience their inner strength on a physical level.
> To help children connect their physical strength to an inner emotional strength.
> To help children become comfortable with standing up for their own beliefs.
> To explore what it feels like to stand alone or to express opinions that may differ from their friends.
> To relate resistance to temptation to resisting violence and weapons.
> To develop a safety plan for dealing with weapons at someone's house.

Activity 1, Resisting Peer Pressure: Resisting the Pull

Overview: Children practice resisting the pulling of the stretch cloth by everyone around them. Their task is to try to not be influenced by the pressure of the cloth, to not get pushed around. This activity is a supplement to Activity 11 Grounding While Standing in a Stretch Cloth from Chapter Three. The resisting children can stand together at first, but then they should stand separately as they might if they had to take a stand against a group pressuring them to steal or take a dare etc. The group discusses strategies and feelings concerning resistance.

Teaching Thoughts: This activity can get out of hand quickly unless clear limits are established as to how hard participants may pull. Try to group children of equal size together and protect weaker members of the class by having them stand next to an adult. If the pulling gets too intense, stop the exercise, but use the opportunity to point out that peer pressure can get very intense sometimes. It is often very hard to stand up for your own values and risk humiliation or rejection.

Activity 2, Resisting Peer Pressure: Taking A Stand

Overview: Children are asked to practice making a choice and standing up for their beliefs by moving to places in the room representing specific viewpoints.

Teaching Thoughts: This is a values clarification activity that helps children get used to choosing a point of view and letting their opinion be known. I've played this activity as an ice-breaker in several situations, I did not create it and I don't know its original source. For the purpose of the curriculum, I will call it "Taking a Stand."

With some of the more emotionally charged topics, children may find themselves alone under a sign. If students get many chances during school to represent their point of view simply by walking over to a sign which represents it, they will get a lot of practice asserting themselves (taking a stand) in low pressure situations. They also will get comfortable with the idea that there are many points of view and that they will not always have the same viewpoint as their friends. If this can then be linked to dealing with peer pressure, children may feel more confident that they can handle this issue in social situations. The *Kids Book of Questions* by Gregory Stock, (1988) can help teachers come up with statements to use in this activity.

Activity 3, Resisting Peer Pressure: Resisting Temptation to Handle or Use Weapons or Violence

Overview: Review ignoring activities from Chapter Four. Repeat Activity 4: Ignoring Temptation. This time include discussion about weapons and peer pressure.

Teaching Thoughts: Many children have fears about weapons and violence that may not emerge if we do not bring up the topic. Developing specific safety plans and brainstorming ideas can help to alleviate this anxiety.

Activity 4, Resisting Peer Pressure: Prolonged Resistance

Overview: Children are challenged to ignore a favorite treat placed on their desk all day long. Discussion follows comparing resisting for five minutes in the Bubbles or Don't Laugh activity with the prolonged resistance of not eating their treat for the entire day.

Teaching Thoughts: The ability to delay gratification is very important in developing into a responsible person. This is a very simple activity that builds this skill. You can repeat this activity with different types of temptations.

SKILLS TO DEAL WITH ISOLATION AND ALIENATION

When I was in Junior High I lived in a community that was still racially segregated. My family participated in protests and, in general, was more politically active than most. The message I got from my peers was clear: if I wanted friends I shouldn't get good grades or study, and I shouldn't talk about my family's values. I decided that I did not want those kinds of friends. While I stood up for myself, I had some very lonely years. Having hobbies helped. I played music and tried to find people through other organizations with similar values. I was not a very happy child during those years.

Parents need to be prepared to support their children in this kind of situations. Planning more family activities helps for some people. Getting connected in clubs outside of school can also help. Loneliness and isolation can cause anger and depression. Be prepared to help support your children by accepting and acknowledging their feelings.

Isolation does not always come from resisting peer pressure. Adolescence is a tumultuous time for many. Loneliness and despair can come in waves. It effects self-esteem and makes one vulnerable to being preyed upon by cults, predators, etc. Building skills in self-settling, sharing feelings, using appropriate assertion, joining groups socially, occupying one's self with individual hobbies and activities, as well as reaching out to others who are perceived as being alone are all important in coping with this issue.

Many of the school shootings of the recent past have been done by people who felt isolated and developed fantasies about revenge for their rejection. Sometimes Internet groups that fuel hatred and violence feed these feelings. Sometimes they develop within when there is no one to empathize and help redirect angry feelings into constructive outlets. I cannot emphasize enough the importance of parents staying in touch with their children and providing adequate supervision. This supervision involves knowing who their friends are, what web sites they frequent on the internet, where they are after school as well as knowing if they have any illegal items in their rooms, what music they're listening to and what video games they play. The community as a whole needs to look at what it takes to provide some of this supervision when parents have to work late hours or are otherwise unavailable. For instance, if a community member observes a neighbor's child involved in a suspicious activity, they should contact the child's parents. Or, if the situation poses a danger to the neighborhood, they should contact the police for intervention. The lack of willingness to intervene and protect the community is a nationwide problem and was one of the factors that brought about the tragic outcome in Littleton, CO.

This violence prevention program is designed for elementary school children. The development of pro-active skills needs to start early to make a significant impact on violence. However, we can't assume that because children have learned certain skills at a young age that they do not need to revisit these skills as they get older. The issues they face become more complex and require different developmental strategies. A good violence prevention program should start in the earliest years and continue in some form all the way through school.

 ## Decreasing Alienation: Skills for Dealing with Isolation and Alienation

Purpose:
> To help children gain pro-active social skills for avoiding or coping with loneliness.
> To help children build empathy for the role of the joiner or outsider.
> To learn and practice strategies for coping with being excluded.
> To establish a caring atmosphere in the classroom.
> To help students become aware of the signs of isolation and loneliness in others and to realize their role in reaching out to them.
> To help each person develop a repertoire of activities to do while alone.
> To help them view being alone for periods of time as a positive option.

Activity 5, Decreasing Alienation: Joining the Group

Overview: Children are taught four steps for joining a group, which they then practice in small groups. Children rehearse being accepted into the group, having to wait before joining, and being turned down.

Teaching Thoughts: These four steps of observing are 1) moving to the periphery of the group and standing or sitting on the same level as the group, 2) watching what the children are doing for awhile, 3) making comments and 4) then asking to join. They can be suggested any time a child reports feeling left out, not just during prevention time. The same four steps can be used for joining individuals when they are occupied with an activity.

Activity 6, Decreasing Alienation: Being Outside a Group:

Overview: Using the stretch cloth to represent a solid barrier, have the class be inside the cloth doing something (pick an activity from the stretch cloth list), while one student sits out and has to watch. If everyone is in the cloth the rejected person will only be able to see outlines and shadows. Explore what that person can do with their feelings of being isolated. Options include trying to enter the group using different techniques such as talking to people or trying to sneak in. The isolated individual might try calling to someone in the group to join them on the outside, initiating a new activity, or s/he might try doing something independently.

Child comes near at the same level and watches.

Teaching Thoughts: When picking a child to play the role of being left out, try not to choose a child who is already isolated by

Child asks what the group is doing.

Child joins group.

their peers, who already stands out with obvious differences, or who is otherwise vulnerable. Wait until there has been a class discussion, participation by other students, and some empathy built before calling on them. In very large classes, or classes including children with emotional difficulties, make sure the offer to pass is understood by all the children, giving them a choice to participate in this role or not. There may be a time where you actually structure this activity so specific children may take their turn with a support person sitting next to them to remind them of what to do. You may also decide not to give certain children a turn because you feel they are just too vulnerable. This has to be done delicately. Give all of the children an opportunity to contribute to the discussion without putting any child on the spot.

Activity 7, Decreasing Alienation: Becoming Aware of Isolation

Overview: A few children at a time are secretly assigned the role of acting lonely. The other children must try to tell who you picked and find ways to show they care.

Teaching Thoughts: The Group Responsibility in Preventing Isolation:
Thus far we have focused on giving isolated or individual children resources for dealing with their problems. It is important, however, that the onus of this issue is not placed solely on the individual. The group and community must take some responsibility for noticing who is isolated and helping them become part of the group. This is similar to the role of the witness. Everyone in the community takes on the responsibility of the health and well-being of its members.

While doing this, it is also important to discuss with older students the potential problems of taking on this role. How will they handle other students teasing them or potentially ostracizing them for connecting to students who are deemed unacceptable? Will they become tainted? This is a place for the class to pull together and make a contract not to do that. Make it clear that isolating someone is a form of bullying. Leave time for students to express anxiety about it or to stand together and make a pact not to exclude anyone.

Activity 8, Decreasing Alienation: What Do I Like to Do When I am Alone

Overview: Develop a list of activities that can be done alone. Have each child make an individual list and possibly illustrate three to five enjoyable activities besides the computer and watching television.

DEALING WITH PREJUDICE

Sometime ago, a kindergarten child I worked with was told by a group of children that he couldn't play with them because he was black. The child was understandably upset, and his mother was angry. How could this happen in a warm, caring school? Of course the offending children along with their parents were talked to and given the opportunity to apologize, but the little boy has not forgotten this issue in over a year's time. He sometimes wishes he were not black so he would be more accepted, and he sometimes feels angry again at what those children said to him, and questions why the color of his skin should make him an unwanted playmate. Sometimes words hurt in a way that cannot be made better with an apology. In this situation, the mother realized that more than apologies were needed. She enrolled her son part-time in a daycare situation that had a majority of non-white children and staff to help instill pride in his own race. She asked the school to further integrate the school-based after school daycare. The school arranged for several slots to be reserved for minority children and put funding aside to provide scholarships if needed. Even in a school where multi-culturalism is celebrated and community-building is emphasized, prejudice still continues. All of the non-white children know each other and tend to hang out together. Of course there are many inter-racial friendships, but it is important to recognize the tendency to stay with the familiar.

It is human nature to see the strange and unknown as scary and to avoid it. In fact, in Chapter Five there is a pro-active intervention to use when faced with potential violence that is based on this tendency. In this intervention, if you feel that you are truly in danger, you can act "as if" you are strange. Most people are scared of individuals who act "weird." The true story about the man in the subway who saved himself from a gang of potential assailants by shrieking, drooling, and ripping his clothes exemplifies this principle in use.

Last year in my son's fifth grade class, a new child joined the class part way through the year. It is difficult enough to be a new student in the middle of the year, but this child was obese and had some special needs. He asked strange questions, and he did not have good social skills. This class was a good group of children. I don't think anyone was outwardly mean to him. I don't think anyone in the class teased him. But I do think he was socially ostracized in subtle ways. I know he put off my son. While I encouraged him to include this new child and actively invite him to play, this was a tall order. I watched the other day as my son and this boy walked home from school. The boy was asking repetitive questions, which my son answered but with reluctance. He clearly didn't want to be having the conversation.

Without realizing it, my son was communicating his feelings by maintaining only minimal eye contact, turning his body away after each question to cut off conversation and using phrasing that was somewhat monotone or dropped at the end of his answers as if to end the interaction. When we spoke later, he was surprised to learn that his body cues were saying, "I don't want to be near you." He thought he was being polite, but really he was barely tolerating this child's presence.

Many children do not feel a responsibility to become friends with someone who is different. They feel it is sufficient to simply not be mean. However, this is what causes isolation and, from what I've seen, this is not an uncommon experience for this type of child. Intrusive and immature behavior results in isolation, and it is this isolation that in some children eventually leads to anger, hatred, and sometimes violence, including murder or suicide. How can these children learn to be more appropriate, and how can other children learn to find the parts of these children that they can respect and accept?

A shift from focusing on what is different or "weird" about someone to what is similar and likeable is needed. But such a shift takes support from the community or school as well as from the individual. The result of such a shift would mean that the small interactions, like the one I witnessed, could have a different flavor. Whose responsibility is it to create such a shift? And what can one do to cause this shift?

Prevention programs need to address this issue as a community problem. Many bullies turn behavior around when they are seen as worthwhile people. If everyone sees the problem as someone else's, nothing will happen. It takes work and commitment at every level. A program or school has to adopt a way of interacting that emphasizes emotional intelligence and the embracing of diversity. Running a classroom when several children have ADHD can be a teaching nightmare. But, what if the quickness and multi-focus ability of these children were seen as an asset? What if they were given tasks requiring those skills and were admired for them? I know teachers who have incorporated the need of children with ADHD to move around by making them messengers, paper distributors, watching the clock for a certain time to remind the class of something. Other children should also get a turn to do these tasks, but a classroom that allows for movement to take place eliminates some of the problems these children might have.

This approach is hardly problem-free. I sometimes get frustrated running a prevention class when children will not settle and pay attention. But I also know what a difference it can make when some acceptance is given.

In a second grade class, there was a lot of resistance when given the assignment to find a rhythm that the whole class could move in. There were children on each end of the energy continuum, from high energy to low energy, that refused to compromise. Instead of getting annoyed or having the class feel like they failed at the cooperation task, we sat and processed how it felt to have an energy that is different from most other people. We asked if this was a common feeling for anyone in the class and empathized how frustrating that must be. The class agreed to try out several different rhythms together. They began with each extreme, tried them out, and discussed what felt good about that rhythm. We then all tried the middle ranges and discussed when each energy pattern might come in handy. As a result of the acceptance the resistant children experienced, they became much more open to trying the middle ranges of behavior at other times. The class made a decision to allow each person a turn to choose the energy or rhythm of an activity.

Both hyperactive and particularly passive children are often excluded because their style of moving is not the norm. The more left out they feel, the more stuck they become in their chosen mode. In order for a child to understand isolation and decide to do something about it, there needs to be the kind of discussion and experience described above.

Dealing with prejudice and learning to accept and respect different cultures, can be approached in many ways. Several movement activities can lead into discussions. For example, in Aliens, the activity described below, children learn how to observe another culture and join with them without expecting the others to be like them. Observing, asking, and discussing differences are all important in creating understanding.

 ## Decreasing Prejudice: Dealing with Prejudice

Purpose:
> To encourage openness to differences among people.
> To gain an understanding of how all parties in a diverse group might feel.
> To practice joining different groups.
> To increase understanding of others and decrease prejudice.
> To discover differences and similarities with others.
> To learn how accepting others can lead to friendship or at least good feelings.
> To increase empathy toward others.
> To increase understanding of other cultures.

Activity 9, Decreasing Prejudice: Aliens

Spaceship lands. Aliens are curious.

Aliens on their planet moving about.

Astronaut leaves the spaceship to meet the alien. She gives the alien some space.

Overview: The stretch cloth becomes a space ship. The children take off in it and fly to a distant planet. There they encounter some aliens (students and adults picked ahead of time). The children must decide how to determine if the aliens are friendly and how to let the aliens know that they are friendly.

Activity 10, Decreasing Prejudice: Getting To Know You

Overview: Children are asked to select as a partner someone they do not usually interact with in the class, someone they would like to get to know better, or even someone who seems very different from them. The pairings then take turns mirroring each other. Discussions focus on exploring what happens in the relationship when they accept and move with each other.

Activity 11, Decreasing Prejudice: Other Activities

Overview: A series of classroom activities that stimulate discussion and understanding of prejudice are presented.

Teaching Thoughts: Sharing or reading aloud stories about other cultures, playing ethnic music or instruments, cooking/bringing in ethnic foods, teaching children folk dances, taking field trips specific to other cultures, and other interactive techniques are fun and educational. Book reports, geography lessons, research projects, and other academic units can incorporate lessons about other cultures. Numerous films are also available for various grade levels and can be used to stimulate discussions. (See the Resources at the back of this book for Suggested Readings.)

In another exercise, children skim through various magazines and find people of color shown in executive positions or go through sports magazines and count the number of women in photos compared with the number of men photographed. These visual activities can lead to lively discussions. The main point to communicate is that all people, regardless of ethnicity or cultural background, share a common bond and that peace is only possible when we are open to accepting what is new or unfamiliar to us. Understanding or respecting other cultures requires education and communication.

> *A boy in one of my son's third grade classes had lived in Japan until he entered first grade. In Japan, children are taught to look down at the floor when talking. The direct eye contact that we as Americans expect when someone is actively listening would be considered rude in Japan. The teacher and children in the American classroom were alerted to this boy's tendency to look down when being spoken to so they wouldn't think he was being disrespectful to them.*

Sometimes we aren't alerted to cultural differences and have to figure out what behaviors are different from ours and then investigate what they might mean to that person. As a dance/movement therapist, I sometimes roleplay a client that I am confused about. Taking on the client's movement behavior helps me become more sensitive to their feelings as well as to options that might feel good in making connections. Sometimes, I have another dance/movement therapist try out different interventions on me while I roleplay my client. This gives me a sense of what might feel helpful from the client's perspective.

Lynn Koshland is a dance/movement therapist and social worker practicing in Salt Lake City, Utah. Adapting ideas from my prevention curriculum, Lynn has developed a movement-based approach to teaching pro-social, nonviolent behavior, using multi-cultural literature to elicit themes. She uses a story, *Angel Child/Dragon Child* by Michele Maria Surat to introduce and explore cultures.

Nancy Beardall, a dance/movement therapist, teacher, and consultant in the Newton, Massachusetts Public Schools has developed a comprehensive health program for middle school students. This program incorporates both movement and the arts and contains several powerful exercises that deal with prejudice (Beardall, 2001). She uses Dr. Seuss' story *Sneetches*, along with movement activities, to facilitate discussions. This story works well with older students. A teacher in the Stoughton, Wisconsin Public Schools uses it successfully with her high school classes.

MEDIA AND CULTURAL INFLUENCES

Violent video games, increased time spent unsupervised on the Internet and watching inappropriate television have had a significant impact on children. Researchers looking only at regular broadcast television, for example, have found that primetime programming averages about 5 violent incidents per hour and that Saturday morning programming for children averages up to 25 acts of violence per hour. "By the time a typical child leaves elementary school, he or she will have witnessed 8,000 murders and 100,000 other acts of violence" (Hughes & Hasbrouck, 1996). Add to this the wide array of computer and video games that simulate killing situations, some with game controllers shaped as guns, and it doesn't seem like a huge leap to connect excessive exposure to simulated violent acts with overly aggressive reactions to people in real life. In addition to aggression or other problem behaviors, children exposed to simulated violence may react with excessive anxiety, with symptoms of trauma, or with overwhelming feelings of hopelessness.

I am always surprised when kindergarten and first grade children tell me about R-rated movies they have seen on television, either when their parents are not watching them or while in the presence of their parents. I worked with several young children who had televisions in their bedrooms. If they woke in the middle of the night, they would watch anything they happened to find. It is very difficult to supervise screen time (television or computer) when it happens in the child's bedroom. Many of these children are deeply disturbed by what they have seen. They make value judgements on the kind of life they should lead based on television scenes that are so arousing that they cannot stop thinking about them. It is sometimes impossible to tell if certain children have been sexually abused or are "just" over-stimulated by having seen explicit sex scenes on TV. And worse, a lot of the sex in these shows is linked with violence in graphic ways. Children who experience overstimulation from viewing explicit, violent sex acts are at increased risk for dangerous, sexualized, acting-out behavior. This kind of overstimulation can also interfere with a child's sexual identity or put them at risk for developing unhealthy relationships as they mature.

One mother had her first grade son watch violent R-rated programs to demon-strate what not to do when he grew up. He would come to school and talk to other children about sex. He hurt people regularly and ended up teaming with another boy to hold down little girls and touch them under their clothes. This case may be extreme, but many children with caring parents, who profess to providing adequate supervision at home, do not seem concerned about what their children are viewing. Other children just seem to find ways to watch shows that are inappropriate for their developmental level without their parents' knowledge.

Children are like sponges; they absorb, all too well, messages that we think may be over their heads. Depending upon their developmental maturity, children may have difficulty in distinguishing between make-believe and reality. Many children are also accomplished mimics, copying behaviors, gestures, and interactions modeled by the people around them, whether those people are real or characters on television. Constant exposure to violent, interpersonal interactions will rein-force the belief that physical force or aggression is a valid option for dealing with anger or frustration. Children who become desensitized to violence tend to have very little empathy or regard for the feelings of others and are at risk for develop-ing anti-social personalities or behaviors.

Parents can take preventive measures to protect their children from being exposed to violence unnecessarily. Having the television set and/or computer in a common space instead of in a child's room will make supervision easier. Parents can also help by interpreting or developing empathetic responses to characters in a televi-sion show (or computer/video game) where someone gets hurt to lessen the im-pact of watching the violence. But even with parents interpreting or discussing the show, some material is just too explicit and overstimulating, which is why there is a rating system for television programming and movies (Vedantam, 2002).

SEXUAL HARASSMENT

Sexual harassment is clearly another issue connected to violence. Since this cur-riculum was designed for elementary school, this topic was not included as a dis-tinct unit. Sexual abuse prevention is addressed in every elementary school class in our school system. Since this is covered thoroughly by the counselors in the schools I work in, I have not felt a pressing need to emphasize it in this curricu-lum. However, I have incorporated it briefly by reading the stories in *Zing and Zipp, the Troggs of Wongo-Wongo Wood* by Gordon and Litt and connecting it to the pro-active interventions.

In one class that heard these stories, a discussion followed which included brainstorming strategies for stopping uncomfortable tickling. (See the example on tickling in Chapter One.) In other classes, children decided that they would use the extreme strategies such as yelling "fire," pretending to vomit, or urinating in their pants if anyone tried to abduct them or touch their private parts. These techniques would help them get away and get help from an adult. We discussed how promising not to tell and then telling was not lying—it is okay to promise anything that will keep you safe and enable you to get help. Many children seemed to appreciate the ability to brainstorm about what to do if they really were in danger. I always emphasize several times that there is no guarantee that any one technique will save them.

Although it would be nice to think that sexual issues would not come up in early elementary school, they can and do. Children who have been sexually abused themselves, or exposed to sexual activity through media or older siblings, may become over stimulated and act out on other children. At an early elementary school level, I see this less as sexual harassment and more as inappropriate touching. Sexual behavior at this young age is a warning sign that a child is troubled or traumatized and needs treatment. By fifth grade, of course, children are reaching an age where sexual exploration may be starting. Prevention programs in middle and high school need to be aware of the impact this issue can have. Sexual harassment is one form of bullying.

Summary

In this chapter we have looked at how the curriculum can be used to help create an atmosphere where each person and culture can be seen as having something of value to contribute to the whole, and where self-control and compassion are seen as goals for all. In order to accomplish this, the topics of isolation, prejudice, sexual abuse and violence with weapons must all be addressed. Although weapons is the topic that brings the most fear to every parent, as well as many children, isolation, alienation, and prejudice play a strong role in creating the rage that precipitates violence with these weapons. These issues therefore have been explored in the same chapter. The Violence Prevention Through Movement curriculum, however, is not without its limits. It is a program that offers movement and cognitive skills that can enable individuals and groups to find new ways to interact peacefully. But it cannot be effective unless the wider community (in the form of teachers, administrators, parents, neighbors and legislators) implements and supports the principles of peace it proposes.

Anger and rage exist for many reasons, and the easy availability of guns makes them a very tempting way to deal with this anger. Media and cultural influences that glamorize violence also have a measurable impact on the number of violent incidents that occur. While there is no way to guarantee anyone's safety in any given situation, there are ways to optimize one's chances for a successful outcome. Some of these ways depend on individual skills, some on the skills of the community, and some on society as a whole.

The following table lists some of the social issues that must be addressed if we really hope to have a nationwide impact on school violence, and includes the social or community skills necessary to avoid resorting to weapons to deal with conflict.

SOCIAL ISSUES

- Prejudice and Social Isolation
- Lack of Societal Support for the Importance of Emotional Intelligence
- Too Many People Living in Poverty
- Lack of Recognition by Adults of the Serious or Intense Feelings of Children
- Lack of Adequate Gun Control
- Lack of Pro-Active Social Skills
- Fascination of Media with Graphic Violence
- School Policies that Demand Punishment Instead of Empathy Building and Restitution for Anti-Social Behaviors
- Lack of Adult Supervision over Television, Internet and Video Game Use
- Lack of Training for Teachers and Group Workers on Recognizing:
    - Bullying
    - Precursors to Violence
    - Cues that Signal Social Isolation
- Lack of Societal Controls over the Advertising and Accessibility of Inappropriately Violent Television, Computer & Video Games Geared toward Children
- Societal Problems with Impulse Control and Anger Management
- Lack of Community Commitment and/or Responsibility for Eliminating Violence, Prejudice and Poverty
- Lack of Clear Behavioral Expectations and Consistent Limit Setting by Parents and Other Adults in Charge

SOCIAL SKILLS

- Recognition and Acceptance of Diverse Cultures
- Adequate Support and Training in Emotional Intelligence
- Adequate Job Training and a Living Wage
- Stricter Gun Safety and Control Laws
- Safe Ways to Deal with Conflict
- Reduced Availability of Weapons
- Ability of Parents to Supervise Their Children's Internet and Media Contact (No Televisions or Computers in Children's Bedrooms Where Unsupervised Use is Common)
- Ability to Recognize Exclusion of Others, Along with the Skills to Reach Out or to Bring this to an Adult's Attention
- Impulse Control and Anger Management for Families
- Impulse Control or the Ability to Resist Temptation
- Ability to Notice One's Own Anger Building and Safe Ways to Deal with it before it Gets to an Explosive Level
- Ability to Modulate Arousal or Intense Feelings
- Social Skills that Include Appropriate Ways to Join Groups of People
- Appropriate Ways to Become Inclusive and Learn about Differences Instead of Avoiding Them
- Early Intervention that Deals with Emotional Intelligence
- Ability of Older Children in Charge of Younger Ones, or the Adults in Charge of Any Children, to Recognize the Precursors to Violence

A thorough look at the **Violence Prevention through Movement** curriculum would not be complete without describing activities that utilize props. While some of these activities have been described earlier in the book, others are new. We feel that props deserve their own chapter, particularly for those readers who are not experienced in leading movement-based groups. Information is provided regarding safety rules, best uses, benefits, connections to social skills, and ways to use props to enhance specific unit topics. Patterns for making some of these props are provided as well as sources for purchasing them. Because the chapter on props is not part of the actual curriculum, activities are not described in the detail found in the other chapters. Instead, the chapter is presented in outline form providing an overview of each activity and added detail where necessary.

CHAPTER EIGHT

The Use of Movement Props in Violence Prevention Activities

A second grade class showed great difficulty in forming a cohesive group. Some of the children in the class had special needs and many of the children indulged in attention-seeking behaviors, particularly tantrums, when they didn't get their way or when the teacher's attention was diverted to an individual child. Most activities started off with gusto and then inevitably fell apart as one then another child experienced disappointment and dissolved into tears or angry shouting. To work on empathy and to encourage connection with each other, we introduced mirroring activities. The children were paired, one leading by initiating slow arm movements, the other imitating the movements as closely as possible. The children worked toward the goal of being in such close harmony with their partner that observers would not be able to tell who was leading and who was following. Once the children had practiced this and reached a level of success, they were given scarves as a prop to help expand their movement options. Surprisingly, all of the children in the class showed engagement and concentration in their task. When given the option to join other partners and form larger groups, the children displayed cooperation in their ability to include others and originality in the ways they could connect their scarves together. For a period of almost 30 minutes, this normally disjunctive class became a cohesive whole. The transformation seemed magical. Following this group, the teacher began using mirroring activities in the classroom whenever he needed to refocus the children. He reported seeing a significant increase in concentration and cooperation during class time.

Throughout the preceding chapters, there have been activities that use props such as the stretch cloth or stretch sacks, music or scarves. This chapter will elaborate on the use of props, provide resources for making or buying them, and describe additional activities you may want to use to supplement the violence prevention curriculum. The use of props is very popular with children. It allows a freedom of expression that some people find hard to achieve without the prop. It unifies a class group by giving them something fun to focus on together. It gives you, the teacher, parent, or group facilitator, something to hold out as an incentive for working on new behaviors.

This chapter is activity-based with little or no theoretical background. If you can afford only one prop, I would recommend you buy or make a stretch cloth. Having worked in many classrooms, I know there are frequently one or two children for whom the curriculum would help the most, and yet they seem the most resistant to working on it. They cheerfully sabotage your lesson plans. While it sometimes takes a few weeks of working to get these children involved, it does not hurt to have a carrot to hold out as incentive.

Stretch Cloth

I. Made of Lycra-Spandex

A. Comes thirty or sixty inches wide.

1. Sixty inches is the most versatile width (If you can afford only one, get a sixty inch one).
2. Thirty inch.
    a) small groups (two to eight children)
    b) small space like an office
    c) small children, under four years of age

B. Sewn together with one strong seam, makes a continuous band of cloth, a circle.

C. Length needed;

1. 1/3 to 1/2 a yard per person (an eight yard cloth fits a group of fifteen to twenty-five people)

II. How to Obtain a Stretch Cloth

A. Purchasing

1. Body Band - 5 ft. wide by 16 to 32 ft. around. (These stretch cloths are made of the same type of Spandex you can buy at your local fabric store. You can order the size and color you want. If you do not plan to make

your own, this type of band most closely matches those that I use in my program.) To order: 410-583-8437, Marjorie Falk, 9207 Satyr Hill Road, Baltimore, MD. 21234-1408

2. SporTime "Co-oper Blanket™" (These stretch cloths are made of heavy duty Spandex that lasts a long time. They are significantly smaller than the stretch clothes I use. They are very stretchy and offer more resistance. This increased resistance has made safety more of an issue in my work with whole classrooms, so I do not use it that way. However, Kimberly Dye, who makes them, has agreed to experiment with larger ones, approximately 8 yards around. I suggest you contact her by email to see if these are available. Call 1-800-283-5700, visit www.sportime.com, or contact Kimberly Dye, MS, ADTR via e-mail at kim71955@aol.com

B. Making your own

1. Call fabric stores for availability of swimsuit material (or use the internet).
2. Buy by the bolt or from the remnant table. (You can sew several remnants together to make a circular piece the size you want.)
3. Spring is the best time of year for finding the material.
4. Must be sewn with a stretch stitch (going over the seam several times) or with a surger.

III. Maintaining Cloth

A. Machine washable, gentle cycle, no bleach.

B. Air dry for best results or use lowest setting on dryer.

C. Expected life is 3-5 years

D. For runs or holes, repair using a stretch stitch.

IV. Safety Considerations (Because safety is a major issue with this particular prop, this topic is repeated in its entirety in the Activity Book.)

A. Spandex is very stretchy, like a giant rubber band. This makes it exciting and potentially dangerous. (If the children get wild, it is easy to pull someone off balance).

1. Discuss safety rules before beginning an activity

a) No pulling on the cloth while directions are being given.
b) Stop or freeze immediately if someone falls.
c) Allow anyone to call a STOP TIME if scared or off balance.
d) No stepping or standing on the cloth. It is slippery.
e) Participants must be able to pull gently and must be sensitive to neighbors' safety (medium pulling used when appropriate, hard pulling used only in sitting activities).
f) If you fall, bend your knees to go down gently on your bottom.
2. Safe use of the stretch cloth is crucial. Children can get hurt.
a) Start with sitting activities to provide a lower center of gravity.
b) Promptly remove any child from an activity who does not follow the rules.
c) Do not allow more than one chance to rejoin group appropriately in any given period.
d) Use the 4B's or abdominal breathing between each activity.
e) Build up to more exciting activities as groups demonstrates control.
f) Place children next to similar size peers. This allows the cloth to best cover each child and helps activities work better.

Stretch Sacks

I. **Stretch Sacks for One-Third to One-Half of Your Class.** Every activity can be divided into participants and observers.

II. **Made of Lycra-Spandex** (60 inch Spandex folded over determines width of sack)

A. Rectangular shape with opening in front and Velcro™ closures.

B. Choose length to accommodate size of children.

1. approximately 3 to 3 1/2 feet for pre-school child
2. approximately 3 1/2 to 4 1/2 feet for children in grades K-2nd
3. approximately 4 1/2 to 5 1/2 feet for children in grades 3rd-5th
4. approximately 5 to 6 feet for older children and adults

III. How to Obtain a Stretch Cloth Sack

A. Purchasing

    1. SporTime "Body Sox™" Call 1-800-283-5700, visit www.sportime.com, or contact Kimberly Dye, M.S., ADTR, via e-mail at kim71955@aol.com

B. Making your own

    1. Refer to sewing pattern in Appendix 1 of the Activity Book.
    2. Buy swimsuit material by the bolt or from the remnant table if suitably sized remnants are available.
    3. Buy cotton ribbing (the fabric used on t-shirt necklines) and several tabs of Velcro™ closures for the sack opening.
    4. Must be sewn with a stretch stitch (going over the seams several times) or with a surger.

IV. Maintaining Cloth

A. Machine washable, gentle cycle, without bleach OR hand wash in cold water.

B. Air dry for best results.

C. Important note: Every time a stretch sack is taken off, the Velcro™ closures should be secured to each other to prevent snagging the fabric.

D. To increase the life of the material, have children take their shoes off before climbing into the sack.

Scarves

I. Made of Chiffon

A. Various sizes available.

B. Either solids or patterns work well as long as the fabric is translucent.

II. How to Obtain

A. Purchasing

1. Dancing Colors
   Emily Day & Dancing Colors
   PO Box 61 / 301 6th Street, Langley, WA 98260
   Web: www.dancingcolors.com
   Phone: (360) 221-5989, Email: emilyday@dancingcolors.com
2. SporTime "Dancing Colors™"
   Call 1-800-283-5700 or visit their website at www.sportime.com
3. West Music
   P.O. Box 5521 / 1212 5th Street, Coralville, IA 55241-0521
   Web: www.westmusic.com
   Phone: (800) 397-9378

III. Maintaining Scarves

A. For best results, keep scarves folded or hanging up when not in use.

B. If folded, keep in a bag separate from other props so they do not snag.

C. Wash in gentle cycle, air dry OR follow manufacturer's instructions.

Percussion Instruments

I. Percussion Instruments: Various Drums, Bells, Blocks, Clackers, Maracas, Tambourines, etc.

A. Many activities benefit from the use of a good sounding drum (higher quality than a child's drum).

B. While it is not necessary to have any percussion instruments to implement this curriculum successfully; they can provide alternative ways to work on certain goals when space is restricted.

II. How to Obtain

A. Purchasing

1. Music stores, children's educational stores, and other specialty stores.
2. Various catalogues.

a. West Music
   P.O. Box 5521 / 1212 5th Street, Coralville, IA 55241-0521
   Web: www.westmusic.com
   Phone: (800) 397-9378
3. Thrift stores and yard sales.

Music

I. Pre-Recorded Music

A. While not a necessity for this curriculum, music can enhance many of the activities as well as build a mood, particularly if you plan to practice relaxation or guided imagery with your class.

B. For low energy moods, try baroque music, new age music, or any other music that has either a slow beat (adagio speed) or no discernable beat.

C. For high energy moods, try upbeat music (andante speed) with a definite beat. Some cultural music is particularly well-suited such as Brazilian music, Cajun music, Latin salsa music, African music, etc.

D. Generally, music with vocalists can be distracting. If you do choose vocal music, consider pre-screening it, paying attention to the lyrics.

II. How to Obtain

A. Music stores, specialty stores, catalogues, off the internet. (In particular, Narada Music offers a wide range of high quality selections in both soothing instrumental and world music.)

B. Used CD stores, thrift stores, yard sales.

III. Specific Music Suggestions

A. For a calming, relaxing mood:

   1. *Woodlands* – new age (Tingstad, Rumbel, Lanz/Narada Lotus)
   2. *Cristofori's Dream* – new age (Lanz/Narada Lotus)

3. *Floating on Evening, Songs from Otter River* (Coyote Oldman/Coyote Oldman Music – Xenotrope Music)

B. For an upbeat, high energy mood:

1. *Mondo Beat, Masters of Percussion* (Nljeilu/Narada)
2. *I Am Walking, New Native Music* (Collection/Narada)
3. *Skyline Fire Dance* (Lanz/Narada)
4. *Willie and Lobo* (Siete/Narada World)

C. For both upbeat and relaxing, in turn:

1. *Kali Ma, Dances of Transformation* (Desert Wind/Alan Scott Bachman)

CONCLUSION

This chapter has outlined the various props utilized in the Violence Prevention through Movement curriculum. General facts, resources, tips and suggestions for acquiring and successfully using the props have been presented. This information is provided as a foundation as well as a springboard for new activities that you might develop.

In the final chapter the use of the curriculum in therapeutic and other small group settings is explored, offering suggestions for approaching developmental issues with the various skills taught in the curriculum. This chapter also summarizes activities that would work well in an office or other relatively small setting, and ends with a section geared for dance/movement therapists, detailing how this curriculum can benefit them in their professional work.

CHAPTER NINE

Applications of the Violence Prevention through Movement Program

for Mental Health Professionals, Special Education Teachers, & Dance/Movement Therapists

It's lunchtime, early November at an elementary school in Wisconsin. A fifth grader named Sue, a good student behaviorally and academically, has just left drawings on her teacher's desk. One is a picture of the school with the words "This school sucks. I hate it here." The other has two figures drawn, a girl in the middle of the page and a second much smaller person to the left holding what looks like a gun up to the girl's head. The teacher wisely decides that she needs help investigating and dealing with this issue. The school counselor is called in to help.

As it turned out, three boys in the class decided to make Sue the target of their teasing. She was new to the school and had not yet made new friends. She was vulnerable emotionally, having lived with several families before being permanently placed with her aunt and uncle (now mom and dad) four years ago. She showed a lot of resilience, she had attached to her current family, done well in her previous schools, and made long lasting friends. Sue was a sweet child, always willing to help at school, kind to other people, although, inclined to want things to go her way. She tended to become whiney and have minor accidents when feeling vulnerable. She did not show her anger directly.

Usually Sue's teacher has a special jar on her desk, a place for her students to deposit written accounts of problems they are having. The teacher would read the comments each day and help the students deal with what was bothering them. Sue regularly made use of this jar, but since the end of October, it had been gone. Unable to express her anger directly, Sue turned it inward. The boys had made some comments about her, suggesting that the class would have been better off if she had never joined it, better yet, if she had never been born. Sue began to feel that maybe they were right. Both of the figures in the drawing were Sue. She was killing her own soul so she would no longer be there. Sue had no real plans of killing herself. The pictures served as a warning to those who worked with her that she was desperate and was asking for help, more help than the teacher could be expected to provide.

People who engage in therapy usually do so because they have problems with behavioral or emotional issues. These problems may be based on trauma, as in the example above, or may be due to organic causes, physical or mental limitations, environmental causes and/or relationship conflicts. The client may realize the problems and initiate treatment, or treatment may be that it is initiated by others, parents, school personnel, courts, etc. Sometimes the problems are minor, and short-term help is all that is needed. Sometimes much more involved treatment is recommended.

This chapter examines applications of the Violence Prevention Through Movement Curriculum within the field of mental health. It can be used as a resource for dance/movement therapists, social workers, psychologists, counselors, nurses, special education teachers, occupational and physical therapists, other creative arts therapists, etc. Professionals leading group or individual sessions dealing with anger management, social skills, impulse control, perceptual motor issues, self-esteem, mood disorders, trauma, parenting skills, etc. will be able to utilize aspects of this curriculum to achieve treatment goals. It is pertinent to clients of all ages.

Training in this curriculum would also benefit paraprofessionals such as school aides and support staff for residential treatment centers. While paraprofessionals may not be leading sessions, they are in the trenches, so to speak, and regularly encounter many of the issues listed above. Learning the vocabulary and techniques for helping clients de-escalate and feel validated can be invaluable.

This chapter is divided into three sections. The first section looks at some of the developmental tasks children face, the movement parameters that are associated with each task, and how they relate to the violence prevention curriculum. Examples are provided to illustrate these concepts. The second section discusses how specific activities from the curriculum can be used in group and individual therapy. The last section is specific to dance/movement therapists. It examines how this curriculum can be used to develop new therapeutic skills and to broaden career opportunities.

As previously stated, it is important to remember that the Violence Prevention through Movement curriculum is not a form of therapy. It is an educational program with components that can be used therapeutically. It does not train or prepare individuals to be dance/movement therapists; rather, it introduces movement experiences that have broad-based applications. With that said, it may be helpful for mental health professionals to know my own theoretical background, as a way of understanding how this curriculum makes sense therapeutically.

Section 1: Developmental Tasks

I work from a developmental framework, drawing on the theories of Mahler, Winicott, and Erikson's stages of development to understand the issues that my clients are dealing with. I also have a strong background in movement observation that enables me to relate movement behaviors to developmental issues. When I work with clients, however, I am more interested in the "here and now" perspective, drawing on the work of Rogers, Yalom, and Pearls in the field of psychology and Marion Chase in the field of Dance/Movement therapy. In therapy, of course, there are no lesson plans. How much flexibility a therapist uses is dependent upon his/her style. I try to work with whatever issues the clients bring up as they bring them up.

This "here and now" perspective influences my work in the Violence Prevention Through Movement program as well. Children may come to class with specific issues that are bothering them such as teasing. I might then change my lesson plan to work on the problem at hand. Yet another way in which this approach might affect my lesson plan would be by convincing me to stay with a skill or topic as long as a class seems to need it.

Since several of my earlier positions involved clients dealing with learning disabilities, I also developed a style that works on two levels. The "felt experience," which involves doing movement, gives clients new types of feelings in their bodies and new opportunities to have an impact on the environment. The "symbolic level" of verbalization lets clients explore how this new experience or skill can be used (put back into a felt experience) in other places. I use this technique continually in the Violence Prevention through Movement Curriculum. For example, during the ignoring activities, students try to ignore provocation. After the activity, we discuss how it felt and what strategies worked for each person. We might then try the activity one more time using the strategies that each person felt would work for them. This is followed by yet another discussion, evaluating how effective the strategy was and how it could be used or adapted to situations where ignoring is necessary.

The Violence Prevention through Movement Curriculum offers movement activities that address the tasks necessary to master each of the early stages in development. Children who have a wide repertoire of coping behaviors available to them have the skills necessary to deal with the complexities of a modern world in a peaceful manner.

One of an infant's first developmental tasks is bonding with the primary caregiver and developing a sense of trust that his/her primary needs will be taken care of. This results in an overall feeling that the world is a safe place. On a movement level, bonding requires attunement as the caregiver moves with the baby and the baby learns to move with the caregiver (see Attunement Activities in Chapter Six). During this phase, babies also spend a lot of time learning where things are in the environment. First they discover their own hands. Next they develop a growing awareness that the caregiver and food are things separate from themselves. Developing spatial awareness is a major task in this phase, incorporating both direct staring (at their own hands, people, and objects) and indirect scanning (to find things or learn about where things are). In addition to a sense of trust and safety, the precursors of attention span and focusing ability also develop during this stage.

> *In the foregoing example, Sue exhibited behaviors, which indicated that she had some trust in the environment. She regularly turned to the adults in charge to help her solve problems. She was able to focus on work and play activities with an appropriate attention span. She regularly took comfort from her aunt (now adopted mother) and could share both fear and joy with her. While Sue had been in four homes in addition to her birth home, they had all been loving and somewhat consistent. During a period of reunification with her birth mother at five years of age, there had been concern about attachment and hyperactivity. Sue was given Ritalin, and she and her birth mother participated with me in dance/movement therapy sessions geared toward developing attachment. Mom was shown how to play with Sue by following Sue's lead. These play sessions continued over the course of a year. Mom was able to show affection, comfort, and a willingness to be with Sue at Sue's level. Additional sessions with Sue's older sister and younger brother were also provided. A year later, when Sue had to leave her birth home a second time, sessions were continued with the aunt to help her with the transition. During her time at the aunt and uncle's home, Sue became more and more secure in her attachment to her new family. She was able to discontinue Ritalin and showed no signs of ADHD.*

The second developmental task of childhood is to individuate from the caregiver. The "terrible twos" are part of this process as the child struggles to assert individuality. In movement terms, children learn to use the vertical plane, up and down movements associated with standing and climbing. Even when toddlers walk, their first walk is more an emphasis on the vertical plane (staying upright) than the usual forward movement associated with walking. The world becomes a playground to be climbed upon. Everything is "mine." This is the stage of assertion (see Assertion Activities in Chapter Five). Children explore how they are going to act upon their environment. They are so small in their world that everything seems more powerful than they are. They want to gain some of this power. To individuate successfully, they must be allowed to make choices whenever possible and have secure boundaries to keep them safe during their quest. Children need to learn to stand up for themselves without feeling ashamed. Children learn to talk during this period. Identification of basic feeling states should become associated with the correct labels (see Feeling Identification Activities in Chapter Six). Children can learn the beginnings of "being mad safely" in this period, if this is modeled for them (see the Mad Safely Formula in Chapter Six).

This is the stage of development that is giving Sue difficulty in the earlier example above. The boys in her class are being mean to her and she is unable to stand up for herself. This does not imply that the bullying is her fault; however, the bullying needs to stop, and the school needs to take some action toward that end. But I am looking at this from the perspective of Sue's developmental issues for the moment. Later in this chapter, I deal with the school's role in working with bullies.

In her history of changing homes, attaching and reattaching, Sue has never learned to assert herself. To do so might risk another loss. Some children might have responded to this history by acting angry all of the time. Sue responded by making herself loveable. She internalized tension and showed it by getting injured or whining and crying for help. The task in therapy was to help Sue feel empowered. We practiced saying "Stop!" and "No" with a strong voice, face, and body. The adoptive mother and I made traps for her to escape from in which she had to use all her strength. We also practiced ways of redirecting the teasing by being friendly to the boys, walking away when they started to say mean things, and reaching out to some of the girls to make friends with them. (See list of strategies for redirecting aggression in Chapter Four.) The questions that I had Sue address were: "How am I going to deal with what they are doing?" "Am I going to let them trap me into feeling bad about myself, or am I going to use my wits and body to get out of the trap?" The image of traps and escaping worked for Sue and gave her a feeling of empowerment.

The third developmental task of childhood is gaining mastery of one's body and learning to make an impact on the environment. Erikson calls this stage "initiative versus guilt." In movement terms, children use the sagittal (arrow-like) plane, which is related to traveling forward or backward in space. The children are always on the go, busy and doing things. At the beginning of this stage, they can become impulsive in their love of moving and will sometimes do dangerous things like forgetting to slow down at the top of a flight of stairs or running impulsively into the street. They bear close supervision during this phase.

As they gain mastery, there is a growing awareness of time and when something is supposed to happen allowing the children to anticipate events. This is an ideal time to teach safety rules, but don't expect that they will remember to follow them. Children experiment with time. They may go in sudden bursts or dawdle endlessly. The result of this increasing awareness and ability to anticipate allows children to use self-talk strategies for self-settling (see Self-Settling Techniques in Chapter Three). The child at nursery school who is beginning to panic over missing his mother can say something like, "Mommy comes after snack time." Parents can use phrases like "First Nathan will go, and then Sammy will have a turn." Children at this stage can learn to take a deep breath and calm down. They can make a simple plan with a friend and carry it out. The ability to anticipate means children can begin to defer gratification. They can wait for at least short periods of time. This is the period in which many of the basic social skills can be taught and in which strategies for positive problem-solving can be introduced and used with support (see Chapter Six, Positive Problem-Solving). **This is the stage where violence prevention programs should begin.**

Just because a child fails to master one developmental task does not mean that she cannot move on to work on another. Sue was able to anticipate things. She was able to think about possible solutions to her problem and anticipate fairly accurately how the boys would react. This helped her devise a plan of action to protect herself even though she was not yet ready to stand up for herself directly. She decided it would be easiest for her to make friendly comments to the boys, acting toward them "as if" they were nice boys who would never intentionally do anything mean. We practiced timing her intervention, doing it before they had a chance to gang up on her, in other words, acting in a friendly way to each boy separately. Sue had a chance to try out this solution and then come back to therapy and work out the kinks.

Meanwhile, immediately after learning about Sue's pictures, Sue's mother and I made an appointment to meet with the classroom teacher and school counselor. It wasn't fair to expect Sue to handle this on her own. The school needed to provide a sense of safety.

The school was very responsive to all suggestions. In fact, as a result of our meeting they decided to implement the Violence Prevention Through Movement Curriculum. In the short term, they agreed to several interventions for Sue. First, in an attempt to help Sue make friends, they had already picked her to be in a small group of girls who met weekly to make greeting cards for the staff at the school. The other girls in the group were also lacking a large circle of friends but were not overly troubled children. While this was a great idea, children usually like to pick their own friends. I asked the school counselor if she could arrange for Sue to have a special lunch bunch once a week for several weeks with two or three girls that she liked. The ability to choose gave Sue more power along with the prestige of having a special privilege that only a few children could join. I also asked if the teacher could implement a kindness jar. Children would be asked to describe something in writing whenever they witnessed someone else doing a kind act. These events would be described on slips of paper put in the kindness jar. The teacher could read them to the class and keep track of how many kind acts were being noticed. The class could have a kindness party when the jar was full. I also asked the teacher what had happened to the shark jar, the one used for sharing feelings. It had gotten broken. She subsequently replaced that jar, which Sue had found very helpful as a positive outlet for her concerns.

I also discussed consequences for the boys who were doing the teasing. The teacher and counselor agreed to have them perform a kind act as restitution each time they did something mean. Suggestions included arranging bookshelves or reading to a kindergarten class. Even though recess was withheld until they completed restitution, the kind acts would help build their sense of self worth and empathy. The teacher also agreed to discuss bullying and its effects with the class as well as to examine and practice positive responses to bullying such as assertion and changing the subject. Children were to be given a strong message that teasing was not acceptable. I left the meeting feeling that Sue was fortunate to have such a responsive and skilled school staff working with her.

The last developmental task that we will address is one that encompasses the elementary school years. This is the task of becoming productive beyond the "whims and wishes of play" (Erikson, 1960, p.259). Of course, in the early elementary years, a wise teacher incorporates play into the lesson plan. Nonetheless, sitting at a desk for reading and math is different from the play of early childhood. Without the ability to anticipate and defer gratification, children are at a loss as to how to succeed both socially and academically.

On a movement level, all of the basic tasks of locomotion have been mastered. Children are now combining skills in order to learn some of the more complex motor skills required in sports and academics. They are learning to follow the rules of fair play. Movement phrases with clear beginnings, middles, and endings are beginning to develop. This phrasing decreases impulsivity. At the same time, children have more control over individual body parts, and they can now use gestures to release tension instead of having to use the whole body. An increase in body integration allows the appropriate amount of tension to be used for completing a task.

For some children, this is the first time attention problems become apparent. As children compare themselves to others in the class environment, those who cannot function feel inadequate. This feeling can, of course, lead to difficulty with taking risks, which creates more inadequacy and reinforces the feelings of being inferior. Inferiority can also evolve because of racial or ethnic differences. Many schools have in place cultural awareness programs for reducing prejudice. Despite these programs, there are still some teachers who have different expectations based on unconscious biases. Tensions that arise from prejudice or cultural differences must be carefully considered.

Many schools work very hard to help children gain the early academic and social skills necessary for school success. Children may be pulled out for special reading or math help. They may receive a special group experience to work on anger management. At Lapham Elementary School, where I have done most of my work, these groups can be very helpful. Even so, some children have their feelings of inferiority reinforced by that special assistance.

Because academic success relies on mastering many movement tasks, some of the problems that arise at this stage require movement work before academic interventions can be successful. Impulsiveness and difficulties with focusing are skills that are built into the violence prevention curriculum. Spatial awareness and gestures that specifically help to calm individuals and groups, also help to decrease violence and make classroom management easier.

Because she had many academic and social competencies, Sue was able to make a plan and follow through. Just two weeks after the incident, she was already feeling much more positive. She started her lunch bunch and felt like she finally had some girlfriends. She was able to keep the idea of finding ways to escape traps fresh in her mind and wanted to keep playing the trap game with her mother and me in our sessions. She began treating the boys as if they were friendly, nice guys. The boys began to act friendlier, both to Sue and to others in the school. Additionally, due to the work of the teacher and counselor, class members have also began to stand up for each other, telling anyone who was teasing someone else in a mean way to stop. And, of course, Sue continued in dance/movement therapy with me.

Section II: Applications of the Prevention Curriculum to Small Group and Individual Settings

This section provides examples of using the activities in small group or individual settings. These activities do not require previous movement training or a large movement space to be successful.

Chapter Two: Spatial Awareness and Implications for Safety

contains two activities that many therapists find useful: Activity 1, Spatial Needs: Approach and Stop, and Activity 2, Appropriate Distancing: Safe Distancing. Since spatial intrusiveness or isolation is a major issue for many individuals who have been victims of trauma as well as for those who are aggressive, this theme is useful in many groups. One member of the group can approach another who is at the opposite side of the room and who stops the approaching member at a distance that feels safe. By giving everyone a turn, the group will be able to see that different people have different spatial preferences. Group members can also experiment with stopping someone at one arm length away (a common distance for polite interaction) and two arm lengths away (the minimum distance you want to maintain from a hostile person). This activity is useful for people of all ages. Since it requires only walking, it does not tend to make people self-conscious. In addition to developing spatial awareness, these activities can be used to increase perception of early warning signs as well as the ability to interpret emotions in others by having group members approach each other while expressing different states of mind.

Another useful task that can be explored in a small group setting is developing awareness of the different amounts of space needed for a variety of activities. Use the Space Bubble handout and worksheet in Chapter Two for this purpose.

Being sensitive to spatial needs of clients is a way to empower them. I usually spend time creating a safe space with any clients dealing with trauma. A list of ways this can be handled in therapy sessions is included below (Kornblum, 2000).

1. Allow client(s) to explore where they feel most comfortable, for example, against a wall, in the middle of the room, with a lot or a little space around them, with others across from them or to the side, on the floor, or on a chair.
2. Ask your client(s) where they would like you, the therapist, to be. Allow them to try placing you in different locations in reference to them.

Have them check in with themselves, on both a body and an emotional level, to see how these different spatial relationships feel.

3. Ask client(s) to draw a picture of what a safe space for them would be like: a large or small room, with windows or no windows, with doors or no doors, how many of each, and where in relation to them. What would be in the space: chairs, cushions, other objects, other people? Where would the space be: at home, in the woods, in a meadow, in the mountains, etc.? Where would they be in the space? You can draw the sketch as directed by a client, or the client can make the drawing and then discuss it with you.

4. If your client(s) could make the meeting space feel safe, how would they arrange things and people? Give them a chance to try doing it.

5. Allow client(s) time to make a safe space using props in your room. Have pillows, beanbag cushions, stuffed animals, and different scarves or pieces of material available. They can decorate the space, making it complete with pillows or tables defining boundaries. Allow enough time for the client to experiment with different arrangements while still leaving time to indulge in being in their space. Drawing, creating a journal, or verbal processing could follow.

6. Allow clients, if you have a group, to make a group space. The space might have individual sections, some of which might be partially enclosed and some of which might be open. Other props such as instruments, puppets, or stuffed animals might be a part of it. You may not want to use this activity with children if unsafe touching may be an issue. Sharing each person's perspective on the process of making the space and how each person feels about the completed space can follow the activity. Are there places in the space where someone feels uncomfortable, most comfortable, ownership, etc.

The activities from Chapter Two address not only spatial awareness but also establishing boundaries for clients. I have included some additional movement experiences for establishing boundaries. (Some clients may have a difficult time participating in these experiences. They will need adequate preparation and a sufficient time in therapy before they can participate in a meaningful way.)

1. Have the clients pair up, with one partner assigned the role of approaching his/her partner and the other as the one being approached. The partner being approached guides the approaching client. The goal is to experiment with speed, direction, level (walking, crawling), body orientation (front, side, back), and spatial direction (straight on or meandering) to see what feels comfortable and what does not. Allow enough time to experiment with several different approaches. Switch roles so everyone gets a

chance to both approach and be approached. Leave time to process how the different approaches felt.

2. Using crepe paper streamers, have clients outline their personal space. How big a space do they want around themselves? (If you try this on different days, the size may vary.) In what way are they most comfortable allowing you or someone else to enter their space? Is there a way two spaces could share a boundary with each other? If not, respect that need. How could two people sharing a boundary move back and forth between their spaces with both parties remaining comfortable?

3. With children, a safe space can be seen as a nest, and they can hatch as different creatures, born in a comfortable, safe place. They can venture out into general space and return back to their nest. They can experiment with visiting other nests, always getting permission first. They can work on respecting others' boundaries and on learning social skills as these different creatures.

4. They can also develop assertion while learning to protect their space. You can approach a client's space and have the client tell you "Stop" or "No" in an assertive voice. Model an assertive facial expression and a strong body stance (see handout on Asserting Yourself in Chapter Five).

Chapter Three: Self-Control and Stress Management
contains activities that need adaptation for use in an office setting. Activity 1 and 2: Statues can be done as long as there is space for everyone to stand with a medium to large space bubble around them. Activity 3: Introduction to Self Control involves moving with high energy, but in control. This can only be done in an office-size space if the high energy movements are done in place, without moving. You can't quite get the same effect, but in some ways, it requires even more control. "In control" is defined, and abdominal breathing is introduced as a way to calm down. There are activity sheets in Chapter Three, which clarify the amount of energy needed for different types of tasks and help clients monitor and adjust their internal thermostat. Activity 5: Energy Modulation in Place: The Storm can work in any size space. Again, developing skill in energy modulation is the goal. Activity 7B: Putting on the Brakes, Part 2 works on the ability to stop quickly when agitated and helps to improve impulse control.

ACTIVITY 8: The 4 B's of Self-Settling is a crucial part of this chapter. This intervention offers a ritualized way of calming down, which has proven very effective. There is a handout, which demonstrates the movement sequence. This can be done anywhere but is best learned if taught in conjunction with the other energy modulation activities.

In a six-week anger management group run by the school counselor and psychologist, children were exploring ways they could calm down if they started to get mad. The whole group stated affirmatively, "We could do the 4 B's." These children had incorporated this technique from their violence prevention classes and readily saw its application for helping them to control their anger.

ACTIVITY 9: The 4 C's of Self-Control is an activity that can be done anywhere. It works on increasing attention span and developing the ability to resist temptation. Activity 13 introduces relaxation techniques. Sample scripts are provided.

Chapter Four: Awareness of and Response to Dangerous Situations divides activities into three sections. The first section includes alerting activities, which help children develop a greater awareness of early warning signs. Activity 2: Breaking Balloons and Activity 3: Friendly or Not, Here I Come can both be done in any size space and can help clients assess accurately who is in their environment. The second section has to do with scanning the environment and developing the ability to be multi-focused. These activities are more difficult in a smaller space, but Activity 6: Following the Changing Leader and Activity 7: Who is Different? are possible if you have enough space for everyone to form a circle, either sitting or standing, with a medium space bubble around them. These two activities take a lot of concentration and may require the skills involved in paired mirroring to be developed first. The third section in this chapter deals with ignoring provocation. Activity 8: Don't Laugh, Activity 10: Breaking the Rules, and Activity 11: Resisting Temptation can all be done in a small space. Breaking the Rules, however, would need to be restricted to a sitting task.

Lonny is a second grade boy who has great difficulty with focusing. He is easily distracted by both external and internal stimuli and has a very short attention span. Lonny talks out loud to himself and seems constantly agitated. He is participating in a dance/movement therapy group with five other boys who also have focusing and attention problems. I adapted the Don't Laugh activity by having the boys work on a verbal task, counting out loud by twos, while being distracted by their peers. This activity requires the utmost concentration from Lonny. Following an activity like this, Lonny becomes calm and settled. This settled behavior continues into his next class, which is in the computer lab. He was failing this class at the beginning of the school year and is now able to be successful.

Chapter Five: Movement Strategies for Dealing with Conflicts and Aggression contains activities that fit the same framework

of the Approach and Stop activity in Chapter Three. All of the pro-active strategies introduced in Chapter Five can be demonstrated in any size space. After practicing the body posture and facial expressions that are used with the different interventions, clients can try using them as someone approaches pretending to be hostile. There are several handouts that illustrate the interventions and a worksheet to help each client develop his/her own repertoire.

In one therapy group, children were dealing with anger issues. These were all children who had experienced domestic violence in their homes. Although it was a dance/movement therapy session, we had a very small space to work in. The children were introduced to assertion and changing the subject as possible ways to deal with tense situations. Before we practiced these techniques, we had each child find a spot against a wall, having at least a medium space bubble around them. We practiced these techniques as a group and then had each child try them individually as one of the dance/movement therapists approached them. This was followed by a discussion about which situations these techniques might or might not be helpful in diffusing. Children need to have realistic expectations of what these skills can do. The goal in the group was to help these children develop nonviolent ways to deal with their own feelings, not to leave the group feeling that they will be able to stop the adult violence from happening at home.

Chapter Six: Managing Anger and Developing Empathy or-

ganizes activities into four sections addressing feeling identification, anger management, empathy, and empowerment. There are many handouts and activity sheets to supplement the movement activities. Activity 1: Guessing Games, Activity 2: What is My Body Showing? Activity 6: Double Dip Feelings, and Activity 7: Feeling Approaches all work very well in therapy settings. In fact, most of these activities work best in small groups. For an additional activity to augment the others, have clients pick a situation, which happened to them and roleplay their feelings evoked by that situation. After other members of the group try to guess the feelings, the situation may be shared with the group if the client chooses to do so. All four of the anger management activities can be done in a small space. It is important to remember that managing anger involves many of the skills that have already been covered in the curriculum such as self-settling, ignoring provocation, and awareness of arousal. These basic skills form a foundation for successful mastery of anger management. Activity 9: Matching Intensity, Activity 10: Who is the Mirror? Activity 11: Group Mirroring, Activity 13 & 14: Paired and Circular Pushing, Activity 18: Making Waves, and Activity 21: See-Saw can all be done in a small space. Activity 17: Animal Babies could work in a dyad situation but would require a large office, living room size, to use with a small group. Activity 28A & B: I Didn't Get My Way and Activity 29: I Can Be Mad Safely are actually easier to do with small groups than with a classroom.

Occasionally, working on these techniques can cause over-arousal. Therapists need to be vigilant in protecting boundaries and maintaining safety while children are practicing these skills.

> One such incident occurred in a dance/movement therapy group for three elementary school boys needing to work on anger management and self-control. One of the boys, Reese, had a very short fuse and could be disruptive in class and at home with his angry outbursts. He was also very articulate and, as the group progressed, he showed openness to exploring and expressing his feelings. He regularly used the dance/movement therapists and other group members as resources to brainstorm problems he was having at home or in the class. Due in part to his enthusiasm and intense feelings, Reese could quickly become immersed in an activity to the point of losing his sense of boundaries and moving recklessly. Over several months, the boys had been working actively on anger management skills. They had learned the "mad safely formula" and had done anger roleplays. Their favorite thing to follow this work was an adaptations of the Baby Animals activity. With three boys and three therapists, each boy paired up with a therapeutic "mom." After a rough weekend, Reese had a harder time than usual dealing with his feelings. Nothing his therapeutic "mom" did was right. Reese was acting out his disappointment from home and he became immersed in the feelings. Although he began by showing these feeling safely, he got lost in the moment and hit the dance/movement therapist in the face with a pillow. Almost immediately he realized he had overstepped the boundaries for safety and took a time-out to calm down, using abdominal breathing to help himself regain control. Within a few minutes, he was once again grounded and rejoined the group. A discussion followed, dealing with both his feelings from the weekend and his loss of control.

Chapter Seven: Additional Issues utilizes activities from several other chapters along with several new activities. Activity 2: Taking a Stand, Activity 5: Joining a Group, Activity 8: What Do I Like to do When I'm Alone?

can all be done in a small space. Activity 6: Being Outside a Group, could be adapted by replacing the stretch cloth with an art activity or rhythmic game. Have the clients sit in a circle with one person outside of the group, excluded from the activity. The exploration and techniques for dealing with being isolated would be the same as described in this chapter. Activity 8: What I Like to do When Alone involves developing a individual list to remind each child of activities they can do when alone.

Section Three: Applications of the Violence Prevention through Movement Program Specific to Dance/Movement Therapists

This section lists and discusses ways that the Violence Prevention through Movement program may benefit Dance/Movement Therapists in their professional practice.

1. Violence Prevention through Movement is a curriculum that dance/move ment therapists are especially suited to implement because of their body awareness and training in developing movement themes. Since school violence is a major concern throughout the country, dance/movement therapists familiar with this curriculum can promote the profession and develop positions doing prevention work in schools or community agencies.

2. Due to the importance and urgency of preventing violence in schools and communities, there are numerous opportunities to apply for grants in this area. The Violence Prevention Through Movement Checklist provides pre- and post-measures as well as specific vocabulary to aid in the writing of these grants. The Challenge Sheets also provide concrete measures of the children's application of the curriculum outside the sessions. Granting agencies as well as teachers appreciate how easy it is to notice and track changes.

3. While this is not a "cook book" for therapy, it does include movement experiences that work on and can stimulate further ideas for interventions regarding specific client issues. The cross-reference chart on "Issues" de- lineates which activities are recommended.

4. Many clients who come to therapy have issues around violence, having either perpetrated it or been victim to it. This book provides background information on bullying and resources for skill-building to help bullies, vic- tims, and witnesses of violence.

5. Part of being an effective therapist is the ability to communicate with others. When working with clients dealing with bullying issues, it may be very important for you as a therapist to meet with school staff in order to support your client. This book provides vocabulary and ideas for these meetings. (See example of Sue in Section 1 of this chapter.)

6. Some children need direct connections between learning a movement skill and applying it outside the session. This book provides vocabulary to describe movement skills in ways that link them to cognitive/emotional issues. Children can then define a problem, try out solutions, and transfer their new skills to other situations.

7. While many of the activities in this curriculum may already be part of a dance/movement therapist's repertoire, the sections on alternative modes for redirecting aggression and for developing ignoring and focusing skills are unique ideas, not usually part of a dance/movement therapists' training. The hand-outs and worksheets that accompany these activities make them readily accessible to clients as well as to therapists. While I initially developed these activities specifically for the prevention program, I now find myself using them regularly in therapy sessions.

8. The handouts and workbook sheets can be used to aid communication between therapy and home as well as between dance/movement therapists and other professionals.

9. Throughout the book, dance/movement therapists will find various measures and vocabulary for use in charting therapy sessions and tracking progress toward treatment goals.

Summary

This chapter has explored applications of the Violence Prevention through Movement Curriculum to small group settings, both therapeutic and educational. Activities that are appropriate to do in small spaces were summarized. Almost all the skills taught in this curriculum can be accomplished in an office space; although, larger spaces give clients the chance to practice skills in the type of spatial environment they might need to use these abilities such as the playground or school building. The skills presented in the curriculum were connected to therapeutic themes and illustrated with case vignettes. Applications specific to dance/movement therapists were also described along with suggestions for marketing and grant-writing.

References

CHAPTER ONE: GETTING STARTED

Beane, A. L. (1999). *The bully free classroom: Over 100 tips and strategies for teachers K-8.* Minneapolis, MN: Free Spirit Publishing, Inc.

Dusenbury, L., Falco, M., Lake, A., Brannigan, R., & Bosworth, K. (1997). Nine critical elements of promising violence prevention programs. *Journal of School Health, December,* 67 *(10),* 409-414.

Fried, S. & Fried, P. (1996). *Bullies and victims.* New York, NY: M. Evans and Company, Inc.

Hoover, J. H. & Oliver, R. (1996). *The bullying prevention handbook: a guide for principals, teachers and counselors.* Bloomington, IN: National Education Service.

Kellerman, A., Fuquawhitley, D., Rivara, F., & Mercy, J. (1998). Preventing youth violence – what works. [Review] *Annual Review of Public Health, 19, (1):* 271-292.

Kocs, K. J. (1998). *All about bullying: Information and reproducibles for students, parents, schools and communities.* Madison, WI: Prevention Resource Center of the Wisconsin Clearinghouse for Prevention Resources.

Nowicki, S., Jr. and Duke, M. P. (1992). *Helping the child who doesn't fit in.* Atlanta, GA: Peachtree Publishers, Ltd.

Olweus, D. (1993). *Bullying at school: What we know and what we can do.* Cambridge, MA: Blackwell Publications.

Rigby, K. (1997). *Bullying in schools and what to do about it.* Melbourne, Australia: The Australian Council for Educational Research.

Ritter, M., & Low, K. G. (1996). Effects of dance/movement therapy: A meta-analysis. *The Arts in Psychotherapy, 23 (3):*249-260.

Webster-Doyle, T. (1992). *Why is everybody always picking on me.* Middlebury, VT: Atrium Society Publications.

Crime and violence in our schools – an overview of the statistics. (1996) Washington, D.C.: United States National Institute on Justice.

Chapter Two: Spatial Awareness

Hall, E. (1966). *The Hidden Dimension*. New York, NY: Doubleday.

Nowicki, S & Duke, M. (1992). *Helping the Child Who Doesn't Fit In*. Atlanta, Georgia: Peachtree Publishers.

Chapter Three: Self-Control and Stress Management

Davis, M., Eshelman, E.R., & McKay, M. (1995). *The relaxation and stress reduction workbook, fourth edition*. Oakland, CA: New Harbinger Publications, Inc.

Elias, M.J., Tobias, S.E., & Friedlander, B.S. (1999). *Emotionally intelligent parenting: how to raise a self-disciplined, responsible, socially skilled child*. New York, NY: Three Rivers Press.

Goleman, D. (1995). *Emotional intelligence*. New York, NY: Bantom Books.

Kurcinka, M. S. (1992). *Raising your spirited child*. New York, NY: Harper Perennial.

Sapolsky, R. M. (1994). *Why zebras don't get ulcers: a guide to stress, stress-related diseases, and coping*. New York: NY: W. H. Freeman and Company.

Chapter Four: Awareness of and Response to Tense or Dangerous Situations

De Becker, G. (1997). *The gift of fear: And other survival signals that protect us from violence*. New York, NY: Dell Publishing.

West, P. F. (1989) *The basic essentials protective behaviors anti-victimization and empowerment process*. Burnside, South Australia: Essence Publications PTY LTD.

Chapter Five: Movement Strategies for Dealing with Conflict and Aggression

Cohen-Posey, K. (1995). *How to handle bullies, teasers and other meanies*. Highland City, FL: Rainbow Books, Inc.

De Becker, G. (1997). *The gift of fear: And other survival signals that protect us from violence*. New York, NY: Dell Publishing.

CHAPTER SIX: MANAGING ANGER AND BUILDING EMPATHY

Beland, K. (1991). *Second step, preschool-kindergarten.* Seattle, WA: Committee for Children.

Ekman , P., & Friesen, W. (1975). *Unmasking the face.* Palo Alto, CA: Consulting Psychologists Press, Inc.

Frederich, W. (1990). *Psychotherapy of sexually abused children and their families.* New York, NY: Norton & Co.

Goleman, D. (1995). *Emotional intelligence.* New York, NY: Bantam Books.

Morris, D. (1995). *Body talk: The meaning of human gestures.* New York, NY: Crown.

Nowicki, S. & Duke, M. (1992). *Helping the child who doesn't fit in.* Atlanta, Georgia: Peachtree Publishers.

Pudney, W. & Whitehouse, E. (1996). *A volcano in my tummy: Helping children to handle anger, a resource book for parents, caregivers and teachers.* Gabriola Island, British Columbia, Canada: New Society Publishers.

Stern, D. (1987). *The interpersonal world of the infant.* New York, NY: Basic Books.

CHAPTER SEVEN: ADDITIONAL ISSUES: GUNS AND OTHER WEAPONS, ALIENATION, PREJUDICE, MEDIA AND CULTURAL INFLUENCES

Beardall, N. (2001). *Creating a peaceable school: Confronting intolerance and bullying (unit guide).* Newton, MA: Newton Public Schools.

Cappello, D. (2000) *Ten talks parents must have with their children about violence.* New York, NY: Hyperion.

Erickson, D. & Brinkman, P. (2000). Truancy law seen as no big deal, new penalties won't stop school skipping, students say. *Wisconsin State Journal, January 6, 2000.* Madison, WI: Madison Newspapers, Inc.

Gordon, S. & Litt, S. (1988). *Zing and Zipp, The Troggs of Wongo-Wongo Wood.* Burnside, South Australia: Pagel Books Ply Ltd for Essense Publications.

Hughes, J. & Hasbrouck, J. (1996). Television violence: Implications for violence prevention. *School Psychology Review, 25 (2),* 134-151.

Mayer, G. R. (1995). Preventing antisocial behavior in the schools. *Journal of Applied Behavior Analysis, 28 (4),* 467-478.

Surat, M.M. (1983). *Angel child/dragon child.* Milwaukee, WI: Raintree Publishers, Inc.

Suess, D. *The sneetches.*

Vendantam, S. (2002, March 29) "Watch TV now, get into fights later." Madison, WI: The Capital Times Newspaper.

CHAPTER NINE: APPLICATIONS OF THE VIOLENCE PREVENTIONS THROUGH MOVEMENT PROGRAM FOR MENTAL HEALTH PROFESSIONALS, SPECIAL PROFESSIONALS, SPECIAL EDUCATION TEACHERS, AND DANCE/MOVEMENT THERAPISTS

Erikson, E. (1963). *Childhood and society, second edition.* New York, NY: W. W. Norton & Company, Inc.

Kornblum, R. (2000). *Safe spaces in therapy settings empowering clients. In Sixteenth Annual Midwest Conference Proceedings on Child Sexual Abuse and Incest, held October 22-26, 2000 held in Middleton, WI.* Madison, WI: Co-sponsored by the University of Wisconsin, Madison, Division of Continuing Studies, Professional Development and Applied Studies; and Family Sexual Abuse Treatment, Inc.

Mahler, M., Pine, F., & Bergman, A. (1975). *The psychological birth of the human infant.* New York, NY: Basic Books, Inc.

Perls, F. (1971). *Gestalt therapy verbatim.* New York, NY: Bantom Books.

Rogers, C. (1951). *Client-centered therapy.* Boston, MA: Houghton Mifflin Company.

Sandel, S., Chaiklin, S., & Lohn, A. (Eds.). (1993). *Foundations of dance/movement therapy: The life and work of Marian Chace.* Columbia, MD: The Chace Foundation, American Dance Therapy Association.

Winnicott, D. W. (1965). *The maturational processes and the facilitating environment: Studies in the theory of emotional development.* New York, NY: International Universities Press.

Yalom, I. (1995). *The theory and practice of group psychotherapy, fourth edition.* New York, NY: Basic Books, Inc.

Resources

Recommended Reading Resources for Adults

(There are innumerable good books out there that illustrate the skills needed in violence prevention. I have offered you a sampling of books I enjoy and use. If one of these is no longer in print, feel free to ask the librarian or book clerk to help you find one that is comparable.)

EDUCATIONAL

Aikins, N. (1997). *Teaching children protective behaviors.* Madison, WI: Safety Education Unit, Madison Police Department.

Allen, J. S. & Klein, Roger J. (1996). *Ready...set...relax: A research based program of relaxation, learning and self esteem for children.* Inner Coaching: Watertown, WI.

Beane, A. L. (1999). *The bully free classroom: Over 100 tips and strategies for teachers K-8.* Minneapolis, MN: Free Spirit Publishing, Inc.

Beland, K. (1991). *Second step, preschool-kindergarten.* Seattle, WA: Committee for Children.

Beland, K. (1989). *Second step, grades 4-5.* Seattle, WA: Committee for Children.

Beland, K. (1988). *Second step, grades 1-3.* Seattle, WA: Committee for Children.

Chisholm, J. (1998). Understanding violence in the school: Moral and psychological factors. *Journal of Social Distress and the Homeless, 7 (2),* 137-157.

Davis, M., Eshelman, E.R., & McKay, M. (1995). *The relaxation and stress reduction workbook, fourth edition.* Oakland, CA: New Harbinger Publications, Inc.

De Becker, G. (1997). *The gift of fear: And other survival signals that protect us from violence.* New York, NY: Dell Publishing.

Drug Strategies. (1998). *Safe schools, safe students: A guide to violence prevention strategies.* Washington, D.C.: Drug Strategies.

Education Committee for Turn Off the Violence. (1993). *Turn off the violence now!* Minneapolis, MN: Turn Off the Violence.

Fried, S. & Fried, P. (1996). *Bullies and victims.* New York, NY: M. Evans and Company, Inc.

Fried, S. (1997). Bullies and victims: Children abusing children. *American Dance Therapy Journal, 19, (2),* 127-133.

Fried, S. & Weyforth, M. (1999). *On target to stop bullying: A program guide for addressing bullying and violence in our schools.* Kansas City, MO: STOP Violence Coalition, Inc.

Fried, S. (2000). *Bullies and victims (newsletter).* Shawnee Mission, KS: SuEllen Fried.

Golding, C. & Todd, F. (1994). *Protective behaviours through drama.* South Australia: Windows on Practice Publications.

Hendricks, G. & Wills, R. (1975). *The centering book: Awareness activities for children, parents, and teachers.* Englewood Cliffs, NJ: Prentice-Hall, Inc.

Hoover, J. H. & Oliver, R. (1996). *The bullying prevention handbook: A guide for principals, teachers and counselors.* Bloomington, IN: National Education Service.

Kocs, K. J. (1998). *All about bullying: information and reproducibles for students, parents, schools and communities.* Madison, WI: Prevention Resource Center of the Wisconsin Clearinghouse for Prevention Resources.

Mason, K. C. (Ed.). (1974). *Focus on dance VII, dance therapy.* Reston, VA: American Alliance for Health, Physical Education, Recreation and Dance.

Masson, J. M. and McCarthy, S. (1995). *When elephants weep: The emotional lives of animals.* New York, NY: Dell Publishing.

Madison Metropolitan School District. (1988). *S.A.V.E. Student Anti-Victim Education: A protective behaviors program designed to empower children in kindergarten - grades 1-2-3.* Madison, WI: Madison Metropolitan School District.

Olweus, D., Limber, S., & Mahalic, S. (1998). *Bullying prevention program.* Boulder, CO: Center for the Study and Prevention of Violence, Institute of Behavioral Science, University of Colorado.

Olweus, D. (1993). *Bullying at school: What we know and what we can do.* Cambridge, MA: Blackwell Publications.

Posner, M. (1996). *Youth violence: Locating and using the data.* Newton, MA: Education Development Center, Inc.

Rigby, Ken. (1997). *Bullying in schools and what to do about it.* Melbourne, Australia: The Australian Council for Educational Research.

Thraves, B. & Williamson, D. *Now for the dance: Integrating dance and movement in primary and early childhood learning.* Australia: Phoenix Education.

West, P.F. (1989). *The basic essentials: Protective behaviours anti-victimisation and empowerment process.* Burnside, South Australia: Essence Publications Pty. Ltd.

PARENTING

Beekman, S. & Homes, J. (1993). *Battles, hassles, tantrums and tears: Strategies for coping with conflict and making peace at home.* New York, NY: Hearst Books.

Brazelton, T.B. (1992). *Heart start: The emotional foundations of school readiness.* Arlington, VA: National Center for Clincial Infant Programs.

Brazelton, T.B. (1989). *Toddlers and parents: A declaration of independence.* New York, NY: Delta/Seymour Lawrence.

Brazelton, T.B. (1984). *To listen to a child: Understanding the normal problems of growing up.* Reading, MA: Addison-Wesley Publishing Company, Inc.

Brett, D. (1986). *Annie stories: A special kind of storytelling.* New York, NY: Workman Publishing.

Canter, L. & Hausner, L. (1987). *Homework without tears.* New York, NY: Harper and Row.

Cappello, D. (2000). *Ten talks parents must have with their children about violence.* New York, NY: Hyperion.

Carter, J. (1989). *Nasty people: How to stop being hurt by them without becoming one of them.* Chicago, IL: Contemporary Books, Inc.

Chess, S. & Alexander, T. (1989). *Know your child: An authoritative guide for today's parents.* New York, NY: Basic Books, Inc.

Clarke, J.I. (1978). *Self esteem: A family affair.* Minneapolis, MN: Winston Press, Inc.

Crary, E. (1996). *Without spanking or spoiling, second edition.* Seattle, WA: Parenting Press.

Dinkmeyer, D. & McKay, G. (1989). *The parent's handbook: Systematic training for effective parenting (STEP).* Circle Pines, MN: American Guidance Service.

Elias, M.J., Tobias, S.E., & Friedlander, B.S. (1999). *Emotionally Intelligent parenting: How to raise a self-disciplined, responsible, socially skilled child.* New York, NY: Three Rivers Press.

Elium, J. & Elium, D. (1997). *Raising a family: Living on planet parenthood.* Berkeley, CA: Celestial Arts Publishing.

Faber, A. & Mazlish, E. (1990). *Liberated parents/ liberated children: Your guide to a happier family.* New York, NY: Avon Books.

Faber, A. & Mazlish, E. (1988). *Siblings without rivalry.* New York, NY: Avon Books.

Faber, A. & Mazlish, E. (1982). *How to talk so kids will listen and listen so kids will talk.* New York, NY: Avon Books.

Garbarino, J. (1995). *Raising children in a socially toxic environment.* San Francisco, CA: Jossey-Bass.

Garbarino, J. (1993). *Let's talk about living in a world with violence.* Chicago, IL: Erikson Institute.

Goleman, D. (1995). *Emotional intelligence.* New York, NY: Bantom Books.

Hendricks, G. & Wills, R. (1975). *The centering book: Awareness activities for children, parents, and teachers.* Englewood Cliffs, NJ: Prentice-Hall, Inc.

Keen, S. (1992). *Inward bound: Exploring the geography of your emotions.* New York, NY: Bantom Books.

Kraizer, S.K. (1985). *The safe child: A commonsense approach to protecting your children from abduction and sexual abuse.* New York, NY: Delacorte Press.

Kurcinka, M. S. (1992). *Raising your spirited child.* New York, NY: Harper Perennial.

Pudney, W. & Whitehouse, E. (1996). *A volcano in my tummy: Helping children to handle anger, a resource book for parents, caregivers and teachers.* Gabriola Island, British Columbia, Canada: New Society Publishers.

Rich, D. (1988). *Megaskills: How families can help children succeed in school.* Boston, MA: Houghton Mifflin.

Saunders, A. & Remsberg, B. (1984). *The stress-proof child: A loving parent's guide.* New York, NY: Holt, Rinehart and Winston.

Saunders, C.S. (1994). *Safe at school: Awareness and action for parents of kids grades k-12.* Free Spirit Publishing: Minneapolis, MN.

Schwebel, R. (1989). *Saying no is not enough: Raising children who make wise decision about drugs and alcohol.* New York, NY: Newmarket Press.

Shure, M. (1996). *Raising a thinking child: Help young child to resolve everyday conflicts and get along with others, second edition.* New York, NY: Henry Holt.

Strong, S. (1996). *Strong on defense: Survival rules to protect you and your family from crime.* New York, NY: Simon & Schuster, Inc.

Weinhaus, E. & Friedman, K. (1991). *Stop struggling with your child.* New York, NY: Harper Collins.

Wolfe, A. E. (1991). *Get out of my life, but first could you drive me and Cheryl to the mall?* New York, NY: The Noonday Press.

CLINICAL

American Journal of Dance Therapy. New York, NY: Human Sciences Press, Inc.

The Arts in Psychotherapy: An international journal. Oxford, England: Elsevier Science Limited.

Berg, B. (1990). *The social skills workbook: Exercises to improve social skills.* Dayton, OH: Cognitive Counseling Resources.

Berg, B. (1990). *The anger control workbook: Exercises to develop anger control skills.* Dayton, OH: Cognitive Counseling Resources.

Berg, B. (1990). *The self-control workbook: Exercises to control inattention, impulsivity and hyperactivity.* Dayton, OH: Cognitive Counseling Resources.

Block, J. (1995). On the relation between IQ, impulsivity, and delinquency. *Journal of Abnormal Psychology, 104.*

Crisci, G., Lay, M., & Lowenstein, L. (1997). *Paper dolls and paper airplanes – therapeutic exercises for sexually traumatized children.* Charlotte, N.C: Kidsrights.

Davis, N. (1990). *Once upon a time...Therapeutic stories to heal abused children.* Oxon Hill, MD: Pychological Associates of Oxon Hill.

Friedrich, W. N. (1990). *Psychotherapy of sexually abused children and their families.* New York, NY: Norton.

Garmezy, N. (1987). *The invulnerable child.* New York, NY: Guildford Press.

Goodill, S. (1987). Dance/movement therapy with abused children. *The Arts in Psychotherapy, 14*, No. 1, 59-68.

Hall, E. T. (1973). *The silent language.* Garden City, NY: Doubleday & Company, Inc.

Hall, E. T. (1969). *The hidden dimension.* Garden City, NY: Doubleday & Company, Inc.

Herman, J.L. (1992). *Trauma and recovery.* New York, NY: Basic Books.

James, B. (1989). *Treating traumatized children: New insights and creative interventions.* Free Press, NY: Lexington Books.

Johnson, T. C. (1996). *Understanding children's sexual behaviors: What's natural and healthy.* South Pasadena, CA: New Harbinger Publications.

Kindlon, D. & Thompson, M. (1999). *Raising Cain: Protecting the emotional life of boys.* New York, NY: Ballantine Books.

Kornblum, R. (2000). *Safe spaces in therapy settings empowering clients. In Proceedings of the Sixteenth Annual Midwest Conference on Child Sexual Abuse and Incest, held October 22-26, 2000 in Middleton, WI.* Madison, WI: Co-sponsored by the University of Wisconsin, Madison, Division of Continuing Studies, Professional Development and Applied Studies; and Family Sexual Abuse Treatment, Inc.

Kornblum, R. (1982). *A perceptuo-cognitive-motor approach to the special child.* Harrisburg, PA: Arts in Special Education Project of Pennsylvania.

Kornblum, R. (1981). An individual session with an emotional disturbed, learning disabled adolescent. In T. Leatherbee and S. Wood (Eds.). *A primer for theoretical models and clinical work in dance/movement therapy.* Philadelphia, PA: Hahnemann Medical College of Philadelphia.

Kranowitz, C. S. (1998). *The out-of-sync child: Recognizing and coping with sensory integration dysfunction.* New York, NY: The Berkley Publishing Group.

Leventhal, M., (Ed.). (1980) *Movement and growth: Dance therapy for the special child.* New York University, New York, NY: Center for Educational Research, Press Building.

Levy, F., Fried, J.P., & Leventhal, F. (Eds.). (1995). *Dance and other expressive arts therapies: When words are not enough.* New York, NY: Routledge.

Levy, F. (1988). *Dance/movement therapy: A healing art.* Reston, VA: National Dance Association, American Alliance for Health, Physical Education, Recreation, and Dance.

Lewis, P. (1986). *Theoretical approaches in dance/movement therapy, volume 1.* Dubuque, IA: Kendall-Hunt Publishing Company.

Lewis, P. (1984). *Theoretical approaches in dance/movement therapy, volume 2.* Dubuque, IA: Kendall-Hunt Publishing Company.

Miller, A. (1990). *For your own good: Hidden cruelty in child-rearing and the roots of violence.* New York, NY: Noonday Press.

Mohacsy, I. (1995). Nonverbal communication and its place in the therapy session. *The Arts in Psychotherapy, 22 (1),* 31-38.

Morris, D. (1995). *Body talk: The meaning of human gestures.* New York, NY: Crown.

North, M. (1972). *Personality assessment through movement.* Boston, MA: Plays, Inc.

Nowicki, S., Jr. & Duke, M.P. (1992). *Helping the child who doesn't fit in.* Atlanta, GA: Peachtree Publishers, Ltd.

Pallaro, P. (1996). Self and body-self: Dance/movement therapy and the development of object relations. *The Arts in Psychotherapy, 23 (2),* 113-119.

Patterson, S. (1990). *I wish the hitting would stop: Facilitator's guide.* Fargo, SD: Rape and Abuse Crisis Center of Fargo-Moorhead.

Patterson, S. (1987). *I wish the hitting would stop: A workbook for children living in violent homes.* Fargo, SD: Rape and Abuse Crisis Center of Fargo-Moorhead.

Pert, C. B. (1997). *Molecules of emotion: Why you feel the way you feel.* New York, NY: Touchstone.

Pipher, M. (1994). *Reviving Ophelia: Saving the selves of adolescent girls.* New York, NY: Ballantine Books.

Pudney, W. & Whitehouse, E. (1996). *A volcano in my tummy: Helping children to handle anger, a resource book for parents, caregivers and teachers.* Gabriola Island, British Columbia, Canada: New Society Publishers.

Sandel, S., Chaiklin, S., & Lohn, A. (Eds.). (1993). *Foundations of dance/movement therapy: The life and work of Marian Chace.* Columbia, MD: The Chace Foundation, American Dance Therapy Association.

Sandel, S.L., & Johnson, D.R. (1996). Theoretical foundations of the structural analysis of movement sessions. *The Arts in Pyschotherapy, 23 (1),* 15-25.

Sapolsky, R.M. (1994). *Why zebras don't get ulcers: A guide to stress, stress related diseases, and coping.* New York: NY: W. H. Freeman and Company.

Scheflen, A. (1972). *Body language and social order: Communication as behavioral control.* Englewood Cliffs, NJ: Prentice-Hall, Inc.

Seligman, M. (1996). *The optimistic child: A proven program to safeguard children against depression and build lifelong resilience.* New York, NY: Harper Collins.

Weisberg, L.W., & Greenberg, R. (1988). *When acting out isn't acting: Understanding child and adolescent temper, anger, and behavior disorders.* Washington, D.C.: The PIA Press.

Weltman, M. (1986). Movement therapy with children who have been sexually abused. *American Journal of Dance Therapy, 9,* 46-66.

Williams, M.S. & Shellenberger, S. (1996). *How does your engine run? A leader's guide to the alert program for self-regulation.* Albuquerque, NM: TherapyWorks, Inc.

Websites:

http://safechild.org

http://www.solnet.co.uk/kidscape/kids4.htm

http://www.family.com (Disney's family site)

Resources
Recommended Readings for Children
Pre-School through Second Grade

(There are innumerable good books out there that illustrate the skills needed in violence prevention. I have offered you a sampling of books I enjoy and use. If one of these is no longer in print, feel free to ask the librarian or book clerk to help you find one that is comparable.)

Alborough, Jez. (1992). *Where's my teddy?* Cambridge, MA: Candlewick Press.
A boy and a bear share the same fear, problem and adventure. (Dealing with fear and problem-solving.) For ages 3 and up.

Aliki. (1984). *Feelings.* New York, NY: Greenwillow Books, William Morris & Co.
Children explore a range of feelings through humorous pictures and dialogue. For children pre-school – 2nd grade.

Aliki. (1990). *Manners.* New York, NY: Greenwillow Books, William Morris & Co.
Children explore manner and how their behavior effects others people through humorous pictures and dialogue. For children in K – 3rd grade.

Artis, Vicki Kimmel. (1974). *Gray duck catches a friend.* New York, NY: G.P. Putnam's Sons.
Gray ducks discovers new ways to make friends. For children K - 2nd grade.

Baker, Keith. (1999). *Sometimes.* New York, NY: Green Light Readers, Harcourt Brace & Company. This brightly illustrated story explores the range of feelings children may experience and offers a self-affirming message. For children in K - 1st grade.

*Berenstain, Stan & Jan. (1995). *The Berenstain bears and too much teasing.* New York, NY: Random House, Inc.
This story illustrates the concept that while teasing may be a part of life, it really isn't a good idea. Bear experiences all the different sides of teasing and uses positive problem solving skills to deal with a gang that teases. A "First Time Book" for early elementary school reading.

Blume, Judy. (1981). *The one in the middle is the green kangaroo.* New York, NY: Bradley Press.
Freddy deals with being a middle child, feeling left out, and then feeling better when he gets a part in the school play. For 1st - 3rd grade.

Bonsall, Crosby. (1965) *The case of the cat's meow.* New York, NY: Harper & Row, Publishers.
Four friends become detectives to solve the disappearance of a cat. Deals with friendship, multi-cultural, name-calling, problem-solving. Read It Myself Book beginning 2nd grade reading level. (See more of this author's beginning reading books.)

*Bosch, C. W. (1988). *Bully on the bus*. Seattle, WA: Parenting Press, Inc.
A fifth grader on the school bus is picking on other children. The reader chooses a scenario and creates their own story. A book in "The Decision Is Yours" series for elementary school children.

Cameron, Ann. (1981). *The stories Julian tells*. New York, NY: Bullseye Books/Alfred A. Knopf. Julian's tall tales glow with imagination as he learns the consequences of exaggeration. For children in 2nd - 4th grade.

Cameron, Ann. (1995). *The stories Huey tells*. New York, NY: Bullseye Books/Alfred A. Knopf.
A collection of short stories that deal with sibling relationships, courage, building self-esteem and other social issues looked at from the perspective of young boy. For children ages 7 and up.

Capucilli, Alyssa S. (1996). *Biscuit*. New York, NY: Harper Collins Publishers.
A little girl shows empathy for the needs of her puppy, which mirror the emotional needs of small children. (Deals with empathy, friendship.) For pre-school, kindergarten, or beginner readers.

*Carlson, Nancy. (1983). *Loudmouth George and the sixth-grade bully*. New York, NY: Viking Penguin, Inc.
George is confronted by a bully and suffers alone until a friend finds out and helps him come up with a pro-active plan. A "Picture Puffin" book for ages 3rd - 8th.

Chardiet, Bernice & Maccarone, Grace. (1990). *Brenda's Private Swing*. New York, NY: Scholastic, Inc.
Children use negotiating skills and positive problem solving to deal with a bully. 1st – 2nd grade reading level.

Cole, Joanna. (1996). *Monster and muffin*. New York, NY: Grosset and Dunlap.
Two very different dogs become best friends. An "All Aboard Reading" book for ages 3rd - 5th.

*Cole, Joanna. (1989). *Bully Trouble*. New York, NY: Random House, Inc.
Best friends use trickery to escape being picked on. A "Step into Reading" book for grades 1st - 3rd.

*DePaola, Tomie. (1986). *Kit and kat*. New York, NY: Scholastic Inc.
A brother and sister deal with a bully and use positive problem solving skills. An "All Aboard Reading" book for beginning readers.

*DePaola, Tomie. (1979). *Oliver button is a sissy*. New York, NY: Harcourt Brace Jovanovich. Oliver is teased about his differences and finds a way to remain true to himself. (Deals with ignoring, despair, positive-problem solving.) For 1st - 2nd grade readers.

Doleski, Teddi. (1983). *The hurt*. Ramsey, NJ: Paulist Press.
A book for young elementary school children that deals with a fight between friends, hurt feelings, and how to feel better.

Dooley, Norah. (2000). *Everybody loves soup*. Minneapolis, MN: Carolrhoda Books, Inc.
Part of a series about a child's multi cultural neighborhood for pre-school - 1st grade.

Dragonwagon, Crescent (1984). *Always, always*. New York, N: Macmillan Publishing Co.
A young girl hates her brother or does she? Deals with feeling left out, not being believed, name-calling, sibling relationships, anger, conflicted feelings, etc. For children pre-school - kindergarten.

Fisher, Iris. (1987). *Katie-bo: An adoption story*. New York, NY: Adama Books.
A family with two boys is waiting to adopt a baby girl from Korea. All the feeling associated with a new sibling are explored as well as learning about a new culture. Pre-school-1st grade.

Friedman, Ina R. (1984). *How my parents learned to eat*. Boston, MA: Houghton Mifflin & Co.
An American man and a Japanese woman each secretly try to learn the other's way of eating. A good cultural awareness book.

Gilmore, Rachna. (1999). *A screaming kind of day*. Toronto, Canada: Fitzhenry & Whiteside.
This is a beautifully written book about an angry day of a hearing impaired child. The internal dialogue is realistic and shows a full range of feelings. Her feelings will resonate with all children. Pre-school – 2nd grade.

Grahame, Kenneth. (1988). *The reluctant dragon*. USA: Troll Associates.
A boy finds a dragon that is friendly but has trouble convincing the villagers and the knight not to kill it. For pre-school through 1st grade.

Graves, Kimberlee. (1994). *Mom can fix anything*. Cypress, CA: Creative Teaching Press, Inc.
A little girl believes in herself and creatively uses her Mom's tools. For pre-schoolers or very young readers.

Hall, Kirsten. (1995). *A bad, bad day*. New York, NY: Scholastic, Inc.
Explores the events and feelings around having a bad day. A "Hello Reader!" book with flash cards for ages 3 - 6.

Havill, Juanita. (1986). *Jamaica's find*. Boston, MA: Houghton Mifflin Company.
A little girl does not want to take a stuffed animal she found to the lost and found. She struggles with honesty and thinking about her actions. Good for Pre-school – 1st grade.

Hazen, Barbara Shook. (1987) *Fang*. New York, NY: Atheneum; Macmillan Publishing Company.
A large, fiece looking dog is really quite fearful and has to deal with others perceptions of him as he deals with his fear. For children in pre-school - 1st grade.

Herman, Gail. (1995). *Otto the cat*. New York, NY: Scholastic, Inc.
A housecat is upset by the new dog but finally learns to accept him. A picture reader with flash cards for preschool - 1st grade.

Herman, Ronnie A. (1996). *Pal the pony*. New York, NY: Scholastic, Inc.
A pony who is too little to compete in a rodeo feels bad about himself, but then he finds out that he is a good friend for children. An "All Aboard Reading" book for preschool - 1st grade.

Hoban, Lillian. (1981). *Arthur's funny money*. New York, NY: Harper and Row, Publishers, Inc.
When a penniless chimpanzee goes into business, he learns to problem solve and negotiate. An "I Can Read Book" for young children, and part of a series of books about Arthur that are very popular with young children.

Hoban, Russell. (1970). *A bargain for Frances*. New York, NY: Scholastic, Inc.
A story that highlights positive problem-solving and negotiating between friends. For 1st grade and up.

Hoban, Russell. (1969) *Best friends for Frances*. New York, NY: Harper & Row, Publishers.
Frances learns to appreciate her younger sister while trying to teach her friend about friendship. Deals with making friends, sibling relationships & loneliness. Part of a series of books about Frances. Good for kindergarten - 2nd grade.

*Howe, J. (1996). *Pinky and Rex and the bully*. New York, NY: Aladdin Paperbacks.
A second grade boy is bullied about his preferences and is helped to accept himself. A Ready to Read Alone Book at a 2nd grade level.

Hubbard, Woodleigh. (1990). *C is for curious, an ABC of feelings and 2 is for dancing, a 1 2 3 of actions (2 books in 1)*. San Francisco, CA: Chroncicle books.
A zany alphabet and action book that explores a wide range of feelings and movements. Pre-school – 1st grade.

Janssen, Larry. (1984). *My sister is special*. Cincinnati, OH: The Standard Publishing Company.
A positive look at how one little boy interacts with his sister, who has Down's Syndrome. For pre-school - 1st grade.

Jenness, Aylette. (1990). *Families: a celebration of diversity, commitment, and love*. Boston, MA: Houghton Mifflin Company.
Seventeen children talk about their families. Includes single parent households, gay parents, foster parents, divorced parents and stepfamilies along with traditional two-parent families.

*Johnston, Tony. (1997). *Sparky and Eddie: the first day of school*. New York, NY: Scholastic, Inc.
Two very different boys are best friends and after dealing with the disappointment of not being in the same classroom, they decide they like school afterall. A "Hello Reader!" book for grades 1 - 2.

Keats, Ezra Jack. (1969). *Goggles*. New York, NY: Aladdin Books.
Peter and a friend use positive problem-solving to deal with bullying after they find some goggles that an older group of boys wants. For children in pre-school - kindergarten.

Lasker, Joe. (1974). *He's my brother*. Chicago, IL: Albert Whitman & Company.
A boy shares his experiences with his brother who has a learning disability. We are introduced to things he can and cannot do and learn to empathize with his problems. Young elementary school children.

Lawson, Robert. (1936). *Ferdinand the Bull*. Cedar Grove, NJ: Rae Publishing Co., Inc.
This book tells the story of a bull who would rather sit and smell the flowers than fight and how he convinced people to allow him to be non-violent. For all ages.

Levy, Elizabeth. (1995). *The snack attack mystery*. New York, NY: Scholastic, Inc.
A new girl deals with making a diverse group of children her friends. She is overwhelmed and scared. Then she is accused of stealing when her classmates try to solve a mystery. A "Hello Reader!" chapter book for grades 2 - 3.

Lionni, Leo. (1985, 1986). *It's mine*. New York, NY: Random House Inc.
A storm helps three foolish frogs learn the value of sharing. Pre-school.

Maccarone, Grace. (1994). *Pizza party!* New York, NY: Scholastic Inc.
A group of friends cooperate to make a pizza together. A "Hello Reader!" book for preschool - 1st grades.

Marchall, James. (1972). *George and Martha*. Boston, MA: Houghton Mifflin Company.
Two friends learn about the the value of friendship, dignity, honesty and trust. George and Martha stories are enjoyed by children pre-school - 2nd grade.

Marchall, James. (1988) *George and Martha*. Boston, MA: Houghton Mifflin Company.
These two friends learn that joking is fine as long as it is not at the expense of others, and that friends can disagree and still be friends. Pre-school - 2nd grade.

Marzollo, Jean. (1987). *Cannonball Chris*. New York, NY: Random House, Inc.
A boy overcomes his secret fear of deep water with a little help from his Dad. Excellent book for children on overcoming fear and evaluating risks. A "Step into Reading" chapter book for grades 2 - 3.

McCourt, Lisa. (1997). *Chicken soup for little souls: the goodness gorillas*. Deerfield Beach, FL: Health Communications, Inc.
A story adapted from "Practice Random Acts of Beauty" by Adair Lara, this book deals with spreading kindness and how to incorporate that concept into dealing with a bully. For elementary school children.

McGrath, Bob. (1989). *Dog lies*. Los Angeles, CA: Price Stern Sloan.
One of a series of books called Bob's Books, designed to read together with a child, about a different ethic. This one is obviously about lying. Designed for pre-schoolers it could also be used with early elementary school children.

Medearis, Angela S. (1995). *We play on a rainy day*. New York, NY: Scholastic, Inc.
A group of friends overcome disappointment and have fun in the rain. A "Hello Reader!" book for preschool - 1st grade.

Minarik, Else H. (1960). *Little bear's friend*. New York, NY: Harper Collins Publishers.
A baby bear makes friends with other animals and a little girl. An "I Can Read Book" for beginning readers.

Minarik, Else H. (1968). *A kiss for little bear*. New York, NY: Harper Collins Publishers.
A baby bear's generosity touches all of his friends in a positive way. An "I Can Read Book" for beginning readers.

Minarik, Else H. (1958). *No fighting, no biting*. New York, NY: Harper Collins Publishers.
An amusing story about two children and two alligators who need to learn about keeping out of a fight. This is a beginning reader story that is fun for pre-schoolers to have read to them and for older children to read themselves.

Moore, Eva. (1996). *The day of the bad haircut*. New York, NY: Scholastic, Inc.
With help from her brother, a little girl overcomes her disappointment when mom cuts her hair too short. A "Hello Reader!" book for K - 2nd grades.

*Naylor, Phyllis R. (1994). *King of the playground*. New York, NY: Aladdin Books, Macmillan Publishing Company.
A little boy learns to use humor to handle threats of a bully. For beginning readers.

Sharmat, Marjorie Weinman. (1973). *Nate the Great goes undercover*. New York, NY: Coward, McCann & Geoghegan, Inc.
One of a series of books on a 2nd grade level in which a young boy tries to solve cases and deals with a scary dog and his owner at the same time. Good books on problem solving,, friendship, and feelings.

*Slater, Teddy. (1995). *Who's afraid of the big, bad bully?* New York, NY: Scholastic, Inc.
A little boy and his friends discover that once they can stop being scared of Big Bertha, a girl who bullies children, she can stop being a bully. A "Hello Reader!" chapter book for grades 1 - 2.

Seuss, Dr. (1989). *What was I scared of?* New York, NY: Scholastic, Inc.
The main character learns that the being he fears is not only afraid of him, but even deserving of friendship.

Steptoe, John. (1987). *Mufaro's beautiful daughters*. New York, NY: Lothrop, Lee & Shepard. This is an African folktale about two sisters who are very different, one is very jealous of the other. Good for Kindergarten - 2nd grades.

Stinson, Kathy. (1984). *Mom and Dad don't live together any more*. Toronto, Canada: Annick Press Ltd. A book, with simple text, for young children dealing with divorce. It brings up many of the conflicting and confusing feelings while maintaining its simplicity.

Suess, Dr. (1961). *The sneetches and other stories*. New York, NY: Random House. Two types of Sneetches, imaginary characters, deal with prejudice showing the effects on victims and the rediculousness of the prejudicial ideas in the first place. Good for people of all ages.

*Surat, M.M. (1983). *Angel child/dragon child*. Milwaukee, WI: Raintree Publishers, Inc. A Vietnamese girl attending school in the U.S. is lonely for her mother, left behind in Vietnam, and makes a new friend who presents her with a wonderful gift.

Udry, Janice May. (1961). *Let's be enemies*. New York, NY: Harper & Row, Publishers. Two friends have a big fight. After much arguing they become friends again. Pre-school.

Van Leeuwen, Jean. (1990). *Amanda Pig on her own*. New York, NY: Dial Books for Young Reader.
Amanda pig finds out that there are positives and negatives to living on her own. Children see her dealing with problem-solving, communicating feelings, understanding cause and effect, and learning anger triggers. This I Can Read It Myself book for early elementary age children. There are other Amanda Pig books too.

Van Leeuwen, Jean. (1979). *Tales of Oliver Pig*. New York, NY: The Dial Press.
This book contains five tales that show Oliver dealing with a bad day, comforting others, feeling left out, and handling anger. It is an, I Can Read It Myself book for early elementary children. See the other Oliver Pig books too.

Viorst, Judith. (1972). *Alexander and the terrible, horrible, no good, very bad day*. New York, NY: Scholastic, Inc.
A little boy learns that some days are better than others and demonstrates that self-talk, especially if negative, can influence how the day turns out. For children in early grades.

Widmer, Katherine. (1975). *Feeling shy*. New York, NY: Macmillan Publishing Company, Inc. A seven-year-old boy and his mother overcome shyness to make new friends. A Beginner Reader Book, mid-first grade level.

Wilt, J. (1979). *Handling your ups and downs*. Columbus, OH: Weekly Reader Books. A children's book about emotions specifically designed for ages 4 - 8. Wilt proposes a four-step procedure for children to follow when they experience uncomfortable feelings. This book is one of a series of books about handling different issues.

Yashima, Taro. (1955). *Crow boy*. New York, NY: The Viking Press.
A boy who is different from his classmates goes to school in Japan for six years before a teacher appreciates him for who he is and teaches other students to appreciate his differences.

Ziegler, Sandra. (1989). *Understanding*. Chicago, IL: Children's Press.
Children are introduced to different ways of showing that they care.

Zolotow, Charlotte. (1969). *The hating book*. New York, NY: Harper Collins Children's Books.
A book about friendship and the fear a young girl has of reaching out to her angry friend in case she is rejected. Pre-school - 1st grade.

Resources

Recommended Readings for Children
Grades 3 - 5

(There are innumerable good books out there that illustrate the skills needed in violence prevention. I have offered you a sampling of books I enjoy and use. If one of these is no longer in print, feel free to ask the librarian or book clerk to help you find one that is comparable.)

American Girl Library. (1996). *The care and keeping of friends*. Middleton, WI: Pleasant Company Publications.
Advice for making and keeping friends for girls ages 8 and older.

Anno, Mitsumassa et al. (1986). *All in a day*. New York, NY: Philome Books.
Illustrations and a brief text communicate about children in eight different countries, emphasizing the commonality of people in general while also showing differences.

Banks, Lynne Reid. (1980). *The indian in the cupboard*. New York, NY: Avon Books, A Division of the Heart Corporation.
This is one of a series, each one placing the reader in other people's shoes through an intriguing story of plastic figures coming to life as miniature people of their own time. Good story to evoke empathy and the responsibility one must take when one feels it.

Bauer, Marion Dane. (1994). *A question of trust*. New York, NY: Scholastic, Inc. Apple Paperbacks.
Two brothers find a cat and decide to keep it without telling anyone. This leads to all kinds of problems requiring problem-solving and cause and effect relationships. These issues are dealt with in an intense way that keeps the reader involved.

Blume, Judy. (1972). *Otherwise known as Sheila the Great*. New York, NY: E. P. Dutton.
Sheila deals with her fears of dogs, thunderstorms, swimming, etc.

Blume, Judy. (1980) *Superfudge*. New York, NY: E. P. Dutton.
Sibling relationships are tense as seen through the eyes of an older brother, Peter, as he deals with his four-year-old brother. Lots of feeling issues are dealt with in a humorous, down to earth way. There are other books about Peter and his brother that are equally good. Blume is well known as a dynamic children's author.

Bosch, C. W. (1988). *Bully on the bus*. Seattle, WA: Parenting Press, Inc.
A fifth grader on the school bus is picking on other children, the reader chooses a scenario and creates his/her own story. A book in "The Decision Is Yours" series for elementary school children.

Boyd, Candy Dawson. (1984). *Circle of gold*. New York, NY: Scholastic Inc.
Mattie wants to make things right in her family by buying her mother a beautiful pin. On the way she has to deal with the temptation to lie and cheat as well as deal with gossip, frustration, put downs, etc. A moving story.

Bruchac, Joseph. (1997). *Eagle song*. New York, NY: Dial Books for Young Readers.
Danny Bigtree must deal with Native American sterotypes after moving to Brooklyn, NY from a Mohawk Indian Reservation. He has to deal with anger management, making friends, positive problem-solving and prejudice.

Cameron, Ann. (1987). *Julian's glorious summer*. New York, NY: A Stepping Stone Book, Random House.
Julian deals with his fear of bikes by lying and avoiding his best friend. All of the Julian and Huey books deal with feelings and conflicts in a humorous and realistic way.

Carrick, Carol. (1985). *Stay away from Simon*. New York, NY: Clarion Books.
Two siblings are afraid when a child with special needs follows them home one day. They deal with their fear, accepting differences, fairness, etc.

CastaÒeda, Omar S. (1991). *Among the Volcanoes*. New York, NY: Bantam Doubleday Dell Publishing Group, Inc.
This book offers a look into the culture of Guatemala and lives that are very different from those of most young people in the USA. It shows a young girl trying hard to hold onto her dream and work toward her goal of being a teacher against what seems like insurmountable odds.

Cleary, Beverly. (1984). *Ramona forever*. New York, NY: William Morrow.
Third grader, Ramona, has many new things to deal with; fighting with a sibling, waiting for a baby, being a latch key child. The Ramona series is great for dealing with all kinds of feelings. For ages 8 and older.

Coatsworth, Elizabeth. (1930). *The cat that went to heaven*. New York, NY: Scholastic Press Inc.
A Newbery Medal book that gives a sense of Japanese culture back in history as well as portraying the conflict of the desire for money and success versus love and dedication. A short read that elicits much thought.

Cohen, Barbara. (1994). *Make a Wish, Molly*. New York, NY: Bantam Doubleday Dell Publishing Group, Inc.
Molly is new to America and her Russian background hasn't prepared her for birthday parties or prejudice. Fortunately, her mother knows how to handle both issues and helps Molly to learn a valuable lesson. A "Yearling Book" for 3rd grade readers and older.

Cohen, Barbara. (1983). *Molly's pilgrim*. New York, NY: Bantam Doubleday Dell Publishing Group, Inc.
Molly and her family move from Russia to America. Molly is afraid she'll never fit in with her 3rd grade classmates. A "Yearling Book" for 3rd grade readers and older.

Conrad, Pam. (1988). *Staying nine*. New York, NY: Harper & Row, Publishers.
A nine year-old-girl does not want to turn ten but finally sees that growing up is not so bad.

Dodds, Bill. (1993). *My sister, Annie*. Honesdale, PA: Boyds Mills Press, Inc.
A boy struggles with the challenges of having a sister with Down's Syndrome. He deals with anger, peer pressure, and a desire to feel accepted by his friends.

Estes, Eleanor. (1944, 1972). *The hundred dresses*. San Diego, CA: Voyager Books-Harcourt Brace Co.
A polish girl encounters prejudice, teasing, and isolation in a new school. After she moves away, the other children begin to understand about the effect of their teasing and some of the talents this quiet girl had all along. Bullying, dealing with peer pressure, cause and effect, and the role of the witness are all dealt with in this story.

Fang, Linda. (1995). *The ch'i-lin purse, a collection ancient chinese stories*. Canada and USA: A Sunburst Book, Farrar Staus Giroux.
A book dealing with cultural awareness, and filled with kind and clever characters that have to deal with difficulties.

Filipovic, Zlata. (1994). *Zlata's diary*. New York, NY: Viking Penguin Books.
The diary of a thirteen-year-old girl living during the war in Sarajevo. It is reminiscent of *Anne Frank's Diary* showing both the pain and suffering and the eternal hope of youth.

Gorman, Carol. (1992). *The biggest bully in Brookdale*. St. Louis, MO: Concodia Publishing House.
This book is part of the Tree House Kids Series. A 4th grade bully moves to town and terrorizes the children. The children make plans to get a 6th grader to beat him up but a grown-up in the neighborhood advises against using violence. She suggests the children pray to God for help. The children end up using kindness, which changes the dynamic in a positive way.

Greenfield, Eloise. (1978). *Honey, I love and other love poems*. New York, NY: HarperCollins Publishers.
This book consists of a set of poems that express the joy in friendship and caring for other people. These poems are short and wonderful to read aloud. They are wonderful examples of positive feelings about life.

Greenfield, Eloise. (1974). *Sister*. New York, NY: HarperCollins Publishers.
Thirteen-year-old Doretha shares pages from the journal that she has kept since she was nine-years-old. There are happy times like learning about her freedom fighting, ex-slave ancestor and sad times like when her father dies. An unpretentious book opening up the life of an Afro-American girl.

Hesse, Karen, (1998). *Just juice*. New York, NY: Scholastic, Inc.
A nine-year-old girl faces difficulties with learning and how to help her father earn the money to pay the back taxes. Its absorbing and convincing, showing love and endurance.

Holyoke, Nancy. (1996). *More help! Another absolutely indispensable guide to life for girls.* Middleton, WI: Pleasant Company Publications.
Tips for dealing with stepfamilies, picky parents, and other issues for girls ages 8 and older.

*Holyoke, Nancy. (1995.) *Help! An absolutely indispensable guide to life for girls.* Middleton, WI: Pleasant Company Publications.
Tips for dealing with bullies and other problems for girls ages 8 and older.

Hughes, Langston. (1994). *The dream keeper and other poems.* New York, NY: Scholastic Inc.
A collection of poems that give us the feelings of the Afro-American culture that Langston Hughes grew up in as well as universal themes of life that all of us experience. Wonderful collection for children.

Keehn, Sally M. (1995). *Moon of two dark horses.* New York, NY: Bantam Doubleday Dell Publishing Group Inc.
Two boys, one white and one Indian, are best friends. As tension builds between the two groups their friendship is put to the test. Children are introduced to the culture of the Delaware Indians and see courage and loyalty portrayed in both boys.

Kherdian, David. (1979). *The road from home; the story of an Armenian girl.* New York, NY: Puffin Books, Viking Penguin Inc.
A Newbery Honor book that illustrates an almost forgotten part of history through the diary of a young girl, Vernon, in 1915, during the death march into the desert in Armenia.. For children ages 10 - 14.

Koller, Jackie French. (1993). *A dragon in the family.* New York, NY: Pocket Books, a division of Simon & Schuster.
This book is part of a trilogy that illustrates standing up to bullies, changing people's minds, peer or community pressure versus standing up for what is right, family loyalty, etc. It is a tradition for boys of a certain age to hunt and kill a dragon. Dragons are seen as the enemy and are to be feared and destroyed. Then a young boy discovers that dragons are not aggressive after all. He must stand up first to his family and then to his community to change their prejudice. The trilogy consists of *Dragonling, A Dragon in the Family* and *Dragon Quest.*

Krulik, Nancy. (1998). *Don't stress! How to keep life's little problems little.* New York. NY: Scholastic Inc. A little book with advise for how to deal with stress.

Lewis, Barbara A. (1992). *Kids with courage, true stories about young people making a difference.* Minneapolis, MN: Free Spit Publishing, Inc.
This book relates the stories of young people making a difference in their neighborhood, community, or the world by helping in such areas as crime, life-saving and the environment.

Lowry, Lois. (1989). *Number the stars*. Boston, MA: Houghton Mifflin Company.
This book deals with an entire countries heroism in working together to save the Jewish population. The pro-active role of the witness conquers the oppression of the Nazis as seen through the eyes of a ten-year-old girl.

Mills, Claudia. (1997). *Losers, Inc.* New York, NY: Scholastic, Inc.
Boys who identify themselves as loosers face the possibility of having a different identity.

Mohr, Nicholasa. (1979). *Felita*. New York, NY: Puffin Books, Penguin Putnam Books for young readers.
A book about a Puerto Rician girl who's family leaves their neighborhood for a better neighborhood and faces prejudice. Excellently written work, you really have a feel for the neighborhood and its cultural heritage as well as the conflicts and tensions facing this family. Written for children ages 7 – 11.

Naylor, Phyllis R. (1999). *Saving Shiloh*. New York, NY: Aladdin Paperbacks.
Addresses sibling rivalry, empathy, and bullying. Third book in a trilogy. Ages 8 - 12.

Naylor, Phyllis R. (1996). *Shiloh*. New York, NY: Cornerstone Books.
Addresses sibling rivalry, empathy, and bullying. First book in a trilogy. Ages 8 - 12.

Naylor, Phyllis R. (1996). *Shiloh season*. New York, NY: Atheneum Books.
Addresses sibling rivalry, empathy, and bullying. Second book in a trilogy. Ages 8 - 12.

Naylor, Phyllis Reynolds. (1973). *To walk the sky path*. New York, NY: Dell Publishing, a division of Bantam Doubleday Publishing Group, Inc.
Billie, a ten-year-old Seminole Indian, learns to deal with the Indian and white world as he is the first in his family to go to school. The reader is introduced to the Seminole way of life as well as the conflict Billie faces as he learns more and more of the white culture.

Park, Barbara. (1987). *The kid in the red jacket*. New York, NY: Bullseye Books, Alfred A. Knopf.
A ten-year-old boy moves to a new school and deals with making new friends, peer pressure, empathy and self-talk. He tries to deal with a six-year-old who follows him everywhere and interferes, he thinks, with his chance of being accepted by his peers. A good growing up book.

Patterson, Katherine. (1992). *The king's equal*. USA: HarperCollins Publishers.
A Prince who is arrogant and rich but unfit to wear the crown is told by the king that he must find a woman who is his equal before he can rule. A poor farmer's daughter is equal to the task and through trickery and ingenuity she creates a place where both are equal to each other. Positive problem-solving as a way to turn the tables on a bully will leave the readers chuckling.

*Romain, Trevor. (1997). *Bullies are a pain in the brain*. Minneapolis, MN: Free Spirit Publishing, Inc.   A guide to handling problems bullying problems.

Rodowsky, Colby. (1976). *What about me?* Toronto, Canada: Collins Publishers. United States: Sunburst edition.
This book illustrates the relationship between fifteen-year-old Dorrie and her eleven-year-old brother, Fredlet, who is developmentally delayed. Shows the conflict of loving and resenting him.

Russell, Ching Yeung. (1994). *First Apple*. New York, NY:Puffin Books, Penguin Group.
The story of a young girl, Ying, who lives in China and wants to buy an apple for her grandmother. Apples are so expensive that only rich people can afford to buy them. Ying has to deal with a bully among other problems in her quest.

Shreve, Susan. (1993). *Joshua T. Bates takes charge*. New York, NY: Alfred A. Knopf.
Joshua struggles with the role of witness as he watches a new boy getting bullied. He is afraid to add to his own problems by standing up for him. Joshua deals with conflicting feelings, fear, peer pressure, self-talk, and courage.

Snyder, Zilpha Keatly. (1990). *Libby on Wednesday*. New York, NY: Bantam Doubleday Dell Publishing Group Inc.
Libby must learn to socialize after have been tutored at home her whole life. She ends up dealing with a bully and learns how to accept others. Snyder has several other excellent books, three of which are Newbery Honor books. Her writing encourages readers to look at life through other children's viewpoint and develop empathy for them.

Speare, Elizabeth George. (1958, 1986). *The witch of blackbird pond*. New York, NY: Bantam Doubleday Dell Books for Young Readers.
A young girl comes to New England to live with Puritan relatives. Prejudice, bigotry, and witch hunts are all part of this coming of age book.

Stolz, Mary. (1963). *The bully of Barkham Street*. New York, NY: Harper and Rowe, Publishers.
A sixth-grade boy struggles with the perception that he is a bully and succeeds in changing his behavior. For ages 8 - 12.

*Surat, M.M. (1983). *Angel child/dragon child*. Milwaukee, WI: Raintree Publishers, Inc.
A Vietnamese girl attending school in the U.S. is lonely for her mother, left behind in Vietnam, and makes a new friend who presents her with a wonderful gift.

Tamar, Erika. (1995). *The junkyard dog*. New York, NY: Alfred A. Knopf Inc.
An eleven-year-old girl is trying to deal with her mother's recent marriage when she finds a dog in a junkyard that is mistreated. The plight of the dog helps Katie do what she would not ordinarily have the courage to do. The book brings up empathy and the role of the witness. It is an intense book but has a happy ending.

Taylor, Mildred D. (1976). *Roll of thunder, hear my cry*. New York, NY: Bantam Doubleday Dell Publishing Group, Inc.

A year in the life of Cassie Logan, a black child raised to be independent and strong in an area where prejudice and racism are common place.

Treffinger, Carolyn. (1995). *Li Lun: Lad of courage.* New York, NY: Walker Publishing Company, Inc.
A young Chinese boy growing up in a fishing village must prove his bravery when his family banishes him for being afraid of the sea. This book originally won a Newbery Honor Award in 1948. For children ages 8 and older.

Warner, Sally. (1998). *Sort of forever.* New York, NY: Scholastic, Inc.
Two girls have been friends forever when the more outgoing, daring and giving of the pair is struck with cancer. Cady has to dig inside herself to become the stronger one who now supports Nana. They find even in the midst of this crisis, their friendship can have laughter and joy.

Westridge Young Writes Workshop. (1994). *Kids explore America's Japanese American heritage.* Sante Fe, New Mexico: John Muir Publication.
This book celebrates the many contributions Japanese Americans have made to our country from a child's point of view. It is part of a series that includes exploring African American Heritage, Hispanic Heritage, and gifts of children with special needs.

Wojciechowski, Susan. (1994). *Don't call me beanhead!* Cambridge, MA: Candlewick Press.
A collection of short stories that feature a little girl who is a worrywart. She learns to be her own person and stand up for herself. For readers 8 years and older.

Yates, Elizabeth. (1950). *Amos Fortune, free man.* New York, NY: Puffin Newbery Library, Penguin Books Inc.
This is a Newbery medal book that describes the life of Amos Fortune, captured by slave traders at the age of fifteen, he lived in Massachusetts as a slave and a free man. It shows what slavery was like in the north and never looses sight of the importance of freedom. For children ages 8 – 12.

Resources

Guides and Reference Books
for Children and their Therapist and/or Parents

(There are innumerable good books out there that illustrate the skills needed in violence prevention. I have offered you a sampling of books I enjoy and use. If one of these is no longer in print, feel free to ask the librarian or book clerk to help you find one that is comparable.) For your convenience I have divided these books into topics. Some of these resources are repeated in the readings for children from pre-school through grade two and from grades three to five. I wanted to give parents, teachers and therapists choices of books to read to illustrate or evoke discussion in specific areas.

ABUSE (DOMESTIC, VERBAL, PHYSICAL AND SEXUAL) AND TRAUMA

Bernstein, Sharon C. (1991). *A family that fights*. Morton Grove, IL: Albert Whitman & Company. Presents a difficult family situation from a young boy's perspective and offers a list of things children can do in situations of domestic violence. (To be read with a therapist or support group. This book is a favorite of mine to introduce this topic.)

Cain, Sandra & Speed, Margaret. (1999). *Dad's in Prison*. London, England: A & C Black Publishers Ltd.
Two children experience their father being taken away to jail. The book is set in England but the feeling are universal. The children visit their father and deal with the trauma.

Davis, D. (1984). *Something is wrong at my house: A book about parent's fighting*. Seattle, WA: Parenting Press, Inc.
A book for elementary school children about domestic violence and what they can do if they're experiencing problems at home. (To be read with a helping adult.)

Gil, Eliana. (1986). *I told my secret: A book for kids who were abused*. Rockville, Maryland: Launch Press.
A book about abuse for children and adults to read together. Written in language for middle elementary school students. (It could be read alone, but it would be better to have an adult to discuss it with.)

Holmes, Margaret. (2000). *A terrible thing happened*. Washington, D.C.: Magination Press.
This books describes a racoon who witnessed some type of trauma and is afraid to talk about it. The reader sees the after effects of bad dreams and angry, acting out behavior and then sees him work with a therapist to deal with what he saw. (Good for children who have witnessed any kind of violent or traumatic event.)

Jacobson, Lee Carolynn. (1994). *Pitterpat.* Norfolk, VA: Hampton Roads Publishing Company, Inc.
An illustrated book which approaches the topic of sexual abuse in a non-threatening manner. (To be used with sexually abused children by parents, teachers, therapists and other concerned adults.)

Jessie. (1991). *Please tell! A child's story about sexual abuse.* United States: Hazeldon Foundation.
This story was written and illustrated by a pre-teen survivor of sexual abuse. It communicates to children that the abuse was not their fault and explores things they can do to get the help they need.

Katz, Illana. (1994). *Sarah.* Northridge, California: Real Life Storybooks.
A book about incest, written simply enough for young children but profound enough for older children to get something from it. (I recommend that this book be read with an adult.)

Lee, I. & Sylwester, K. (1996). *When Mommy got hurt.* Charlotte, NC: Kidsrights.
A book about domestic violence. (To help parents, teachers and therapists talk to young children, early childhood and kindergarten, about this topic.)

Loftis, C. (1995). *The words hurt.* Far Hills, NJ: New Horizon Press.
A story about the power of words and the role that communication plays in both hurting and healing. A story about emotional abuse. (For upper level elementary children and their therapist or counselor.)

Patterson, Susan. (1990). *I wish the hitting would stop. A workbook for children living in violent homes and the facilitator's guide.* Fargo, ND: Red Flag Green Flag Resources. Rape and Abuse Crisis Center.
A workbook and guide that provides activities for children living in violence. Good for elementary and possibly middle school students.

Sanford, Doris. (1989). *Lisa's parents fight.* Portland, OR: Multnomah.
A little girl talks to God about the problems in her family and turns to her teacher for help in dealing with the verbal and physical abuse at home.

Sweet, Phyllis. (1981). *Something happened to me.* Racine, WI: Mother Courage Press.
A sensitively written book exploring the feelings of children who have been sexually abused. (For therapists, parents and other adults working with sexually abused children.)

Trottier, Maxine. (1997). *A safe place.* Morton Grove, IL: Albert Whitman & Company.
A child describes her experience of going to a safe house and dealing with domestic abuse. The fear of leaving home with nothing but a stuffed animal, missing her father, dealing with other children, and getting ready to leave are all explored. (For therapist and parents working with children needing to be in a shelter.)

Wilgocki, Jennifer & Wright, Marcia Kahn. (2002). *Maybe days. A book for children in foster care.* Washington, D.C.: Magination Press.
This book for children ages 4 – 10 explores some of the questions and feelings children have in foster care. (There is an extensive section for adults working with these children.)

Anger Management

Berg, B. (1990). *The anger control workbook: Exercises to develop anger control skills.* Dayton, OH: Cognitive Counseling Resources.

Moser, Adolph J. (1994). *Don't rant and rave on Wednesdays! The children's anger-control book.* Kansas City, MO: Landmark Editions, Inc.
A book to help children understand their own feelings of anger and learn how to deal with those feelings in a productive ways.

Pudney, W. & Whitehouse, E. (1996). *A volcano in my tummy: Helping children to handle anger, a resource book for parents, caregivers and teachers.* Gabriola Island, British Columbia, Canada: New Society Publishers.

Bullying (Teasing and Violence)

Adams, Lisa K. (1997). *Dealing with someone who won't listen.* Center City, MN: The Conflict Resolution Library. A Hazelden/PowerKids Press Book.

Berry, Joy W. (1982). *Let's talk about teasing.* Newark, NJ: Peter Pan Industries.
This story provides information about why people tease and strategies for stopping it. (Can be read by a child or by a parent, teacher, or therapist.)

Bosch, C. W. (1988). *Bully on the bus.* Seattle, WA: Parenting Press, Inc.
A fifth grader on the school bus is picking on other children, the reader chooses a scenario and creates their own story. A book in "The Decision Is Yours" series for elementary school children.

Burnett, Karen Gedig. (2000). *Simon's hook: A story abut teases and put downs.* Roseville, CA: GR Publishing.
A fun book for elementary school students. Simon is teased by his classmates. Grama Rose comes to the rescue by showing him how to avoid taking the bait. (This book is a valuable resource for teachers, parents, children and therapists.)

Chardiet, Bernice & Maccarone, Grace. (1990). *Brenda's private swing.* New York, NY: Scholastic, Inc.
Children use negotiating skills and positive problem-solving to deal with a bully. 1st –2nd grades.

Cohen-Posey, Kate. (1995). *How to handle bullies, teasers and other meanies*. Highland City, FL: Rainbow Books, Inc.
A handbook for children and adults with information and strategies for dealing with bullying, prejudice, and teasing. (Can be read alone by older children but some of the strategies can be utilized by all ages with the help of an adult.)

Garbarino, James. (1993). *Let's talk about living in a world with violence*. Chicago, IL: Erikson Institiue.
This is an activity book for school age children on dealing with the impact that violence has in their world. It defines violence and looks at the feelings of those doing and those receiving the violence. It relates these concepts to the society we live in.

Johnson, J. (1996). *(How do I feel about) bullies and gangs*. London, England: Aladdin Books.
In this book the author uses the word "gang" as synonymous with cliques, clubs, or peer groups as opposed to criminal gangs. This may need to be distinguished for children.

Park, Barbara. (1987). *The kid in the red jacket*. New York, NY: Bullseye Books, Alfred A. Knopf.
A ten-year-boy moves to a new school and deals with making new friends, peer pressure, empathy and self-talk. He tries to deal with a six-year-old who follows him everywhere and interferes, he thinks, with his chance of being accepted by his peers. A good growing up book.

*Petty, Kate and Firmin, Charlotte. (1991). *Being bullied*. Huppauge, NY: Barron's Educational Series, Inc.
A little girl learns to assert herself and ignore teasing to solve a bullying problem at school.

*Romain, Trevor. (1997). *Bullies are a pain in the brain*. Minneapolis, MN: Free Spirit Publishing, Inc. A guide to handling problems bullying problems.

Suess, Dr. (1961). *The Sneetches and other stories*. New York, NY: Random House.
Two types of Sneetches, imaginary characters, deal with prejudice, showing the effects on victims and the ridiculousness of the prejudicial ideas in the first place. This book is good for people of all ages. This is a perfect story to supplement the alien activity.

Thomas, Pat. (2000). *Stop picking on me*. "A first Look At Book." Hauppauge, NY: Barron's Educational Series, Inc. http://www.barronseduc.com
A book for young children through 2nd grade that explores bullying.

Webster-Doyle, Terrence. (1992). *Why is everybody always picking on me?* Middlebury, VT: Atrium Society Publications.

DEALING WITH DEATH

Boulden, Jim & Joan. (1992). *Saying goodbye; Bereavement activity book*. Weaverville, CA: Boulden Publishing.
A book for pre-school and young elementary school students on death and grief. Coloring and drawing activities are interspersed with the text. (To be used with an adult.)

Carrick, Donald. (1976). *The accident*. New York, NY: Clarion Books, Houghton Mifflin Company.
A young boy, Christopher, must deal with the death of his dog. He deals with feelings of guilt, anger and acceptance. There are other stories about Christopher dealing with other issues. (This book could be read alone or with an adult.)

Frost, Dorothy. (1991). *Dad! Why'd you leave me?* Scottdale, PA: Herald Press.
A young boy deals with his grief over the unexpected death of his father and turns to his family, friends and God for comfort. Shows a full range of emotions. (Could be read alone by an child 10 or older, but if they are dealing with grief it would be good to read with an adult.)

Mellonie, Bryan & Ingpen, Robert. (1983) *Lifetimes; The beautiful way to explain death to children*. New York, NY: Bantam Book, A division of Bantam Doubleday Dell Publishing Group, Inc.
A book with beautiful illustrations and a simple text that can be used by people of all ages.

Moser, Adolph J. (1996). *Don't despair on Thursdays! The children's grief-management book*. Kansas City, MO: Landmark Editions, Inc.
Gives children information on loss and grief and offers ways to cope with painful feelings.

Mundy, Michaelene. (1998). *Sad isn't bad: A good-grief guidebook for kids dealing with loss*. St. Meinrad, IN: Abbey Press.

Thomas, Pat. (2000). *I miss you*. Hauppauge, NY: Barron's Educational Series, Inc. http://www.barronseduc.com
"A First Look At Book" for young children through 2nd grade explores the issue of death.

DIVERSITY (DIFFERENT CULTURES, DIFFERENT ABILITIES)

Anno, Mitsumassa et al. (1986). *All in a day*. New York, NY: Philome Books.
Illustrations and a brief text communicate about children in eight different countries, emphasizing the commonality of people in general while also showing differences.

Bruchac, Joseph. (1997). *Eagle song*. New York, NY: Dial Books for Young Readers.
Danny Bigtree must deal with Native American sterotypes after moving to Brooklyn, NY from a Mohawk Indian Reservation. He has to deal with anger management, making friends, positive problem-solving and prejudice.

Carrick, Carol. (1985). *Stay away from Simon*. New York, NY: Clarion Books.
Two siblings are afraid when a child with special needs follows them home one day. They deal with their fear, accepting differences, fairness, etc.

CastaÒeda, Omar S. (1991). *Among the volcanoes*. New York, NY: Bantam Doubleday Dell Publishing Group, Inc.
This book offers a look into the culture of Guatemala, and lives that are very different from those of most young people in the USA. A young girl tries hard to hold onto her dream and work toward her goal of being a teacher against what seems like insurmountable odds.

Dodds, Bill. (1993). *My sister annie*. Honesdale, PA: Boyds Mills Press, Inc.
A boy struggles with the challenges of having a sister with Down's Syndrome. He deals with anger, peer pressure and a desire to feel accepted by his friends.

Dooley, Norah. (2000). *Everybody loves soup*. Minneapolis, MN: Carolrhoda Books, Inc.
Part of a series about a child's multicultural neighborhood for pre-school through 1st grade.

Geller, Rita. (1995). *Victoria's smile*. New York, NY: Scholastic.
A young girl survives cancer only to face rejection because the cancer damaged her facial muscles. Children in her class learn to accept Victoria for her bravery and personality. Good for children young and old.

Greenfield, Eloise. (1974). *Sister*. New York, NY: HarperCollins Publishers.
Thirteen-year-old Doretha shares pages from her journal that she has kept since she was nine-years-old. There are happy times like learning about her freedom fighting, ex-slave ancestor and sad times like when her father dies. An unpretentious book opening up the life of an Afro-American girl.

Janssen, Larry. (1984). *My sister is special*. Cincinnati, OH: The Standard Publishing Company.
A positive look at how one little boy interacts with his sister, who has Down's Syndrome. For pre-school - 1st grade.

Jenness, Aylette. (1990). *Families: A celebration of diversity, commitment, and love*. Boston, MA: Houghton Mifflin Company.
Seventeen children talk about their families which include single parent households, gay parents, foster parents, divorced parents and stepfamilies, along with traditional two-parent families.

Lasker, Joe. (1974). *He's my brother*. Chicago, IL: Albert Whitman & Company.
A boy shares his experiences with his brother who has a learning disability. We are introduced to things he can and cannot do and learn to empathize with his problems. Young elementary school children.

McConnell, Nancy. (1982). *Different and alike*. Colorado Springs, CO: Current, Inc.
A book that explains various handicaps for elementary school children.

Mitchell, Lori. (1999). *Different just like me*. Watertwon, MA: A Talewinds Book, Charlesbridge Publishing. www.charlesbridge.com

Powers, Mary Ellen. (1986). *Our teacher's in a wheelchair*. Niles, IL: Albert Whitman & Co.
Children meet a nursery school teacher who requires the use of a wheel chair and still lives an active life. Good for pre-school through kindergarten.

Osofsky, Audrey. (1992). *My buddy*. New York, NY: Henry Holt & Company.
Children are introduced to helping dogs and how one of these dogs helps a boy with muscular dysrophy do things he cannot do himself.

Sobol, Harriet L. (1977). *My brother, Steven, is retarded*. New York, NY: Macmillan Publishing. An eleven-year-old girl shares her thoughts and feelings on what it's like living with her mentally retarded brother.

Stern, Judith & Ben-Ami, Uzi. (1996). *Many ways to learn: Young people's guide to learning disabilities*. New York, NY: Magination Press.
Written especially for children who have learning disabilities, this book presents information, real life stories, and practical suggestions for reassuring and encouraging children, ages 8 - 14.

Surat, M.M. (1983). *Angel child/dragon child*. Milwaukee, WI: Raintree Publishers, Inc.
A Vietnamese girl attending school in the U.S. is lonely for her mother, left behind in Vietnam, and makes a new friend who presents her with a wonderful gift.

Weiss, Nicki. (2000). *The world turns round and round*. Hong Kong, China: South China Printing Co. www.harperchildrens.com
A book about children from around the world that is good for exploring diversity. For pre-school - 1st grade.

DIVORCE

Brown, Laurene K. & Brown, Marc. (1986). *Dinosaurs divorce, a guide for changing families*. Boston, MA: Little, Brown and Company.
A winner of many awards, this is a great book for children dealing with divorce. (Can be read alone but reading it with an adult allows for questions and discussion.)

Lansky, Vicki. (1998). *It's not your fault, Koko Bear*. Minnetonka, MN: Book Peddlers.
This is a read together book for young children dealing with divorce. It shows that difficult feelings are normal and that they can change over time. It offers suggestions to parents on how to discuss divorce and the accompanying feelings as well as offering ways to provide consistency and support.

Mayle, Peter. (1979). *Divorce can happen to the nicest people*. New York, NY: Macmillan Publishing.
An illustrated handbook that offers reassurance, sympathy and practical advice on coping with in family that is splitting up.

Seward, Angela. (2001). *Goodnight, Daddy*. Buena Park, CA: Morning Glory Press.
A story about a child whose absent father does not always make his scheduled visits. (For pre-school and elementary school, to be read with an adult.)

Sinberg, Janet. (1978). *Divorce is a grown-up problem*. New York, NY: Avon Books, a division of The Hearst Corporation.
This is a book about divorce written for young children and their parents. The young child in the book is shown how to express a full range of feelings about divorce safely.

Stinson, Kathy. (1995). *Mom and Dad don't live together anymore*. Buffalo, NY: Annick Press Ltd. Firefly Books.
A book on divorce for pre-school and early elementary school children.

DRUG AND ALCOHOL ABUSE

Al-Anon Family Group. (1977). *What's "drunk," mama?* New York, NY: Al-anon Family Group Headquarters, Inc.
A book about alcoholism for elementary school children dealing with the confusion and pain a child feels about her father's drinking and her parents fighting. (This could be read alone or with an adult so the feeling it brings up can be discussed.)

Heegaard, Marge. (1993). *When a family is in trouble*. Minneapolis, MN: Woodland Press.
This workbook allows children to illustrate the text of the book. It's purpose is to help children cope with the feelings brought on from dealing with drug and alcohol addiction in their family. (A good book for a therapy group or individual counseling on this issue.)

Langsen, Richard C. (1996). *When someone in the family drinks too much*. New York, NY: Dial Books for Young Readers, A Division of Penguin Book.
A book written for elementary school children to help them understand alcoholism and it's affects on the family. There are suggestions for coping with this problem in addition to normalizing the feelings children have in response to this issue. (I recommend this book be read with an adult.)

Vigna, Judith. (1988). *I wish Daddy didn't drink so much*. Niles, Illinois: Albert Whitman & Company.
A young child shares her experience of living with a father that drinks too much. (A good book to read together.)

O'Neill, Catherine. (1990). *Focus on alcohol*. United States of America: Twenty-First Century Books.
This book discussed the history, use, and dangers of alcohol, the problems of alcoholism, and peer pressure related to drinking. (It is written for older elementary school and middle school students and can be read alone or with an adult.)

FEELING EDUCATION

Aliki. (1984). *Feelings*. New York, NY: Greenwillow Books, William Morris & Co.
Children explore a range of feelings through humorous pictures and dialogue. For children pre-school – 2nd grade.

Baker, Keith. (1999). *Sometimes*. New York, NY: Green Light Readers, Harcourt Brace & Company.

This brightly illustrated story explores the range of feelings children may experience and offers a self-affirming message. For children in K - 1st grade.

Berry, Joy Wilt. (1982). *Let's talk about teasing*. Newark, NJ: Peter Pan Industries.
Part of a series, called Let's Talk About It, that deals with all types of problem behaviors that pre-school and young elementary children exhibit. It helps children explore their feelings and learn socially acceptable ways of dealing with them.

Cain, Barbara. (1990). *Double dip feelings*. Washington, D.C.: American Psychological Ass.
A book that discusses having more than one feeling at a time. Good to read to pre-school and early elementary children.

Conlin, Susan & Friedman, Susan Levine. (1989). *All my feelings at home, Ellie's day*. Seattle, WA: Parenting Press, Inc.
This book introduces a wide range of feelings as they are felt by Ellie during the different events in her day. Pre-school – Kindergarten.

Crary, Elizabeth. (1991). *Dealing with feelings series*. Seattle, Washington: Parenting Press, Inc. This series of books discusses specific feelings in easy to understand scenarios with positive ways to express and deal with these feelings. The following titles are included in the series: *I'm mad, I'm frustrated, I'm proud, I'm furious, I'm scared, I'm excited*. For children in pre-school - 1st grade. Elizabeth Crary also has several other good books dealing with pro-social behaviors such as: *I can't wait, I'm lost, I want it, I want to play, Mommy don't go, My name is not dummy*. These are all published by Parenting Press, Inc.

Doleski, Teddi. (1983). *The hurt*. Ramsey, NJ: Paulist Press.
A book for young elementary children that deals with a fight between friends, hurt feelings, and how to feel better.

Gilmore, Rachna. (1999). *A screaming kind of day*. Toronto, Canada: Fitzhenry & Whiteside.
This is a beautifully written book about an angry day for a hearing impaired child. The internal dialogue is realistic and shows a full range of feelings. Her feelings will resonate with all children. (Pre-school – 2nd grade)

Lachner, Dorothea. (1995). *Andrew's angry words*. New York / London: North-South Books Inc.
A fanciful book for children through 2nd grade that shows the affect that people's words can have on others.

Leonard, Marcia. (1988). *How I feel; Scared*. New York, NY: Bantam Books, Bantam Doubleday Dell Publishing Group, Inc.
A book for pre-school - kindergarten on feeling scared and what you can do about it.

McGrath, Bob. (1989). *Dog lies*. Los Angeles, CA: Price Stern Sloan.
Part of a series of books, called Bob's Books, designed to read together with a child about different ethic. This one is obviously about lying. Designed for pre-schoolers it could also be used with early elementary children.

McConnell, Nancy. (1988). *Dusty D. Dawg has feelings, too!* Colorado Springs, CO: Current, Inc.
This book explores a wide range of emotions through the sharing of a dog, including feeling angry and feeling sorry. For children in pre-school - kindergarten.

Moser, Adolph J. (1991). *Don't feed the monster on Tuesdays! The children's self-esteem book.* Kansas City, MO: Landmark Editions, Inc.
Discusses how to develop and maintain a positive attitude and healthy self-esteem.

Nruia, Roca & Curto, Rosa M. (2002). *Scared? From fear to courage.* Hauppauge, NY: Barron's Educational Series, Inc. http://www.barronseduc.com
This book is good for pre-school - 2nd grade. It normalizes fear, introduces the concept of early warning signs, and teaches ways to turn fear around. There is a section for parents with guidelines on dealing with fear at the end of the book.

*Payne, Lauren M. (1994). *Just because I am: A child's book of affirmation.* Minneapolis, MN: Free Spirit Publishing, Inc.
For children ages 3 - 8, this book deals with self perception, self-esteem, self-acceptance, body image, and feeling identification.

Payne, Lauren Murphy. (1994). *A leader's guide to just because I am; A child's book of affirmation.* Minneapolis, MN: Free Spirit Publishing, Inc.
This guide to the book described above includes thirteen lesson with reproducible sheets.

Simon, Norma. (1974). *I was so mad!* Morton Grove, IL: Albert Whitman & Company.

Wilt, J. (1979). *Handling your ups and downs.* Columbus, OH: Weekly Reader Books.
A children's book about emotions specifically designed for ages 4 - 8. Wilt proposes a four-step procedure for children to follow when they experience uncomfortable feelings.

PREVENTION AND EDUCATION

Freeman, Lory. (1982). *It's my body.* Seattle, WA: Parenting Press, Inc.
A book to teach young children how to resist uncomfortable touch.

*Golant, M., with Crane, B. (1987). *Sometimes it's okay to be angry! A parent/child manual for the education of children.* New York, NY: Tom Doherty Associates, Inc.

Gordon, Sue & Litt, Sandy. (1988). *Nolly and Groogle, the Gillows of Crimpley Creek.* Burnside, South Australia: Pagel Books Pty. Ltd. for Essence Publications.
Two young Gillows, bird like creatures, learn to listen and respond to early warning signs through a series of events. Good for low to mid elementary children. (Should be read with an adult to help process messages.)

Gordon, Sue & Litt, Sandy. (1988). *Zing and Zip, the Troggs of Wongo-Wongo Wood.* Burnside, South Australia: Pagel Books Pty. Ltd. for Essence Publications.
Two Troggs, imaginary creatures, deal with several scary situations and strategies for staying safe. These situations are more involved than the Nolly and Groggle book above including domestic and sexual abuse. Good for elementary students. (Should be read with an adult to process and generalize messages.)

Lenett, R. & Barthelme, D. with Crane, B. (1986). *It's okay to tell secrets! A parent/child manual for the protection of children.* New York, NY: RGA Publishing Group, Inc.
Sections of the book are for adults and other sections present stories for discussion with children. Deals with educating and protecting children from sexual abuse focusing on disclosure. For elementary age children and their parents or teachers.

Lenett, R. with Crane, B. (1985). *It's okay to say no! A parent/child manual for the protection of children.* New York, NY: RGA Publishing Group, Inc.
Sections of the book are for adults and other sections present stories for discussion with children. Deals with educating and protecting children from sexual abuse, focusing on prevention. For elementary age children and their parents or teachers.

Mason, Donald Brooks. (1998). *The dolphin's dream, healing stories for young people.* Shaker Heights, Ohio: Prairie Schooner Publishing Company.
Stories that use metaphor to help children heal from all types of challenges, fear, loss, neglect, etc. For children of all ages.

Moncure, J. B. (1988). *Yes, no, little hippo.* Mankato, MN: The Child's World.
A book about being safe and developing safety rules. For pre-school – 1st grade.

Stock, Gregory. (1988). *The kid's book of questions.* Workman Publishing Company, Inc.: New York, NY.
Poses a variety of thought-provoking questions regarding issues of trust, fear, ethics, family problems, social pressures and friendship.

Wachter, Oralee. (1986). *Close to home.* New York, NY: Scholastic, Inc.
A collection of stories dealing with child abduction that distinguish what is safe from what is not. For elementary children.

Wachter, Oralee. (1983). *No more secrets for me.* New York, NY: Scholastic, Inc.
A collection of stories dealing with inappropriate touching and what actions children can take. For elementary children.

STRESS MANAGEMENT

Garth, Maureen. (1991). *Starbright, meditations for children.* San Francisco, CA: Harper, a division of HarperCollins Publishers.

Meditations and visualizations that parents, teachers and therapist can use to help children sleep, feel secure, etc.

Garth, Maureen. (1991). *Sunshine, more meditations for children.* NorthBlackburn, Victoria, Autralia: CollinsDove, an imprint of HarperCollins Publishers.
Meditations and visualizations that parents, teachers and therapist can use to help children sleep, feel secure, etc.

Hipp, Earl. (1985). *Fighting invisible tigers: A stress management guide for teens.* Minneapolis, MN: Free Spirit Publishing.
Presents a mini-course in reaching personal potential and provides tools for gaining self control and managing stress. (Could be read alone or with a support group or an adult.)

Moser, Adolph J. (1988). *Don't pop your cork on Mondays! The children's anti-stress book.* Kansas City, MO: Landmark Editions, Inc.
A handbook for children exploring the causes and effects of stress and presenting various techniques for how children can manage stressful situations.